AUSTRALIAN WINE ANNUAL

2000

Published in Australia 1999 by

Jeremy Oliver Pty Ltd trading as OnWine Publications
565 Burwood Rd,
Hawthorn,
Victoria, 3122, Australia.
Tel: 61 3 9819 4400
Fax: 61 3 9819 5322

Printed by	Times Printers Pte Ltd Singapore
Designed by	Artifishal Studios Melbourne, Victoria, Australia
Programming and Layout by	Virgil Reality Melbourne, Victoria, Australia
Cover photograph by	Peter Russell
Distributed to book retailers in Australia by	Pan Macmillan, Free call 1800 684 459 Free fax 1800 241 310

Copyright © Jeremy Oliver 1999.

ISBN 0-9587213-3-5

This book is copyright. Apart from any fair dealings for the purposes of private study, research, criticism or review, as permitted under the Copyright Act, no part may be reproduced by any process or stored in any retrieval system without written permission. Inquiries should be addressed to the publishers.

Introduction

Last year I said it was becoming ridiculous. Looking back, I didn't know what ridiculous meant. I just didn't have a clue. When I started writing about wine some fifteen years ago I actually thought it would be possible for one person to keep fully on top of the Australian wine industry, a sort of walking, talking, tasting vinous encyclopaedia of what's going in, out and in between in Australian wine. I have tried my best, but the goalposts have moved.

Could it be that there are too many wines made in Australia? Of course not, but of the hundreds of bottles that arrive each month on my doorstep, I'm finding I'm recognising fewer and fewer. But it's not only the labels that I struggle to identify at first glance, but the rest of the package as well. This last year has seen Australian wine siphoned into yellow and pink frosted glass, into bottles that would perhaps look more at home in some psychedelic bowling alley, some of which are so tall that you'd think the standard 750 ml of wine would hardly reach their shoulders. There's been a plethora of labels so brazen and so assertive they positively assault the senses with bright, iridescent blues, purples and pastel pinks, the sort of colours previously thought to have much the same effect on wine sales as does saying 'Macbeth' to a thespian.

But I'm sounding jaded, ungrateful and out of touch with the market, to which charges I would plead maybe, maybe not. It's a wonderful challenge personally to taste all the wines that find their way into this book, plus the multitude that doesn't, no matter how many corkscrews I break in the process. At least it won't be too long before those with the connection can hook into this tome over the Internet, where size is less of a problem than with the printed word, rating and label. Keep an eye on my site at www.onwine.com.au, for big things are happening there.

Having just pored over my ratings with the oenological equivalent of a fine-toothed comb, I'm once again in the position at the head of this annual where I do owe something of an explanation. Perhaps it's just because I'm finally becoming harder to please that my Wine Rankings for the Year 2000 edition have been allocated with even a sharper pencil than those given in last year's version. I make no apologies. I figure it's a critic's job to separate the wheat from the chaff and any system deployed to do so should not just exist in name only. I really intend the Wine Rankings to mean something, and as far as I'm concerned any wine that might only score a Fourth or Fifth Ranking has plenty of merit indeed. Australian wine is improving all the time and it's no help to anyone if wines are talked up beyond their worth and clustered at the top end of any rating system.

My approach to rating wine seems to differ from that of most wine critics in that I don't take into account any consideration of price. I don't know how anyone can make a blanket statement concerning value for money, for we all treat the matter of value in our own ways. An Australian cabernet sauvignon priced around $60 might be cheap to some people if a wine of equivalent quality from Bordeaux or the US costs twice that amount. A good Coonawarra shiraz for $20 might well represent dreadful value to the many thousands amongst us who'd never spend more than $10 a bottle. I rate everything on the same scale, be it Jacob's Creek or Grange, for my only aim is to tell you how good or poor each wine is. So it's up to you, the wine buyer, to figure out which wines are good value for you. The Current Price Range symbol which accompanies each wine should help you to make an easy, snap decision.

As I've said before, every now and again somebody re-hashes the argument that wine scores given by critics should not be published in print. Scores, they say, give distorted views about wine and encourage people only to focus on those which rate very highly. Personally, I take each and every score I publish very seriously and hotly dispute the view that scores provide something for the critic to hide behind. To the contrary, I would suggest I put some part of my reputation on the line each time I rate a wine in print. Readers are entitled to real opinions and it's quite plain to any reader exactly how I feel about each wine in this book. I'm never going to be perfect, but in this game, who is? I make no apology about publishing scores, since it would be impossible to convey a meaningful impression about the 9,000-plus vintages included in this book any other way.

It's beyond dispute that verbal descriptions convey much information that scores cannot, but critics often use words to avoid giving a genuine opinion. In my newsletter, *Jeremy Oliver OnWine*, I present both scores and written descriptions for every wine I feature. In a perfect world, I'd present a tasting note with every score in this book, but then you'd need a crane to lift it. I deliberately avoid allocating stars and vintage ratings, glasses, hats and rabbits, each of which is sufficiently ambiguous to make it difficult to ascertain precisely what someone is saying. Or is that really the point?

It's no longer a source of amazement to me that certain types of wine do very much better in wine shows than in my tastings, and vice-versa. The principal role of the wine show system is what Len Evans describes as the 'improvement of the breed' through an exaggerated Darwinian approach of identifying technically faulty wines and making sure they don't get a medal. It's my view that while some wines may not be technically perfect, their personality and expression might make them delicious to drink. That is, after all, why they were made. But I still get dismayed over the soullessness and sameness of so many wine show winners, many of which are simply tricked up and contrived, designed to look at their best for the short period they are exposed to the palates of show judges. It's a fact that many winners of multiple trophies don't perform in the cellar at all.

So, welcome to the third edition of *The OnWine Australian Wine Annual*. It's filled to the brim with more wineries than I ever thought I could cram into 320 pages, with more new wineries and new wines than ever before. I hope that you enjoy using this book and that it helps you find more pleasure than ever before from Australian wine.

Acknowledgments

As ever, this book could never have been published without the help of some very talented, indulgent, but diligent people. My sincere thanks to Frank Ameneiro, John Carabott, Toby Hines, Robyn Lee, Brett Murphy, Stephen O'Connor, Lesley Oliver, Rodney Oliver, Virgil Reality, Jon Williams and to my tolerant wife, Jennifer.

Also, a very special thanks to Jim Hermiston and Harvey Brooks.

Contents

How to use this book	6
Australia's best table wines - the perfect 1's	9
How wine matures	11
1999 Australian vintage report	13
Seasonal variation and wine quality	15
Trends in Australian wine	17
Tasting wine	18
Investing in wine	20
Commercial wine cellaring facilities	22
Australian wineries, wines and vintages	23

How to use this book

Finding the Wine or Winery

It's dead easy to find the listing you're after in *The OnWine Australian Wine Annual*. Each winery or brand of wine is presented in alphabetic order. Under the winery heading, each of its wines or labels is then listed alphabetically. To find Rosemount Estate Roxburgh Chardonnay, for example, simply search for the start of Rosemount Estate's entries, which begin on page 238, after which it's easy to scroll alphabetically down the pages to the Roxburgh Chardonnay, whose entries appear on 240.

Winery Information

The OnWine Australian Wine Annual presents each winery's actual physical address, wine region, telephone number and facsimile number. On those occasions where the entries refer to just a vineyard whose wines are made elsewhere, the address supplied is for the vineyard itself. If you're thinking of visiting a vineyard and wish to be sure whether or not it is open for public inspection, I suggest you telephone the company using the number provided to find out.

Each winery included is accompanied by a listing of its winemaker, viticulturist and chief executive, plus brief details concerning any recent changes of ownership or direction, key wines and recent developments of interest.

The Wine Ranking

The OnWine Australian Wine Annual provides the only current Australian classification of nearly all major Australian wine brands determined on the most important aspect of all: quality. Unlike the very worthwhile Langtons' Classification of Distinguished Australian Wine, which presents a more limited overview of the super-premium market and which is largely based on such aspects as resale price and performance at auction, the Wine Rankings in *The OnWine Australian Wine Annual* are not influenced in any way by price or other secondary factors. Being a secondary market, the auction market is usually slow to respond to the emergence of new quality wines, while in some cases, the release of the Penfolds Yattarna Chardonnay being a fine example, it can produce excessively high prices grossly disproportionate to true wine quality.

The Wine Ranking is your easiest and most convenient guide to wine quality. This book accords to the best wines in Australia a Wine Ranking numeral between 1 and 5, based on the scores received from 20 in my tastings, which are printed adjacent to each entry. The scores from 20 printed in this edition usually relate to the most recent occasion on which I have tasted each wine. Any wines to receive a Wine Ranking must have scored consistently well in these tastings, so each wine with one should be taken seriously, irrespective of whether it is 1 or 5.

To provide a rough basis for comparison, a Wine Ranking of 1 is broadly equivalent to a First Growth classification in France. A large number of wines are included in this book which are not given Wine Rankings, since the minimum requirement for a ranking of 5 is pretty steep.

Here is a rough guide to the way Wine Rankings relate to scores from 20, and how they compare to different medal standards used in the Australian wine show system:

Wine Ranking	Regular Score in Jeremy Oliver's Tastings	Medal Equivalent
1	18.8+	**Top gold medal**
2	18.3–18.7	**Regular gold medal**
3	17.8–18.2	**Top silver medal**
4	17.0–17.7	**Regular silver medal**
5	16.0–16.9	**Top bronze medal**

It is worth noting that wines that score an average of 15.5 out of 20 in Australian wine shows are awarded a Bronze Medal. Those that score 17 are awarded Silver and those that score 18.5 are awarded Gold Medals.

As far as this book is concerned, if a wine improves over time, so will its Wine Ranking. Similarly, if its standard declines, so will its ranking. Since Wine Rankings are largely a reflection of each wine's performance over the last four years, they are unlikely to change immediately as a result of a single especially poor or exceptional year.

Why I Don't Print Meaningless Wine Prices

It is meaningless to print a current price for each vintage of every wine included in this book. Retail prices vary so dramatically from shop to shop that there is no such thing as a standard recommended retail price, even for current release wines. Price guides become even more trite for older releases, since too many factors come into play. Was the wine bought by retailer at auction for resale? In what condition is the bottle? How has it been stored? How keen is the buyer and how desperate is the vendor? What margin does the retailer (or restaurateur) wish to apply and for how long have they had the stock? Since no system has yet been invented which even vaguely approximates the price of older wines and which takes into account all of the factors above, I don't use one. For what value is there in providing worthless information?

Current Price Range

In this book I offer a simple key to help you determine at a glance the approximate retail price of each wine. The Current Price Range, presented in symbol form as described below, provides a reasonable price range for the currently available vintage of each wine, costed at full retail margin.

This price estimation is an approximate guide only and may alter during the period in which a particular vintage wine is for sale. It is largely based around and just under a wine's suggested retail price and does not take into account any special offer or significant discounting.

A wine's Current Price Range can easily be decoded using the table below.

Current Price Range	$5-11	$12-17	$18-25	$26-39	$40+
Symbol	$	$$	$$$	$$$$	$$$$$

When to Drink Each Wine

To the right hand side of every page of wine listings is a column which features the suggested drinking range for every vintage of each wine included, within which I would expect each wine to be drinking at its peak. These drinking windows are my estimations alone, since it's apparent that different people enjoy their wines at different stages of development. Some of us prefer the primary flavours of young wine, while others would rather the virtually decayed qualities of extremely old bottles.

The drinking windows reflect my belief that if a wine shows the necessary potential to develop in the bottle, it should be given some sort of a chance. It's a day-to-day tragedy how few top Australian cellaring wines of all types and persuasions are actually opened at or even close to their prime.

For quick and easy reference, a broad indication of each vintage's maturity is provided with a simple colour background. The chart below illustrates how the colours indicate whether a wine is drinking at its best now, will improve further if left alone, or if it is likely to be past its best.

8 2000 THE ONWINE AUSTRALIAN WINE ANNUAL

Australia's Perfect 1's

Of the thousands of table wines made in Australia today, I have allocated a highest possible Wine Ranking of 1 to a mere sixteen. These are the wines that time and again perform to the highest standard. Each has its particular stamp, its special quality and personal identity. To a major degree, each wine reflects the character of the individual or company whose name it carries. Each certainly reflects vintage variation from year to year, usually without compromising the special qualities associated with the label.

I believe these are the modern benchmarks, the wines against which others can be measured. As a group they are continually improving, but together they define the limits of contemporary Australian wine.

Bannockburn Chardonnay

Gary Farr's complex and ever-so-classical chardonnay: low-yielding fruit from the Bellarine Peninsula given the full Burgundian treatment.

Bass Phillip Reserve Pinot Noir

Australia's best and longest-living pinot noir: a frustratingly rare, full orchestra wine capable of stunning evolution and expression. From Gippsland, by Phillip Jones.

Cullen Cabernet Sauvignon Merlot

An essay in concentration and refinement from Margaret River. The piercing intensity, classically refined structure and enormous potential of Vanya Cullen's premier wine leaves little to the imagination.

De Bortoli Noble One

From the Riverina comes Australia's best and most consistent dessert wine: this sumptuous, concentrated elixir by Darren De Bortoli is an essay in the marriage of late-harvest semillon with noble rot.

Giaconda Chardonnay

My pick as Australia's finest chardonnay, extraordinarily structured and complete, expressing a heritage more Burgundian than Australian. From Rick Kinzbrunner at Beechworth in Victoria.

Grosset Polish Hill

A modern icon in Australian wine, Jeffrey Grosset's standout Clare Valley Riesling stretches the limits of what this most traditional of Australian wines can achieve.

Henschke Cyril Henschke Cabernet Sauvignon

Steven Henschke imparts contemporary attitude to the crop of old Eden Valley vines, fashioning a masterful, complete and sumptuous cabernet sauvignon, steeped in Australian tradition.

Henschke Hill of Grace

In a country full of spectacular single vineyard shiraz wines, Steven Henschke's signature wine from this individual Eden Valley vineyard is the best and most important.

Howard Park Cabernet Sauvignon Merlot

Simply a dream cabernet created by John Wade, sourced from a number of growers in the Great Southern and Margaret River, Western Australia's two most important wine regions.

Leeuwin Estate Chardonnay

At the forefront of Australian chardonnay since its first vintage in 1980, this luscious and long-living Margaret River wine by Bob Cartwright has been for many palates the real 'white Grange'.

Moss Wood Cabernet Sauvignon

A true perfectionist, Keith Mugford makes this classically restrained, reserved and long-living cabernet sauvignon, a corner-stone of Margaret River's reputation for red wine. The latest vintage sees more richness and more oak.

Mount Mary Cabernet 'Quintet'

An inspiration by John Middleton in Victoria's Yarra Valley. The nearest Australian wine to a premier Bordeaux red and a global standard in its own right.

Penfolds Bin 707 Cabernet Sauvignon

The most eloquent expression of Penfolds' approach to red wine, but directed towards cabernet sauvignon. John Duval and his team direct the pick of their entire South Australian cabernet crop towards Bin 707.

Penfolds Grange

Australia's definitive red wine, a model of style, consistency and quality ever since its inception by Max Schubert in 1951. Based on Barossa Valley fruit, with contributions from other South Australian regions, plus cabernet sauvignon.

Petaluma Chardonnay

Brian Croser's highly intellectual approach to chardonnay now pays full dividends in a tightly crafted, infinitely complex and sophisticated wine sourced from a variety of 'distinguished sites' in the Piccadilly Valley.

Pierro Chardonnay

The role model for so many of Australia's more opulent and hedonistically proportioned chardonnays, this stunning expression of Margaret River chardonnay is made by Mike Peterkin.

How wine matures

It's quite forgivable to make a basic misapprehension about the way wine alters with time. Wine doesn't simply become a more intense or expressive version of what it might have been while in its youth, but it actually evolves, sometimes undergoing dramatic changes in colour, smell and taste as it does.

The process of ageing is one of the most complex and least understood of all aspects of wine appreciation. It involves a slow and controlled oxidation and the polymerisation between the many types of molecule initially present in young wine. Oxidation is possible because of the amount of oxygen dissolved in wine prior to bottling and because, so the latest theory goes, tiny amounts of air move down the sides of the cork and into the wine.

Appearance

While the hue of white wines becomes deeper with age, reds go the other way, ultimately losing their deep intensity. So it is considered encouraging to find mature white wines with relatively pale colours and reds with deep colours. As they mature, white wines lose the greenish hues of their youth, becoming straw, then yellow, then gold and eventually amber and brown, by which time they are likely to be too old to enjoy. Wood-aged white wines have received more exposure to oxygen prior to bottling and consequently reveal more developed, yellowish and mature colours than when they were first released.

While most white wines are made after their skins have quickly been removed from the process, red wines acquire their colour from the anthocyanins extracted from grape skins during fermentation. Anthocyanins are firstly oxidised as a consequence of maturation from purple to red, then secondly and more slowly, from red to brown. These processes promote the familiar colour changes in red wines from purple to purple-red, brick red, red-brown and ultimately to an aged tawny colour suggestive of better years gone past.

Aroma and Bouquet

To make it easier to understand and to communicate about, we divide the scent of a wine two ways. Firstly there is the aroma, the smell a wine reveals while fresh in the spring of youth. These smells owe much to the primary fruit flavours of the grapes, plus the other facets often given a wine by its maker, such as nutty, vanilla or toasty influences from oak casks, or the toffee, dairy, bacony or butterscotch flavours which directly result from a secondary (or malolactic) bacterial fermentation. Creamy, yeasty aromas may be derived from extended contact with decaying yeast cells in oak casks; while processes such as whole berry fermentation imbue a wine with a jammy, almost confection-like expression of fruit.

Almost irrespective of where it is grown, cabernet sauvignon tends to exhibit its typical primary flavours of blackcurrants, dark olives and capsicum, while the intense grassy passionfruit and gooseberry aroma of sauvignon blanc is also remarkably consistent from region to region.

The second set of flavours expressed in the nose are known as the bouquet. These flavours, not initially present in young wine, are the result of extended bottle age or extended maturation in oak barrels. The secondary characters which begin to appear are often less distinct and easy to identify than the aroma, although the classic toasty, honeyed and frequently oily characters of bottle-aged Australian riesling are so remarkably different from the flavours encountered in young riesling it's a wonder they actually come from the same wine.

As wines mature, their constituent components of fruit, oak, tannin and acidity alter and marry together, hopefully in a harmonious and pleasing way. Complex volatile esters form when acids combine with ethanol (the alcohol in wine), while aldehydes appear as ethanol is itself oxidised. Ultimately, this esterification reduces and softens the often tart acidity found in young wine.

Good, sound red wines adapt dramatically in the cellar as their ripe primary flavours eventually become more complex and less distinct. You don't have to pay a fortune to find plenty which will. The secondary flavours of cabernet sauvignon can ultimately resemble cedar, violets and cigarboxes. For the gastronomically indulgent, they can even taste like truffles.

How the Palate Matures

Just as their colours become deeper and darker with time, the palate of white wines becomes firstly richer and rounder, before ultimately sliding towards an inevitable decay. Excessive maturation is illustrated by a shortening of the wine's impact on your palate as its level of acidity drops below desirable levels, an over-dominance of oxidised characters resembling toffee, brown apples and vinegar, together with a simultaneous loss of desirable fruit intensity.

While some pinot noirs will 'build' in the bottle throughout their first two years in glass, most red wines begin a gradual process of refinement and ever-increasing restraint as they mature. Their bottle age and development is closely linked to the polymerisation of wine tannins, themselves polymers of polyphenols extracted from grape skins, seeds and the insides of oak barrels. As they combine, molecules which were once relatively small become very large in older wines, reducing their ability to impact with the proteins in the mouth and creating the familiar puckering astringency we associate with wine tannin. As they polymerise, polyphenols and tannins may frequently combine with colour and acid, creating crusts or sediment in maturing wine. As wines become older, their ability to impart a discernible effect from tannin reduces and they become noticeably softer and smoother to drink.

Because they can be too small for the palate to detect, very tiny tannin groups can pass unnoticed on the palate, just like the large, bulky molecules that develop with bottle-age. It take time for these molecules to have evolved to the stage at which the palate can detect them, which is why some apparently insipid and nondescript youthful pinot noirs actually acquire richness, structure and weight with time in the bottle, seemingly defying all logic as they do.

1999 Australian vintage report

In a nutshell, Australia had a massive, but essentially unspectacular vintage in 1999. At a whopping 1,178,673 tonnes, the national crop was 10% up on the industry's expectations, something of great concern with respect to cropping levels and the industry's own ability to forecast accurately. To put this into perspective, the 1998 total was a then-record of 975,669 tonnes. Much of this increase can be attributed to shiraz, which increased its production from 147,300 tonnes to a massive 208,000 tonnes in a single year. Cabernet sauvignon increased from 97,800 to 133,965 tonnes, while chardonnay moved from 173,000 to 237,000 tonnes.

While much of the country was adversely affected by heat then a cool, dampish summer and a continuation of these conditions throughout vintage, several regions will produce exceptional wines. I would be placing orders right now for WA reds, especially Margaret River Cabernet Sauvignon, while the Upper Hunter Valley also experienced a model vintage. On a scarcer note, the pinots from south of Hobart should justify expectations with some special wines.

New South Wales

The Lower Hunter Valley experienced a cooler season than the excellent 1998 vintage, but did substantially better than in 1997. Semillon should be exceptional, being less opulent than the riper 1998s but more in the traditional, leaner style. Overcast conditions and intermittent rain made it difficult to control vegetative growth and ensured that some discipline had to be shown in fruit selection. Fortunately, the rain stopped in time for reds to ripen properly with good balance, colours and around 12.5% alcohol. Richer than traditional Hunter reds, they're not into quite the extra-dimensional league of 1998's drought wines. The Upper Hunter's vintage was perhaps its best ever, with absolutely perfect warm and dry conditions throughout. Late rain in Griffith upset the applecart for growers whose semillon and chardonnay had not already been harvested, as well as later shiraz vineyards and much of the area's cabernet. It was a difficult red vintage, but could be a fine botrytis year for those interested in late-harvest Riverland semillon. NSW's other regions of Hilltops, Cowra, Mudgee and Young didn't receive the strong rains and produced good yields of excellent quality for both red and white table wines.

South Australia

South Australia's 1999 vintage began with several scoringly hot, dry summer months, indeed one of the hottest summers in history. A major frost on October 28 reduced some crops to very low levels, but a warm summer appeared likely to ripen the small bunches and small berries produced by most vineyards. Then the weather intervened again. In the words of Stephen Henschke, it spat the dummy. Rain began in earnest in mid-March, early in the ripening cycle, continuing fairly regularly up to and over Easter. In some regions, Eden Valley, the Adelaide Hills and McLaren Vale in particular, botrytis was a major problem, especially with chardonnay. Some vineyards were not even harvested; others attempted to sort the good from the bad. It was not a year to be caught only with a mechanical harvester. McLaren Vale had a frustrating, disappointing season in which vintage schedules needed constant re-planning due to the weather. Reminiscent of the cool, wet 1992 vintage, 1999 really tested the winemakers.

Provided they were picked before the weather set in, whites should be fine enough, but botrytis was a major issue for those vineyards harvested afterwards. McLaren Vale's shiraz is peppery and spicy but is unlikely to achieve the rich, licorice and chocolate lusciousness of normal vintages. Cabernet was a little better, but essentially lighter than usual.

The better-managed vineyards on the Barossa floor achieved good sugars and flavours, while those who have watered excessively to bump up yields have simply got what they deserved. South Australia's southeast never received the depth of rainfall copped by those regions nearer Adelaide, so there's still genuine optimism in and around Padthaway and Coonawarra, where some growers are proclaiming a truly great vintage. Padthaway chardonnay and cabernet sauvignon have benefited from the low yields, with good flavours and ripeness. Its reworked shiraz vineyards also produced great flavours and sugars.

Tasmania

Things didn't begin well in Tasmania, with a weekly cycle of rainfall that threatened to split and break down fruit. Although summer was warm and unusually humid, and autumn set in early, Tasmania experienced virtually no rain after Easter and prospects improved dramatically. Riesling had an exceptional vintage, while the pinot noirs from south of Hobart should be the best ever. Overall, quality was at least 'good'.

Victoria

It was anything but an easy run home in the premium southern Victorian wine regions. One of the lesser-publicised outcomes of the storms which wreaked such havoc during the Sydney-Hobart yacht race was that they occurred while vines were setting their crops, leading to much lower yields than desirable. The dry summer made matters worse. Then the weather turned quite humid, remaining warm, and in doing so provided first-rate conditions for infections of botrytis, powdery mildew and downy mildew. Finally, the change-of-season hailstorms which typically cross southern Victoria wiped out some crops that remained on certain unlucky vineyards. Again, in the cooler regions south of the Great Divide, it's a vineyard by vineyard affair. Those harvesting lower crops earlier will have done better. The Mornington Peninsula, Yarra Valley and Geelong each had patchy vintages, although fruit tended to ripen around the same time as in the hot 1998. The Western Districts and Pyrenees produced fair, but not great wines, encountering problems with poor cool weather and defoliation before flavour ripeness. With yields reduced by frost, Northeast Victoria had a slightly later vintage than usual, with fully-ripened reds, poor muscat yields and exceptional tokays.

Western Australia

While much of the east coast sweltered under one of the hottest summers of all time, WA's ripening season began as one of its coolest, before culminating in a perfect Indian summer producing some exceptional red wines. Margaret River got out of jail by assiduously missing the cyclonic rainfall that upset most of WA's wine regions and although it received a couple of inches in mid March, the vineyards were never swamped. Its reds should be first-rate, while chardonnay and semillon also performed very well. Pemberton and the Great Southern also had late seasons, producing excellent shiraz, merlot and cabernet. Much Great Southern riesling was harvested before the rain's arrival, but Pemberton's whites were more adversely affected.

Seasonal variation and quality

It's clear just by glancing through this book that the same grapes from the same vineyard invariably produce very different wines from year to year. Although vintage variation in Australia is merely a fraction of that encountered in most European wine regions of any quality, it is still a significant variable which demands consideration when making informed buying decisions.

Even in the event that all other variables are consistent from year to year, which they are certainly not, weather provides the greatest single influence in wine quality and style from season to season. Weather can influence wine in nearly an infinite number of ways, from determining whether conditions at flowering are favourable or not, all the way through to whether final ripening and harvest occur in the warmth of sunshine or through the mists of damaging rains. If viticulturists were to turn pagan, it would be to a god of weather that they would build their first shrine.

Weather-influenced seasonal variation is nearly always more pronounced and more frequent in the cooler, more marginal viticultural regions. While Australia is principally a warm to hot wine producing nation, a significant proportion of the country's premium wine now comes from cooler regions in the south-western and south-eastern corners of the continent. The spectrum of diverse weather encountered in these regions far exceeds that of the traditional Australian wine growing areas like the Barossa Valley, McLaren Vale, central Victoria and the Clare Valley. Paradoxically it seems, the best years in cool climates are actually the warmer seasons which accelerate the ripening period, creating a finer acid balance, superior sugar levels, flavours and better-defined colours.

Variety by variety, this is how Australia's premium wine grapes are affected by seasonal conditions:

White wines

Chardonnay Cool years cause chardonnay and most white varieties to accumulate higher levels of mineral acids and to result in lean, tight wines with potential longevity, provided they have sufficient intensity of fruit. Cool year chardonnays can display greenish flavours and can resemble grapefruit and other citrus fruit, especially lemon. Warmer year wines become richer and rounder, with fruit flavours more suggestive of apple, pear, quince and cumquat. In hot seasons, chardonnays become faster-maturing wines with flavours of peach, cashew, melon and tobacco.

Riesling Although riesling does not need to ripen to the sugar levels necessary for a premium chardonnay, cool-season riesling tends to be lean and tight with hard steely acids, possibly lacking in length and persistence of flavour. Better rieslings from superior years have succulent youthful primary fruit flavours of ripe pears and apples, with musky, citrus rind undertones. Significantly broader and less complex than wines from better seasons, warmer year rieslings tend to mature faster, occasionally becoming broad and fat on the palate after a short time.

Sauvignon Blanc Cool season sauvignon blancs tend to be hard-edged wines with steely acids, with over-exaggerated and undesirable herbaceous flavours of asparagus and cat pee, a description for which I have yet to find a polite alternative nearly as succinct. The warmer the season the riper the fruit becomes and the less grassy and vegetal the aroma. The downside is often a reduction in the intensity of the wine's primary fruit flavours. Expect sweet blackcurrants, gooseberries and passionfruit from sauvignon blancs in good seasons, with at least a light capsicum note. Warmer seasons create broader, occasionally oily and less grassy wines, with tropical fruit flavours suggestive of passionfruit and lychees.

Semillon Semillon tends to react to cooler seasons by creating very tight, lean wines with more obvious grassy influences but without much in the way of primary fruit character. On occasions these rather one-dimensional young wines can develop stunning flavours in the bottle over many years, as classically unoaked Hunter semillon shows time and again.

Red wines

Cabernet Sauvignon A late-ripening grape variety which reacts very poorly to cool, late seasons, cabernet sauvignon has traditionally and wisely been blended with varieties like merlot (in Bordeaux) and shiraz (commonly, until recently in Australia). Cool season cabernet sauvignon makes the classic doughnut wine: intense cassis/raspberry fruit at the front of the palate with greenish, extractive tannin at the back and a hole in the middle. Under-ripe cabernet sauvignon has less colour and a thin, bitter finish. Its tannins are often greenish and under-ripe, tasting sappy or metallic, while its flavour can be dominated by greenish snow pea influences more suggestive of cool-climate sauvignon blanc.

Warmer seasons create much better cabernet, with genuinely ripe cassis/plum flavours, a superior middle palate and fine-grained, fully-ripened tannins, although a slight capsicum note can still be evident. In hot years the wines tend to become jammy and porty, suggestive of stewed, cooked fruit flavours and lacking in any real definition and fineness of tannin.

Pinot Noir Pinot noir does not react well to very cool seasons, becoming herbal and leafy, with a brackish, greenish palate and simple sweet raspberry confection fruit. Warmer seasons produce the more sought-after primary characters of sweet cherries and plums, fine-grained tannins and spicy, fleshy middle palate. Too warm a season and the wine turns out to be undefined, simple and fast maturing, often with unbalanced and hard-edged tannins.

Shiraz Thin and often quite greenish – but rarely to the same extent as cabernet sauvignon – cool-season shiraz often acquires leafy white pepper characters, with spicy, herby influences. Provided there's sufficient fruit, which may not be the case in wine from cool seasons, it can still be a worthwhile wine, although not one likely to mature well in the bottle, especially with metallic, sappy and green-edged tannins. Warmer years create shiraz with characteristic richness and sweetness, with riper plum, cassis and chocolate flavours and fully-ripened tannins. Hot year shiraz is often typified by earthy flavours suggestive of bitumen and leather.

Trends in Australian wine

Right now it's almost possible to hear the wine industry's seams stretching. If you're a medium to large Australian wine company, or have designs on becoming one, the factors you're interested in are the rate of new plantings, the record overseas sales, the opportunities presented by new export markets and the economies of scale offered by large vineyards and wineries. The more vineyards out there, the better, for the cheaper their grapes will have to become. As far as tax is concerned, you're dead scared of a volumetric concept and wish to stick with the ad valorum status quo.

If, on the other hand, you're a small family grape-growing business with a set area under vine, or else a small winery in a good region with a reasonable, but not great profile, you could be worried. You're not so much interested in as preoccupied by the way that Australian grapes are being planted at many times the rate recommended by Strategy 2025, you're scared of an imminent wine surplus, you're waiting for the premium wine bubble to burst in Australia and you're worried about the likely forthcoming decline in grape prices. On the tax issue you're at dead odds with the large companies and are vigorously lobbying for a volumetric tax on wine.

Simply put, there are major issues dividing the Australian wine industry at the moment which are going to seriously test the strength and unity of the industry's representative bodies that in the main provide its access to government and the political decision-making process. Hard times are undoubtedly ahead.

To the year ending May 1999 Australian wine generated an extraordinary $961 million of export revenue. That's an increase of 22% on the previous year and the billion dollar mark is surely just around the corner. Growth by volume was only 11%, a number that isn't increasing as fast as those inserting grapes into the ground would prefer. Strangely, because much of the new plantings being developed are in the warmer irrigated river areas and because the markets both international and local are still so strong for premium wine, there's still a major shortage of quality red wine, but also a significant deficit of top-shelf chardonnay. That's an amazing thing, given the unbelievable volume of chardonnay now being produced in Australia, but is perhaps a sobering reflection that too much of our chardonnay, our shiraz and our cabernet is simply not up to the levels of our past years. There's a message here: Australian wine, especially our red, has done well overseas because of the age of our vines and because of the concentration of flavour delivered by quality fruit from quality regions. Our recent growth has rather changed the coordinates, for our vines are much, much younger, our plantings have shifted disproportionately to river areas and the average standard of most of our lesser-priced wine has actually fallen, and significantly so.

If the Federal Government actually carries out is outrageous idea of taxing cellar door sales above $300,000 it threatens to kill off both a significant employer of trained and untrained rural staff and a major fillup to tourism, an industry on which states like South Australia, Victoria and Tasmania are going to become even more dependent. I cannot believe that a Government elected to rationalise Australia's tax system and establish the settings for the next generation or two could not only perpetuate this idiocy, but establish a Wine Equalisation Tax as well.

Tasting wine

Wine tasting is essentially a play in three parts in which the third part — the tasting itself — is only entered into after a sight and a sniff. We begin by looking at the wine. Use a clear glass, shaped like a tulip and without cuts or grooves. ISO standard glasses are easy to find and strongly recommended. Grab the glass by the stem - that way the bowl stays clear and you won't warm wines above their serving temperature with the heat of your hand. Fill your glass to its widest point (actually very low for a tasting glass) and you're ready to go.

Tilt the glass against a white background, preferably in a well-lit place. The colours in the wine should now be easier to detect. White wines tend to begin life with a green colour, after which with age they move to straw and then yellow, finally to a yellow-amber and brown, at which stage it is usually time to return them to the earth from whence they came. Wood-matured whites are often released with a more advanced colour, resulting from the slow and controlled oxidation they experience in the casks, which is a form of ageing itself.

Reds begin purple, moving to purple-red, red, red-brown, and finally to that tawny brown, usually suggesting that the teeth have well and truly fallen out.

Now check for clarity and brightness. All wines should be filter-bright, as the expression goes, apart from some exceptions from unfiltered pinot noir (rare) and unfiltered chardonnay (rarer). A wine should not look cloudy, hazy, ropy, muddy or any of the colours not previously mentioned. Test this by holding up your glass and looking straight through it from (a) the sides and (b) the top. Bits of cork, crystal or sediment (usually the same colour as the wine itself) in the wine are no cause for alarm. Simply take a little care in pouring or decanting to avoid confronting them later on in the glass.

The nose is next. If you've seen the concentrated sniffing of professional tasters at work you could be forgiven for thinking there was something pretty hypnotic in those glasses. This bit looks terribly impressive, but it works.

Hold the glass by its stem and swirl the wine around once or twice. Put you nose right inside (remember, you didn't fill it to the top) and take a large sniff before the wine has stopped moving. Isn't that more intense? And don't worry, you will soon get used to the way people start looking at you.

A wine's smell can be divided into those flavours derived from its 'grapiness' or 'aroma', and those flavours which result from the wine's own development in the bottle by new flavouring compounds formed as other flavours break down and recombine within the wine, collectively known as the 'bouquet'. Young wines show a dominance of 'aroma' in their nose, while older, more developed wines can reveal almost 100% bouquet. The aromas and bouquets of classic grape varieties, like cabernet sauvignon and riesling, are remarkably consistent from wine to wine and can become quite identifiable by the drinker. It just becomes a matter of becoming familiar with what to look for.

As wine ages, its bouquet becomes less assertive as its different components blend together in a harmonious way. With excessive age, it goes flat, loses its quality and tends to become dominated by a single flavour. Wines that are too old have a dull, toffee-like nose, or may even smell like vinegar, in which case it has gone acetic.

The nose is a great aid in the detection of winemaking faults, for smells of decaying vegetables, old socks, burnt rubber, onion-skins or foreign objects often signal disaster. Some faults are tolerated a little more than others, largely because different people have different threshold level to different smells, while some of us are more tolerant of slight imperfections if the ultimate impression is generally pleasing.

Finally, have a taste. Do this with confidence and a degree of aggression. Take a good mouthful of wine; there's no sense in mucking around with a polite sip. Purse your lips slightly and suck in a little air, which will evaporate volatile wine flavours and shoot them up to the olfactory centre underneath your brain, which is where you detect smell. Once again, it's like turning up the intensity of flavour.

The tasting ability of your mouth is extremely restricted, and most of the perception of wine flavour takes place as I have just described. Apart from being able to detect hot and cool flavours like curry and mint, the tongue can only distinguish four things: sweetness at its tip, saltiness at its front sides, acidity along the sides and bitterness across the very back.

Fruit flavours are generally tasted towards the front of the mouth, where you can also detect if the wine is sweet or dry. Acidity and sweetness are frequently capable of rendering the other less noticeable, often to the point when you wonder if the other is there at all. It is also possible to mistake a wine's fruitiness for sweetness, which is a trap when trying to describe them.

Acid is essential in all wine — for in addition to the freshness and tang it gives to round off flavour, it is also a preservative against bacteria. Wines which lack acid taste fat, flabby and overly broad, before falling away and finishing short in the mouth. Try to think of acid as the punctuation which finishes the taste.

Tannins can be derived from the skins, stalks and seeds of grapes, and some can be picked up from new oak barrels if the wine is matured or fermented in wood. Although wood tannins are generally softer, both are generally detected by the rasping, bitter taste (more of a sensation, really) that puckers up the inside of your mouth as they corrode away the proteins of your mouth lining. Don't be too worried, Nobody has ever required surgery as a result.

Wines should deliver some magnitude of impact from the front of your palate — around your tooth — all the way along the palate to the back of your tongue. Furthermore, the flavour should persist after the wine has been swallowed or, if it's the expected protocol, spat out.

Finally, you should be left with the impression that all of the different facets of the wine, both textural and flavour-related, are in some form of harmony and balance. As such, there shouldn't be any single feature, such as oak for instance, which over-dominates any other. Neither should tannin, acid or any other aspect of the wine. Fruit is of course a legitimate exception to this and is the only facet of a decent wine which can lay an unchallenged claim to centre stage. Fine wines are indeed, as the cliché suggests, a harmonious balance of its constituent components. Although they may seem excessively tannic to drink at a young age, even the traditional Australian cellaring red wines based around shiraz and cabernet sauvignon must be in excellent balance not only to survive, but actually to improve with the test of time.

Investing in wine

While the space it occupies in auction catalogues shows no sign of diminishing, the prices at which Penfolds Grange now trades are considerably more realistic than during the hyped-up period of 'Grangeomania' two years ago. While it appeared that Grange might become a more important economic indicator than either gold or oil, reality has since bitten to the extent that many of the so-called 'wine investors' who bought this wine in the belief they would make an immediate killing are having to think again. Either they accept the marginally lower prices now being offered, excepting of course the absurd prices being asked for the nigh-undrinkable 1951 vintage or, heaven forbid, they might even contemplate having to drink the stuff. Dear me.

And, as I wrote last year, if Grange prices can show a decent wobble or two, there's no Australian wine so sacred it can't experience the same thing. But much to my surprise I admit, other top Australian labels are either holding onto the price gains made at auction two to three years ago, or are still moving up the scale. Wines like Mount Mary Quintet, Hill of Grace, Eileen Hardy Shiraz have shown remarkable consistency at auction, while both Jasper Hill shirazes, Grosset Polish Hill Riesling, Cullen Cabernet Merlot and Leeuwin Estate Chardonnay (1995 especially) have made strong gains very recently. Auctioneers are not expecting a repeat performance of the massive price hikes seen between 1997 and 1998 for any wine.

In facing the question of whether or not to invest in wine, little has really changed over the last twelve months. To do it effectively you need to be resourceful, patient and well equipped. The amateur collectors who are placing their superannuation in Australian wine face considerable disappointment if they lack the resources to care for it properly. You can't just shove it in the garage and start counting the dollars. To become a serious wine investor will still necessitate the taking of significant risks with wines currently rated well below blue-chip status, otherwise you'll just be dabbling in a few bottles of the super-premiums. Clearly, you need to know what you are doing. The issues of cellaring conditions and history are becoming ever more important as the market wakes up to what has been happening.

I have wondered on several occasions how the syndicated wine investment schemes are ever going to be able to get their hands on enough of the super-premiums they need to justify their existence to their stakeholders. It's one thing to have the money to buy some of these wines, but another thing entirely to get your hands on the stock.

With only a few exceptions, the extraordinary increases in retail price of current release premium Australian red wines have not been reflected in similar increases in the prices of older vintages on the auction market. There is no guarantee of high profits, even from mature wines from good vineyards and top years. The few star performers aside, only a handful of Australian wine labels have hitherto been able to guarantee a solid return to the purchaser solely motivated by a return on investment.

Most of the speculative entrants to the wine investment game should not last the distance, since the decline in Grange prices at auction will prevent most from realising the unreal returns that prompted their purchase of a few bottles of Grange, at the expense of genuine wine enthusiasts who might actually have been prepared to uncork them.

With the continuing scarcity of top-notch Australian red wine and the dramatically increased local and international demand for it, the opportunities to make a fast killing are ever diminishing. Although the Asian slowdown and record recent vintages have the potential to bite hard in the middle of the wine market, demand for the best Australian wine still far exceeds supply. Much of the best wine at Australian auctions is now purchased by overseas buyers. So, if your motives are purely financial, it's still highly speculative to buy large volumes of any Australian wine that you can still actually purchase in any significant quantity.

Nobody really expects any dramatic or ongoing plummet in Grange prices. The wine is very good, has a terrific track record and continues to pull the overseas press. A realistic approach to Grange prices in future might see a steady and continued increase in the worth of properly cellared stocks, but at a rate much slower than that witnessed in recent years.

Will there be a spate of so-called 'ultra-premium' super-cuvée wines released as companies seek the prestige and kudos that accompanies a label that performs like a star at auction? While it's difficult to pinpoint that as the sole motive behind certain wines, it was surely a factor behind the Penfolds Yattarna, the Petaluma Tiers and Clarendon Hills' Astralis. Irrespective of their quality, time alone will tell if these wines will be taken as seriously as their makers expect them to be. Australians just can't help slinging off at tall poppies.

Yattarna's release pushed the price for premium Australian chardonnay towards the $100 per bottle mark. It hasn't yet opened the pricing floodgates of other makers following suit, perhaps because there's a significant doubt entering the retail industry concerning the sustainability of current retail prices. The bubble, say many, just has to burst soon. Those makers who apply overly ambitious prices to their product may end up with egg, as well as it all over their faces.

Nobody knows for how long the Australian market can continue to absorb the skyrocketing prices of premium wine. But I have seen the expressions on the faces of regular buyers as they discover new price increases and the time is fast approaching when they won't wear much more. Not only do I anticipate the emergence of a 'new' class of quality wine priced between $20 and $30, but I expect a great deal more activity in imported wine priced between $30 to $60 as buyers look for better value.

Were I a betting man, I'd still take note of the very affordable prices for imported wines at auction and retail today, and stock up on those. Not a day goes by without them looking more and more competitive against the better level of Australian product. It's inevitable that more Australians will taste quality imported wine over the next few years and then it's just a matter of time before they want to buy it themselves. Australian wine might lose some important and influential segments of its own market.

Other than that, I'd watch closely the wines which appear on the Langton's Classification of Distinguished Australian Wine, a mechanism which has unquestionably contributed to the price increases of many Australian wine labels. Langton's claims around 60% of the Australian wine auction market and it makes perfect sense to think carefully about any new labels they promote in this way. Langton's also publishes lists of 'under-performing' companies whose wines are not considered to be realising their full potential. Consider them very seriously.

Commercial cellaring facilities

So, you've just spent the month's pay cheque at the wine auction. You're now the proud owner of an assortment of enviable beverages, say a Henschke or three, a dozen semi-ready Bin 389 from Penfolds, a box of young Dalwhinnie Shiraz and another of Cullen Cabernet Merlot. It's imperative that your investment is protected. It's a fact of modern life that few dwellings are equipped with cellars or have the potential to build one satisfactorily or cost-effectively. You would not risk a similar investment on any other sort of a whim, so it eventually dawns on you that you cannot simply depend on the vagaries of temperature change in your inner-city apartment or 1980s townhouse to safeguard your wine. What can you do?

Fortunately an increasingly large number of professionally operated wine cellaring operations are opening their doors. Several of these offer temperature and humidity-controlled conditions, while others offer a fully computerised stock management schedule with ongoing valuations.

Here's a state-by-state listing of several commercially operating wine storage centres:

New South Wales

Anders Josephson Private Wines, Gwanda Bay Manor, Gwandalan, NSW, 2259, (02) 4972 5100

Langton's Fine Wine Auctions, 52 Pitt St, Redfern, NSW, 2016, (02) 9310 4231

Millers Wine Storage, 866 Bourke St, Waterloo, NSW, 2017, (02) 9699 2300

Wine Ark, 1/3 Esther St, Surry Hills, NSW, 2010, 0417 698 860

Queensland

Millers Wine Storage, 98 Montpelier Rd, Bowen Hills, Qld, 4006, (07) 3257 3224

Millers Wine Storage, 6 Newcastle St, Burleigh Heads, Qld, 4220, (07) 5593 5993

South Australia

Adelaide Lock-Up Self Storage, cnr Adam & Holden Sts, Hindmarsh, SA, 5007, (08) 8346 4948

Glen Ewin Cellars, Lower Hermitage Rd, Houghton, SA, 5131, (08) 9380 5657

Victoria

Chequered Flag Stables, 5-7 Manikato Ave, Mordialloc, Vic, 3195, (03) 9587 6168

Langton's Fine Wine Auctions, 69 Flinders Lane, Melbourne, Vic, 3000, (03) 9662 3355

Liquid Assets, 100 Nicholson St, Abbotsford, Vic, 3067, (03) 9415 8801

Millers Wine Storage, 601 Little Collins St, Melbourne, Vic, 3000, (03) 9629 1122

WineCare Storage Centre, 28 Transport Drive, Somerton, Vic, 3062, (03) 9308 7500

Western Australia

John Coppins, 502 Stirling Hwy, Cottesloe, WA, 6011, (08) 9384 0777

Australian wineries, wines and vintages

Region: Great Southern Winemakers: Michael Staniford, Rod Hallett
Viticulturist: Wayne Lange Chief Executive: Merv Lange

Alkoomi was one of the earliest wineries in the Great Southern area of Western Australia and since its earliest days has struck a chord of consistency and longevity. Its flagship red remains its cabernet sauvignon, a tight-knit, firm, fine-grained and bony expression of the variety. Alkoomi's fragrant and limey offering is one of a collection of excellent rieslings from this emerging region.

CABERNET SAUVIGNON
Great Southern $$$

1996	14.8	2001	2004
1995	15.0	2003	2007
1994	16.8	2002	2006
1993	16.4	1998	2001
1992	16.6	1997	2000
1991	16.7		2003+
1990	17.2		2002+
1989	16.5		2001+
1988	16.0	2000	2005

CHARDONNAY
Great Southern $$$

1998	16.3	2000	2003
1997	17.9	2002	2005
1996	16.5	1998	2001
1995	16.0	1997	2000
1994	17.2	1999	2002
1993	17.5	1998	2001
1992	18.0	1997	2000
1991	18.5	1999	2003

RIESLING
Great Southern $$

1998	17.3	2006	2010
1997	17.6	2005	2009
1996	17.4	2004	2008
1995	17.4	2000	2003+
1994	18.5	2002	2006
1993	16.3	1998	2001
1992	17.6	1997	2000
1991	17.5	1996	1999
1990	16.2	1995	1998

Alkoomi
Wingeballup Road
Frankland WA 6396
Tel: (08) 9855 2229
Fax: (08) 9855 2284

All Saints
**All Saints Road
Wahgunyah Vic 3687
Tel: (02) 6033 1922
Fax: (02) 6033 3515**

SAUVIGNON BLANC
Great Southern $$$

1998	16.5	2000	2003
1997	17.2	1998	1999
1996	15.9	1997	1998
1995	16.2	1996	1999
1994	16.4	1995	1996

Region: NE Victoria   Winemaker: Peter Brown
Viticulturist: Peter Brown   Chief Executive: Peter Brown

From its magnificent vineyard site at Wahgunyah on the banks of the River Murray, All Saints produces a collection of rich, earthy regional red wines with the modern flavours of small new oak, plus a collection of eclectic regional white specialities including the spicy, early-maturing Marsanne and the Late Harvest Semillon.

CABERNET SAUVIGNON
NE Victoria $$$

1997	16.0	2002	2005
1996	15.2	1998	2001
1995	16.6	2003	2007
1994	16.7	2002	2006
1993	15.0	1998	2001
1992	17.0		2004+
1991	16.6	1999	2003

LATE HARVEST SEMILLON
NE Victoria $$

1997	14.5	1998	1999
1996	18.1	2001	2004
1995	16.4	2000	2003
1994	17.3	1996	1999
1993	17.6	1998	2001

MARSANNE
NE Victoria $$

1998	15.2	2003	2006
1997	16.2	1999	2002
1996	16.5	2001	2004
1995	15.8	1997	2000
1994	17.2	1999	2002

SHIRAZ
NE Victoria $$

1997	16.4	2002	2005
1996	16.0	1998	2001
1994	17.9	2002	2006+
1993	17.3	2001	2005
1992	16.4	2000	2004
1989	16.5	1997	2003

VINTAGE PORT
NE Victoria $$$

1996	16.8	2004	2008
1994	15.6	2002	2006
1992	17.0		2004+

Region: Lower Hunter Valley **Winemakers:** Bill Sneddon, Peter Orr
Viticulturist: Bill Sneddon **Chief Executive:** Wally Atallah

Given the vagaries of the Hunter climate, Allandale is a remarkably consistent maker of honest, reliable varietal wines of which the occasional example, like the 1996 Matthew Shiraz and Semillons from 1993 and 1996 are really quite special. Like several other Hunter-based wineries, Allandale is now sourcing cabernet sauvignon from other NSW regions.

CABERNET SAUVIGNON
Mudgee, Hilltops (formerly Lower Hunter Valley) $$

1997	15.0	2002	2005
1996	14.5	1998	2001
1994	17.0	1999	2002
1991	17.0	1999	2003
1990	14.0	1992	1995

CHARDONNAY
Lower Hunter Valley $$$

1998	16.7	2000	2003+
1997	15.7	1999	2002
1996	16.8	1998	2001
1995	17.8	2000	2003
1994	16.6	1996	1999
1993	17.0	1998	2001

Allandale
Lovedale Road
Pokolbin NSW 2320
Tel: (02) 4990 4526
Fax: (02) 4990 1714

Amberley
Thornton Rd
Yallingup WA 6282
Tel: (08) 9755 2288
Fax: (08) 9755 2171

MATTHEW SHIRAZ
Lower Hunter Valley $$$

1996	17.1	2001	2004
1994	14.7	1996	1999
1993	16.0	1998	2001
1991	17.0	1996	1999
1990	17.0	1992	1995

SEMILLON
Lower Hunter Valley $$

1998	15.9	2000	2003+
1997	16.7	2002	2005
1996	17.8	2004	2008
1995	17.0	2000	2003
1993	18.3	2001	2005
1992	17.5	1994	1997

Region: Margaret River Winemakers: Eddie Price, Greg Tilbrook
Viticulturist: Stephen James Chief Executive: Eddie Price

Its fine-grained, earthy Cabernet Merlot from 1997 and restrained, savoury Semillon Sauvignon Blanc from 1998 are two fine new releases from Amberley, whose flavoursome red and white table wines might yet see it take a higher place up the Margaret River food-chain. Amberley offers one of the best winery restaurants in a region known for high quality hospitality.

CABERNET MERLOT
Margaret River $$$

1997	17.2	2005	2009
1995	15.8	2000	2003
1994	16.1		2006+
1993	17.4	2001	2005
1992	17.6	2000	2004
1991	16.6	1999	2003

CHARDONNAY
Margaret River $$$

1997	15.6	1998	1999
1996	15.2	1997	1998
1995	16.2	1997	2000

SEMILLON
Margaret River $$$

1998	15.2	1998	2001
1997	15.0	1998	1999
1996	16.7	2001	2004
1995	16.5	1997	2000
1994	17.3	1999	2002
1993	16.6	1998	2001
1992	16.8	1997	2000
1991	16.2	1992	1993

SEMILLON SAUVIGNON BLANC
Margaret River $$$

1998	17.3	2001	2004
1997	16.6	1998	1999
1996	18.5	1998	2001
1995	14.6	1996	1997
1994	16.8	1996	1999
1993	16.7	1998	2001

SHIRAZ
Margaret River $$$

1997	16.2	1999	2002+
1996	18.0	2004	2008
1995	14.8	1997	2000
1994	14.0	1996	1999

Region: McLaren Vale Winemaker: Phillip Reschke
Viticulturist: Chris Dundon Chief Executive: Ray King

As the bright and zesty 1998 Sauvignon Blanc Semillon reveals, the wines sold under the Andrew Garrett brand are generous, intensely flavoured and genuinely varietal. This Mildara Blass brand is one of the more reliable names in its price bracket.

Andrew Garrett
Kangarilla Road
McLaren Vale SA 5171
Tel: (08) 8323 8853
Fax: (08) 8323 8271

BOLD SHIRAZ
McLaren Vale $$

1997	16.0	1999	2002
1996	15.7	1998	2001
1994	16.3	1996	1999
1993	17.3	1998	2001
1992	17.1	1997	2000
1991	16.8	1996	1999

Annie's Lane

Quelltaler Estate
Quelltaler Road
Watervale SA 5452
Tel: (08) 8843 0003
Fax: (08) 8843 0096

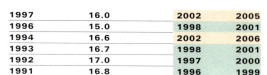

CABERNET MERLOT

Coonawarra, Adelaide Hills, McLaren Vale $$

1997	16.0	2002	2005
1996	15.0	1998	2001
1994	16.6	2002	2006
1993	16.7	1998	2001
1992	17.0	1997	2000
1991	16.8	1996	1999

CHARDONNAY

McLaren Vale, Padthaway $$

1998	16.5	1999	2000
1997	16.0	1998	1999
1996	15.0	1997	1998
1995	17.6	2000	2003
1994	15.8	1996	1999
1993	17.5	1994	1995

SAUVIGNON BLANC SEMILLON (FORMERLY SAUVIGNON BLANC)

Padthaway $$

1998	17.5	1999	2000
1996	14.8	1996	1997
1995	16.5	1996	1997
1994	16.2	1996	1999

Region: Clare Valley Winemakers: David O'Leary, Allen Hart
Viticulturist: Peter Pawelski Chief Executive: Ray King

Annie's Lane has quickly become one of the best Mildara Blass brands. Based around some excellent Clare Valley vineyards and the winemaking skills of David O'Leary, its wines are rich, generous and simply packed with fruit. While each of the Shiraz and Cabernet Merlot are modern, ripe and generously oaked, the reserve 'The Contour' Shiraz from 1995 is exceptional.

CABERNET MERLOT

Clare Valley $$$

1997	16.0	2002	2005
1996	15.0	1998	2001
1995	18.3	2003	2007

THE ONWINE AUSTRALIAN WINE ANNUAL

CHARDONNAY
Clare Valley $$$

1998	16.2	2000	2003
1997	16.9	1999	2001
1996	18.3	1998	2001

SHIRAZ
Clare Valley $$$

1997	16.8	2002	2005
1996	17.0	2001	2004
1995	16.4	2000	2003

Region: Adelaide Hills Winemaker: Stephen George
Viticulturist: Stephen George Chief Executive: Stephen George

Its Riesling is a distinctive, individual wine whose fragrant musky aromas often precede a thick, almost syrupy palate brightly flavoured with lime, apple and pear, but its Pinot Noir is the main cause of my steadily increasing respect for Stephen George's winemaking activities at Ashton Hills. Here's a wine for the Burgundy freak - wild, sappy and supple, with a depth of pure red and black cherry fruit that entirely belies the wine's poise and elegance. Tight, fine-grained and surprisingly firm, it now heads the pack from the Adelaide Hills.

CHARDONNAY
Adelaide Hills $$$$

1997	16.7	2002	2005
1996	15.4	1997	1998
1995	17.0	1996	1997
1993	18.5	1998	2001
1992	15.4	1997	2000

OBLIQUA
Adelaide Hills $$$

1996	16.7	2004	2008
1994	17.6	1999	2002
1992	16.2	1997	2000
1991	18.6	1999	2003
1990	18.3	1998	2002
1989	15.0	1994	1997
1988	15.5	1991	1993

Ashton Hills Vineyard
Tregarthen Road
Ashton SA 5137
Tel: (08) 8390 1243
Fax: (08) 8390 1243

PINOT NOIR
Adelaide Hills $$$$

1997	18.9	2002	2005+
1996	18.6	2001	2004
1995	18.3	2000	2003
1994	18.6	2002	2006
1993	18.3	1998	2001

RIESLING
Adelaide Hills $$

1998	18.1	2006	2010
1997	18.4	2005	2009
1996	17.2	2004	2008
1995	15.0	1997	2000
1994	18.3	1999	2002
1993	18.3	1998	2001
1992	16.5	1997	2000
1991	18.0	1996	1999
1990	17.0	1995	1998

SALMON BRUT
Adelaide Hills $$$$

1995	17.0	1997	2000
1994	15.1	1996	1999
1993	16.4	1998	2001

Baileys

**Taminick Gap Rd
Glenrowan Vic 3675
Tel: (03) 5766 2392
Fax: (03) 5766 2596**

Region: NE Victoria Winemaker: Allan Hart
Viticulturist: Damien de Castella Chief Executive: Ray King

Mildara Blass has revitalised the Baileys label with this traditional expression of northeast Victorian shiraz, whose smoky, chocolate oak gives it something of a contemporary flavour. The 1920s Block Shiraz won't disappoint those buying for well into the future.

1920S BLOCK SHIRAZ
NE Victoria $$$

1997	16.3	2002	2005
1996	16.5	2001	2004
1995	15.8	2000	2003
1994	18.0		2006+
1993	16.2	1998	2001
1992	17.2	2000	2004
1991	18.4		2003+

Region: Bendigo Winemaker: Lindsay Ross
Viticulturist: Lindsay Ross Chief Executive: Lindsay Ross

Balgownie
**Hermitage Road
Maiden Gully Vic 3551
Tel: (03) 5449 6222
Fax: (03) 5449 6506**

The Forrester family recently purchased Balgownie from Mildara Blass, with Lindsay Ross staying on to operate the business, vineyard and winery. The vineyard is shortly to be extended to nearly double its existing area of around 20 acres, to include small parcels of viognier, sangiovese, merlot and petit verdot. I think the future looks very bright for Balgownie, a vineyard still regarded with much respect and affection by those in the know.

ESTATE CABERNET SAUVIGNON

Bendigo $$$

1997	17.6	2009	2017
1996	18.5		2008+
1994	18.0		2006+
1993	17.7		2005+
1992	18.3		2004+
1990	18.6		2002+
1989	17.0	1997	2001
1988	18.5		2008+
1987	16.0	1995	1999
1986	18.0		1998+
1985	17.0		2005+
1984	15.0	1992	1996
1983	14.0	1988	1991
1982	14.5	1987	1990
1981	15.0	1993	1998
1980	19.0	2000	2005
1979	14.5	1984	1987
1978	18.0	1990	1995
1977	16.0	1985	1989
1976	19.0		1996+

ESTATE SHIRAZ

Bendigo $$$

1997	18.2		2009+
1996	18.0	2004	2008+
1995	18.5		2007+
1994	17.3	2002	2006
1993	18.2		2005+
1990	18.4		2002+
1989	16.0	1994	1997
1988	18.0	1993	1996
1987	16.0	1992	1995
1986	17.0	1991	1994
1985	16.0	1993	1997
1984	15.0	1989	1992

Bannockburn

Box 72 Midland Hwy
Bannockburn Vic 3331
Tel: (03) 5281 1363
Fax: (03) 5281 1349

Region: Geelong Winemaker: Gary Farr
Viticulturist: Lucas Grigsby

Since the early 1980s Bannockburn has been at the forefront of Australian chardonnay and pinot noir. Gary Farr's techniques are taken from his regular winemaking experiences in Burgundy and he has adopted Domaine Dujac's approach towards the use of stems during pinot noir fermentation. Most of Bannockburn's pinot noirs reveal a herbal, stalky note during their youth, but this usually eases back and marries with the intense red cherry and spicy plum fruit which its mature vineyards typically deliver.

CHARDONNAY

Geelong $$$$

1997	17.8	2005	2009
1996	18.6	2001	2004
1995	19.1	1997	2000
1994	18.7	2002	2006
1993	18.9	2001	2005
1992	18.5	2000	2004
1991	18.3	1996	1999
1990	18.5		2002+
1989	18.6	1997	2001
1988	18.6	1996	2000
1987	18.5	1999	2004
1986	18.3	1994	1998

PINOT NOIR

Geelong $$$$

1997	19.1	2005	2009
1996	18.7	2004	2008
1995	18.4	2000	2003
1994	18.6	2002	2006+
1993	18.4	1998	2001+
1992	16.5	2000	2004
1991	17.9	1999	2003
1990	18.5	1998	2002
1989	18.6	1994	1997
1988	18.5	1996	2000
1987	17.0	1995	1999
1986	17.5	1994	1998

SERRÉ PINOT NOIR

Geelong $$$$$

1994	18.5	2002	2006+
1993	17.0	2001	2005
1991	13.0	1993	1996

2000 THE ONWINE AUSTRALIAN WINE ANNUAL

SHIRAZ
Geelong $$$$

1997	18.2	2005	2009
1996	18.1	2004	2008
1995	16.0	2000	2003
1994	18.8	2002	2006
1993	17.2	1998	2001
1992	18.7	2000	2004
1991	18.5		2003+
1990	17.0	1998	2002

SRH CHARDONNAY
Geelong $$$$$

1995	18.5	1997	2000
1994	18.2	1996	1999
1993	19.3	1998	2001

Region: Barossa Valley Winemaker: Natasha Mooney
Chief Executive: Bruce Richardson

There's an uncompromising honesty and openness about the E & E red wines, two richly flavoured variants of the traditional Barossa shiraz theme. The Ebenezer wines are consistently generous, flavoursome and uncomplicated, ready to drink on arrival.

E & E BLACK PEPPER SHIRAZ
Barossa Valley $$$$$

1996	17.7	2004	2008
1995	17.7	2000	2003
1994	18.7	2002	2006
1993	18.2	2001	2005
1992	17.2	2000	2004
1991	18.8		2003+
1990	18.0		2002+
1989	17.0		2001+
1988	18.0	2000	2005

E & E SPARKLING SHIRAZ
Barossa Valley $$$$$

1995	17.6	2000	2003
1994	17.9	1999	2002+
1993	16.8	1998	2001

THE ONWINE AUSTRALIAN WINE ANNUAL

Barossa Valley Estate
Heaslip Road
Angle Vale SA 5117
Tel: (08) 8284 7000
Fax: (08) 8284 7219

EBENEZER CHARDONNAY

Barossa Valley $$$

1998	15.9	1999	2000
1997	16.0	1998	1999
1996	16.0	1998	1999

EBENEZER DRY RED BLEND

Barossa Valley $$$

1997	14.5	1999	2002
1996	17.6	2001	2004
1994	16.2	1996	1999
1993	14.0	1994	1995
1992	17.0	1997	2000
1991	17.6	1999	2003

EBENEZER SHIRAZ

Barossa Valley $$$

1996	16.6	2001	2004
1995	17.8	2000	2003
1994	17.5	1999	2002
1993	15.8	1998	2001
1992	16.0	1997	2000

Barwang

Greenacre NSW 2190
Tel: (02) 9722 1200
Fax: (02) 9707 4408

Region: Hilltops Winemaker: Jim Brayne
Viticulturist: Murray Pulleine Chief Executive: Kevin McLintock

The Barwang vineyard in NSW's Hilltops region has become one of the jewels in the McWilliams crown. Its creamy Chardonnay, wild and brambly Shiraz, and tight-knit, dark-fruited Cabernet Sauvignon consistently outpoint many wines several times their prices.

CABERNET SAUVIGNON

Hilltops $$$

1997	18.3	2005	2009+
1996	16.0	2001	2004
1995	16.7	2003	2007
1994	17.3	2002	2006
1993	17.6	2001	2005
1992	17.0	2000	2004
1991	18.6	1999	2003
1990	15.8		2002+

CHARDONNAY

Hilltops $$$

1997	17.2	2002	2005
1996	17.9	2001	2004
1995	16.5	1997	2000
1994	17.5	1996	1999
1993	16.9	1995	1998
1992	16.0	1994	1997

SHIRAZ

Hilltops $$$

1997	18.4	2005	2009
1996	16.3	1998	2001
1995	18.2	2003	2005
1994	17.8	1999	2002
1993	18.3	1998	2001
1992	16.8	2000	2004
1991	17.8	1999	2003
1990	15.5	1998	2002

Region: South Gippsland **Winemaker:** Phillip Jones
Viticulturist: Keith Barrow **Chief Executive:** Phillip Jones

Lesson Number One in how to make yourself unpopular with your friends is to tell them you recently drank a bottle of Bass Phillip. Although its output remains frustratingly small, especially to owner/winemaker Phillip Jones, Bass Phillip continues to amaze for its quality. The incredibly scarce 1997 wines are perhaps the vineyard's best yet and Jones even made two barriques of Reserve! Jones' secrets are incredibly mean yields, an absence of irrigation and careful selection within his multi-clonal vineyard. Pinot noir punters keenly await the day that Jones' new developments around Leongatha come to full fruition.

Bass Phillip
Tosch's Rd
Leongatha South Vic 3953
Tel: (03) 5664 3341
Fax: (03) 5664 3209

PREMIUM PINOT NOIR

South Gippsland $$$$$

1997	18.7	2002	2005+
1996	18.6	2004	2008
1995	18.6	2003	2007
1994	18.4	2002	2006
1993	18.6	1998	2001+
1992	18.5		2004+
1991	18.0	1996	1999
1990	15.3	1992	1995
1989	18.4	1997	2001

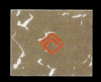

Best's

1Km off Western Highway
Great Western Vic 3377
Tel: (03) 5356 2250
Fax: (03) 5356 2430

RESERVE PINOT NOIR

South Gippsland $$$$$

1997	19.2		2009+
1996	18.8	2004	2008
1995	19.0	2003	2007
1994	19.0	2002	2006
1991	18.8		2003+
1989	18.6	1997	2001
1988	15.4	1996	2000

Region: Grampians/Great Western Winemakers: Viv Thomson, Michael Unwin
Viticulturist: Ben Thomson Chief Executive: Viv Thomson

Here's a vineyard about to burst into the limelight. Given that many of its vines are well over a century old, it's hardly a newcomer to the scene, but Best's is doing something very, very special with shiraz. If you can't afford the simply incredible Thomson Family Shiraz, be sure to find some 'standard' Bin 0. The sheer intensity and fineness of sour cherry and plum fruit, together with spicy, peppery complexity in both of these wines easily rivals that of the most prestigious Australian vineyards.

BIN 'O' SHIRAZ

Grampians, Great Western $$$

1996	18.6	2004	2008+
1995	18.5	2003	2007
1993	17.0	1998	2001
1992	18.1		2004+
1991	17.6	1999	2003
1990	17.8	1995	1998
1989	16.0	1994	1997
1988	18.0		2000+
1987	15.8	1995	1999

CABERNET SAUVIGNON

Grampians/Great Western $$$

1997	17.0	2005	2009+
1996	16.6	1998	2001
1995	17.0		2007+
1993	16.2	2001	2005
1992	18.3		2004+
1991	17.2		2003+
1990	17.8	1998	2002
1989	15.0	1991	1994
1988	17.8	1996	2000

CHARDONNAY
Grampians/Great Western $$$

1997	16.5	2002	2005
1996	16.7	1998	2001
1995	18.1	2003	2007
1994	18.4		2006+
1993	16.0	1998	2001
1992	16.6	1997	2000
1991	17.9		2003+
1990	17.5		2002+

PINOT MEUNIER
Grampians/Great Western $$$

1995	16.4	2003	2007
1994	16.8	2002	2006
1993	15.0	1998	2001
1992	16.8	1997	2000
1991	16.7	1996	1999
1990	16.0	1995	1998
1989	16.5	1994	1997
1988	16.8	1993	1996

PINOT NOIR
Grampians/Great Western $$$

1997	15.0	2002	2005
1996	16.7	2001	2004
1994	15.8	1996	1999
1993	16.2	1998	2001
1992	15.9	1997	2000
1991	15.2	1999	2003

RIESLING
Grampians/Great Western $$

1998	16.5	2003	2006
1997	15.0	1999	2002
1996	16.8	1998	2001
1995	18.3	2003	2007
1994	18.4		2006+
1993	15.1	1995	1998
1992	16.8	2000	2004
1991	16.0	1999	2003
1990	17.5	1998	2002
1989	14.3	1991	1994
1988	17.0		2000+

Bethany

Bethany Road
Bethany via Tanunda SA
5352
Tel: (08) 8563 2086
Fax: (08) 8563 0046

THOMSON FAMILY SHIRAZ

Grampians, Great Western $$$$$

1996	19.1	2008	2012
1995	19.1	2007	2015
1994	18.7	2006	2014
1992	18.8	2004	2012

Region: Barossa Valley Winemakers: Paul Bailey, Geoff & Robert Schrapel
Viticulturists: Geoff & Robert Schrapel Chief Executives: Geoff & Robert Schrapel

Bethany's recent vintages of red wine are earlier maturing wines than those on which the company made its name in the late 1980s and early 1990s, but will certainly appeal to those who enjoy the soft, creamy textures and bright cherry/plum fruit of traditional Barossa red.

CABERNET MERLOT

Barossa Valley $$

1997	14.7	1999	2002
1996	16.5	2001	2004
1995	16.2	1997	2000
1994	17.0	2002	2006
1993	15.0	1995	1998
1992	16.6	1997	2000
1991	18.0	1999	2003
1990	17.2	1998	2002

CHARDONNAY

Barossa Valley $$

1997	14.8	1998	1999
1996	15.8	1998	2001
1995	14.7	1997	2000
1994	17.4	1996	1999

GRENACHE PRESSINGS

Barossa Valley $$

1998	16.3	2000	2003
1996	16.7	1998	2001
1995	15.0	1996	1997
1994	16.2	1996	1999
1993	16.5	1998	2001
1992	16.2	1994	1997

RIESLING
Barossa Valley $$

1997	15.8	1998	1999
1996	17.0	2001	2004
1995	16.2	2000	2003
1994	16.2	1996	1999
1993	17.0	1995	1998
1992	17.5	1997	2000
1991	16.4	1991	1993

SELECT LATE HARVEST CUT RIESLING
Barossa Valley $$$

1997	17.1	2002	2005
1996	17.6	2001	2004
1995	16.0	1997	2000
1994	18.2	1999	2002
1993	17.8	1998	2001
1992	17.5	1994	1997

SHIRAZ
Barossa Valley $$

1997	16.1	2002	2005
1996	16.3	1998	2001
1995	16.0	1997	2000
1994	17.0	1999	2002
1993	16.0	1995	1998
1992	18.2	2000	2004
1991	16.9	1999	2003
1990	18.3	1998	2002
1989	17.0	1994	1997
1988	10.2	1996	2000
1987	16.8	1995	1999

WOOD-AGED SEMILLON
Barossa Valley $$

1996	14.5	1997	1998
1995	16.3	2000	2003
1994	16.3	1996	1999
1993	18.0	1998	2001
1992	16.8	1997	2000
1991	16.5	1993	1996

Bindi

145 Melton Rd
Gisborne Vic 3437
Tel: (03) 5428 2564
Fax: (03) 5428 2564

Region: Macedon Winemakers: Stuart Anderson, Michael Dhillon
Viticulturist: Bill Dhillon Chief Executive: Bill Dhillon

Bindi continues to establish itself as one of the country's most important new chardonnay and pinot noir vineyards. Its terroir encourages musky, spicy flavours to emerge within its velvet-smooth pinot noir, while its chardonnay develops a characteristic spiciness and brightness of fruit, before a long, mineral finish.
These qualities are superbly expressed in the new 'reserve' selections of Block 5 Pinot Noir 1997 and Quartz Chardonnay 1995.

CHARDONNAY
Macedon $$$$

1997	18.1	2002	2005
1996	16.8	1998	2001
1995	18.6	2003	2007
1994	18.3	1999	2002
1993	17.6	1998	2001

PINOT NOIR
Macedon $$$$

1997	18.3	2002	2005
1996	18.3	2004	2008
1995	18.5	2000	2003
1994	18.5	2002	2006

Blackjack

Calder Highway
Harcourt Vic 3453
Tel: (03) 5474 2355
Fax: (03) 5474 2355

Region: Bendigo Winemakers: Ian McKenzie, Ken Pollock
Viticulturist: Ian McKenzie Chief Executive: Ian McKenzie

Blackjack's fine form with the warm 1997 vintage confirms that it is a label to watch for in coming years as more of its vines mature. The early vintages of both red wines reveal encouraging longevity, with ripe dark berry fruit, balanced oak and firm, robust tannins.

CABERNET MERLOT
Bendigo $$$

1997	17.0	2005	2009
1996	16.1	2001	2004
1995	15.5	1997	2000
1994	15.0	1996	1999

SHIRAZ
Bendigo $$$

1997	17.0	2002	2005
1996	17.0	2001	2004
1995	15.0	1997	2000
1994	16.8	2002	2006
1993	16.5	1998	2001

Bleasdale

Wellington Road
Langhorne Creek SA 5255
Tel: (08) 8537 3001
Fax: (08) 8537 3224

Region: Langhorne Creek Winemaker: Michael Potts
Viticulturist: Robert Potts Chief Executive: Michael Potts

A plush, smooth and creamy 1997 Bremerview Shiraz is the highlight of a typically ripe, honest and very consistent range of Bleasdale red wines. This vintage also represents the third excellent release on the trot for the premier Frank Potts label.

BREMERVIEW SHIRAZ
Langhorne Creek $$

1997	17.8	2005	2009
1996	16.7	2001	2004
1995	17.0	2000	2003
1993	15.0	1995	1998
1992	16.6	2000	2004
1991	16.7	1999	2003
1988	16.6	1996	2000

FRANK POTTS BLEND
Langhorne Creek $$$

1997	17.2	2005	2009
1996	17.9	2004	2008+
1995	17.8	2003	2007
1994	16.0	1999	2002
1992	14.8	1994	1997

MALBEC
Langhorne Creek $$

1998	16.5	2000	2003
1997	15.5	1998	2001
1996	15.3	1998	2001
1994	16.4	1999	2003
1992	14.9	1997	2000
1990	16.5	1995	1998
1989	16.5	1994	1997

MULBERRY TREE CABERNET SAUVIGNON
Langhorne Creek $$

1998	16.4	2003	2006
1997	16.4	2002	2005+
1996	16.8	2004	2008
1995	15.0	1997	2000
1993	16.0	2001	2005
1992	16.8	2000	2004

THE ONWINE AUSTRALIAN WINE ANNUAL 2000

Blue Pyrenees Estate

**Vinoca Rd
Avoca Vic 3467
Tel: (03) 5465 3202
Fax: (03) 5465 3529**

Region: Pyrenees Winemaker: Kim Hart
Viticulturist: Kim Hart Chief Executive: Kim Hart

Blue Pyrenees Estate is a remarkable vineyard development in the Pyrenees area of Victoria, not only for its sheer scale in a region mainly populated by small vineyards, but for the extent to which the plantings have been classified and analysed, before being married to specific grape varieties for particular wines. The result is that from a single planting, which varies considerably in altitude and in ripening time, Kim Hart can select from a multitude of fruit components for the vineyard's under-rated still and sparkling wines.

CHARDONNAY
Pyrenees $$$$

1997	18.0	2002	2005
1996	17.6	2001	2004+
1995	16.6	1997	2000
1994	16.8	1999	2002

RED BLEND
Pyrenees $$$$

1996	18.1	2008	2016
1995	18.0	2003	2007
1994	18.6		2006+
1993	18.4	2001	2005
1992	17.8	2000	2004
1991	18.3	1999	2003
1990	18.4	2002	2010
1989	16.8	1994	1997
1988	18.5	2000	2008
1986	18.2	1994	1998
1985	16.1	1993	1997
1984	15.0	1992	1996
1982	16.0	1990	1994

Botobolar

**Botobolar Lane
Mudgee NSW 2850
Tel: (02) 6373 3840
Fax: (02) 6373 3789**

Region: Mudgee Winemaker: Kevin Karstrom
Viticulturist: Kevin Karstrom Chief Executive: Trina Karstrom

Botobolar is an organic vineyard in Mudgee whose wines depend more than most on seasonal conditions around ripening and harvest. Of course this doesn't prevent it from releasing red and white wines that are simply delicious, if indeed a little different.

CABERNET SAUVIGNON
Mudgee $$

1997	16.2	2002	2005
1992	17.5		2004+
1991	18.0	1999	2003
1990	16.7	1992	1995
1989	17.9	1997	2001
1988	14.6	1989	1990
1987	18.0	1995	1999

CABERNET SHIRAZ MOURVEDRE (FORMERLY ST GILBERT DRY RED)

Mudgee $$

1996	15.2	1998	2001
1991	16.0	1999	2003
1990	16.8	1998	2002
1989	17.9	1997	2001

CHARDONNAY

Mudgee $$$

1997	17.0	1999	2002
1995	15.0	1996	1997
1994	16.6	1996	1999
1993	18.0	1998	2001
1992	17.2	1997	2000

MARSANNE

Mudgee $$

1997	15.7	1999	2002
1996	16.8	1998	2001
1995	16.1	1997	2000
1994	16.5	1999	2002
1993	17.8	1998	2001
1992	17.5	1997	2000

SHIRAZ

Mudgee $$

1997	15.2	1999	2002
1996	15.0	1998	2001
1992	18.0	2000	2004
1991	16.0	1999	2003
1990	16.3	1995	1998
1989	18.3	1997	2001

Bowen Estate

Riddoch Highway
Coonawarra SA 5263
Tel: (08) 8737 2229
Fax: (08) 8737 2173

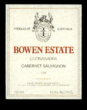

Region: Coonawarra Winemaker: Doug Bowen
Viticulturist: Doug Bowen Chief Executive: Joy Bowen

Doug Bowen deliberately crops well below the Coonawarra average to encourage his ever-expanding vineyard to produce small, concentrated crops which he then fashions into deeply flavoured, expressive wines. The 1997 red wines display fresh, lively fruit flavours, but lack the structure and depth of the excellent and classically proportioned collection from 1996.

CABERNET MERLOT CABERNET FRANC

Coonawarra $$

1997	16.2	1999	2002
1995	15.8	2000	2003
1994	15.0	1999	2002
1993	16.5	1998	2001
1992	18.0	2000	2004
1991	17.8	1999	2003
1990	18.0	1995	1998
1988	16.5	1993	1996

CABERNET SAUVIGNON

Coonawarra $$$

1997	16.6	2002	2005
1996	18.6	2004	2008
1995	15.3	2000	2003
1994	17.1	2002	2006
1993	15.4	1998	2001
1992	18.0		2004+
1991	18.0	1999	2003
1990	18.5	1995	1998
1989	17.5	1994	1997
1988	16.0	1990	1993
1984	18.8	1996	2004

CHARDONNAY

Coonawarra $$

1998	16.0	1999	2000
1996	16.7	2001	2004
1995	14.9	1997	2000
1994	17.5	1996	1999
1993	17.8	1998	2001
1992	16.6	1994	1997

SHIRAZ
Coonawarra $$$

1997	17.3	2002	2005
1996	18.3	2001	2004
1995	17.0	2003	2007
1994	18.0	2002	2006
1993	18.5	2001	2005
1992	18.6	2000	2004
1991	18.3	1996	1999
1990	16.0	1998	2002
1989	17.5	1994	1997
1988	16.5	1993	1996

Region: NE Vic - Alpine Valleys Winemaker: Kel Boynton
Viticulturist: Kel Boynton Chief Executive: Kel Boynton

Hampered by extreme difficulties related to the seals of his 1997 white wines which were not of natural cork, Kel Boynton's cool climate wines are nevertheless polished and refined, especially the flagship Cabernet Sauvignon, which does brilliantly well in warmer seasons like 1994 and 1997.

CABERNET SAUVIGNON
NE Vic - Alpine Valleys $$$

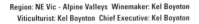

Boynton's Of Bright
**Ovens Valley Highway
Porepunkah Vic 3740
Tel: (03) 5756 2356
Fax: (03) 5756 2610**

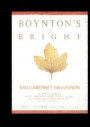

1997	17.4	2005	2009
1996	15.7	2001	2004
1995	13.6	1997	2000
1994	18.3	2002	2006
1993	18.2		2005+
1992	17.9	2000	2004
1991	16.0	1996	1999
1990	18.6	1998	2002
1089	16.0	1994	1997

CHARDONNAY
Ne Vic - Alpine Valleys $$$

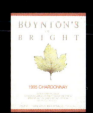

1998	16.2	2000	2003
1996	15.4	1998	2001
1995	14.8	1996	1997
1994	16.8	1999	2002
1993	16.6	1995	1998
1992	16.4	1994	1997

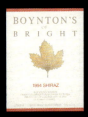

Brand's
Main Rd
Coonawarra SA 5263
Tel: (08) 8736 3260
Fax: (08) 8736 3208

SHIRAZ
NE Vic - Alpine Valleys $$$

1997	16.0	2002	2005
1995	14.0	1996	1997
1994	17.6	1999	2002
1993	17.1	1998	2001
1992	17.5	1997	2000
1991	16.3	1996	1999
1990	18.5	1995	1998
1989	18.0	1997	2001
1988	17.0	1993	1996

Region: Coonawarra Winemakers: Jim Brayne, Jim Brand
Viticulturist: Bill Brand Chief Executive: Kevin McLintock

Brand's has turned the corner with some delicious reds, especially Shiraz and Cabernet Sauvignon from the 1997 vintage. They're a mile from the popular heavyweight public image of Australian red, but simply bursting with bright, translucent dark berry fruits. I'm really interested in the new premium labels of Eric's Blend 1996 (of cabernet sauvignon, shiraz and malbec) and Stentifords Reserve Shiraz 1995, from the company's under-used old vine resources.

CABERNET MERLOT
Coonawarra $$$

1997	16.0	2002	2005
1996	14.9	2001	2004
1995	16.7	2000	2003
1994	16.3	1996	1999
1993	16.0	1995	1998
1992	16.8	1997	2000
1991	18.2	1999	2003
1990	17.4	1998	2002
1988	18.0	1993	1996
1987	16.5	1992	1995

CABERNET SAUVIGNON
Coonawarra $$$

1997	17.2	2002	2005
1996	14.9	1998	2001
1995	16.1	2000	2003
1994	17.4	1999	2002
1993	18.0	1998	2001
1992	14.8	1994	1997
1991	15.5	1993	1996
1990	16.9	1992	1995

THE ONWINE AUSTRALIAN WINE ANNUAL

CHARDONNAY
Coonawarra $$

1997	16.4	1999	2002
1996	15.7	1998	2001
1995	16.4	2000	2003
1994	16.0	1996	1999
1993	17.8	1998	2001
1992	17.8	1997	2000
1991	18.3	1996	1999

SHIRAZ
Coonawarra $$$

1997	17.5	2002	2005
1996	16.7	1998	2001
1995	15.7	1997	2000
1994	14.9	1996	1999
1993	16.3	1995	1998
1992	16.8	1997	2000
1991	16.8	1993	1996

Region: Clare Valley Winemaker: Brian Barry
Viticulturist: Brian Barry Chief Executive: Brian Barry

Brian Barry's rieslings are a Clare Valley benchmark, but stand out as a different, softer, more spicy and appley style from many of his region's counterparts. Typically firm and robust, his Cabernet Sauvignon is made for an extended spell in the cellar.

Brian Barry

**Farrell Flat Road
Clare SA 5343**
Tel: (08) 8363 6211
Fax: (08) 8362 0498

JUDS HILL CABERNET SAUVIGNON
Clare Valley $$$

1996	16.8		2008+
1995	16.6		2007+
1994	16.0		2006+
1993	15.2	1995	1998

JUDS HILL RIESLING
Clare Valley $$$

1998	18.5	2003	2006+
1997	14.6	1998	1999
1996	18.2	2001	2004+
1995	18.0	2003	2007
1994	18.6	2002	2006

Briar Ridge

Mount View Road
Mount View NSW 2325
Tel: (02) 4990 3670
Fax: (02) 4990 7802

Region: Lower Hunter Valley Winemakers: Neil McGuigan, Karl Stockhausen
Viticulturist: Derek Smith Chief Executive: Neil McGuigan

A serious maker of classic regional Hunter Valley styles, Briar Ridge fashions a refined, unwooded semillon, a complex, heavily worked chardonnay and an earthy, astringent shiraz made by Hunter Valley legend Karl Stockhausen, of which the spicy, concentrated 1997 wine is nothing short of a regional classic.

CHARDONNAY
Lower Hunter Valley $$$

1998	17.0	2000	2003+
1997	16.5	1999	2002
1996	18.0	2001	2004
1995	18.0	2003	2007
1994	17.2	1999	2002
1993	18.1	1998	2001
1992	15.8	1994	1997

SEMILLON
Lower Hunter Valley $$$

1998	18.4	2003	2006+
1997	16.6	1999	2002
1996	17.0	1998	2001
1995	16.8	2003	2007
1994	18.2	2002	2006
1993	18.3	1998	2001
1992	17.6	1994	1997
1991	17.8	1996	1999

STOCKHAUSEN HERMITAGE
Lower Hunter Valley $$$

1997	18.5	2005	2009
1996	15.3	2001	2004
1995	17.8	2007	2015
1994	16.4	1999	2002
1993	18.0	2001	2005
1992	17.8	2000	2004
1991	17.7	1996	1999
1990	14.5	1992	1995
1989	17.0	1994	1997
1988	16.5	1993	1996
1987	15.0	1995	1999

Bridgewater Mill

**Mount Barker Road
Bridgewater SA 5155
Tel: (08) 8339 3422
Fax: (08) 8339 5311**

Region: Various SA Winemakers: Brian Croser, Con Moshos
Viticulturist: Mike Harms Chief Executive: Brian Croser

Bridgewater Mill is a bistro-style label made by Brian Croser's team at the Petaluma winery. The ripe, punchy flavours of the Sauvignon Blanc and Chardonnay are ideally suited to early drinking, while no matter how appealing it may be at release, the earthy, bony Millstone Shiraz does reward a short spell in the cellar.

CHARDONNAY
McLaren Vale, Clare Valley, etc $$$

1997	16.6	1999	2002
1996	15.8	1998	2001
1995	17.1	1997	2000
1994	16.7	1996	1999
1993	18.1	1995	1998
1992	17.0	1997	2000
1987	15.0	1992	1995

MILLSTONE SHIRAZ
McLaren Vale $$$

1996	17.2	2001	2004
1995	16.5	2000	2003
1994	17.4	1999	2002
1993	17.8	2001	2005
1992	18.1	1997	2000
1991	16.5	1996	1999

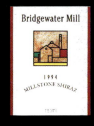

SAUVIGNON BLANC
Coonawarra, Clare, McLaren Vale, Langhorne Creek $$$

1998	16.0		1999
1997	17.5	1998	1999
1996	17.6	1997	1998
1995	16.7	1996	1997

Brokenwood

McDonalds Road
Pokolbin NSW 2320
Tel: (02) 4998 7559
Fax: (02) 4998 7893

Region: Lower Hunter Valley Winemakers: Iain Riggs, Dan Dineen
Chief Executive: Iain Riggs

Brokenwood is an important Hunter Valley winery that gets every possible benefit from the excellent semillon and shiraz vineyards available to it in the Hunter Valley, but isn't afraid to look elsewhere for the material which makes up its Cabernet Sauvignon and Chardonnay. The Graveyard is an Australian benchmark.

CABERNET SAUVIGNON

McLaren Vale, Coonawarra, King Valley $$$

1997	17.0	2000	2005
1996	16.3	2004	2008
1994	17.3	2002	2006
1992	18.0	2000	2004
1991	18.1	1996	1999
1990	17.8	1995	1998
1989	17.0	1994	1997
1988	17.0	1993	1996
1987	16.0	1992	1995

CHARDONNAY

McLaren Vale, Cowra, Padthaway $$$

1998	18.1	2000	2003+
1997	18.5	2002	2005
1995	17.6	2000	2003
1994	15.7	1995	1996
1993	18.5	1998	2001
1991	17.5	1996	1999

GRAVEYARD VINEYARD

Lower Hunter Valley $$$$$

1997	18.2	2005	2009
1996	18.0	2004	2008
1994	18.5		2006+
1993	18.5		2005+
1991	18.2		2003+
1990	17.6		2002+
1989	18.3		2001+
1988	18.0	2000	2005
1987	18.4	1995	1999
1986	18.6	1998	2003
1985	16.7	1990	1993

SEMILLON

Lower Hunter Valley $$$

1998	18.6	2003	2006+
1997	17.6	2002	2005
1995	18.3	2003	2007
1994	18.2	2002	2006
1993	16.5	2001	2005
1992	16.0	2000	2004
1991	18.2	1996	1999
1990	16.7	1995	1998
1989	16.0	1990	1991

Region: NE Victoria Winemaker: Rob Scapin
Viticulturist: Jim Baxendale Chief Executive: John G. Brown

One of the most successful of all Australian wineries, Brown Brothers has set itself the unenviable task of making a wine from virtually every known grape variety, a mission that must leave its technical staff panting with exhaustion. Despite some recent good results at wine shows, the company has still to set the world on fire for its wine quality. Given its resources, I expect more.

BARBERA

NE Victoria $$

1996	16.5	1998	2001
1995	16.0	1997	2000
1994	15.2	1996	1999

FAMILY RESERVE CABERNET SAUVIGNON

NE Victoria $$$$$

1992	15.0	2000	2004
1991	18.1	2003	2011
1988	14.0	2000	2008
1987	15.0	1992	1995
1986	18.2	1994	1998
1978	17.6	1990	1998

FAMILY RESERVE CHARDONNAY

NE Victoria $$$$

1995	15.7	1997	2000
1994	16.5	1996	1999
1993	15.4	1995	1998
1992	16.7	1994	1997

Brown Brothers

**Off main Glenrowan-Myrtleford Road (Snow Rd)
Milawa Vic 3678
Tel: (03) 5720 5500
Fax: (03) 5720 5511**

KING VALLEY CHARDONNAY

King Valley $$

1997	16.6	1999	2002
1996	17.4	1998	2001
1995	16.0	1997	2000
1994	14.2	1995	1996
1993	15.7	1995	1998
1992	15.6	1994	1997

KING VALLEY GEWURZTRAMINER

King Valley $$

1998	16.0	2003	2006
1997	15.6	1999	2002
1996	17.0	1998	2001
1995	17.5	1997	2000
1994	16.8	1996	1999
1992	18.3	1997	2000
1991	17.8	1996	1999
1990	18.0	1995	1998

KING VALLEY RIESLING

King Valley $$

1997	16.0	1999	2002
1996	15.7	1998	2001
1995	15.5	2000	2003
1994	15.5	1999	2002
1993	17.5	1998	2001
1992	17.3	1997	2000
1991	17.5	1993	1996
1990	17.0	1992	1995

LATE HARVESTED ORANGE MUSCAT AND FLORA

NE Victoria $$

1998	14.3	1999	2000
1997	14.8	1998	1999
1996	15.2	1997	1998
1995	16.4	1997	2000

NOBLE RIESLING

NE Victoria $$$$

1996	17.2	2001	2004
1994	15.0	1999	2002
1993	17.8	1998	2001
1992	17.0	1997	2000
1988	15.3	1990	1995
1986	16.7	1994	1998
1985	16.7	1993	1997
1984	17.7	1989	1992

PINOT NOIR CHARDONNAY BRUT

NE Victoria $$$$

1994	16.7	1999	2002
1993	14.3	1995	1998
1992	16.5	1997	2000
1991	18.4	1996	1999
1990	17.3	1995	1998
1989	16.8	1991	1994

SHIRAZ MONDEUSE & CABERNET

NE Victoria $$$

1995	17.5		2007+
1992	17.9	2004	2012
1990	17.5		2002+
1989	17.2		2001+
1988	17.0	2000	2005
1987	17.0	1999	2004
1986	17.5		2006+
1985	17.5		2015+
1984	15.5	1992	1996
1983	17.5		2003+
1980	18.3		2010+

VICTORIA CABERNET SAUVIGNON

Victoria $$$

1997	16.4	2002	2005
1996	17.3	2001	2004
1994	16.9	2002	2006
1993	17.3		2005+
1992	17.9	2000	2004
1991	17.3	1999	2003
1990	16.5	1995	1998
1989	16.5	1994	1997
1988	16.8	1993	1996
1987	15.2	1992	1995
1986	17.5	1994	1998

VICTORIA SEMILLON

Victoria $$

1996	17.5	2001	2004
1995	15.2	1997	2000
1993	16.3	1995	1998

VICTORIA SHIRAZ

Victoria $$$

1997	15.3	1999	2002
1996	16.3	1998	2001
1995	15.8	2000	2003
1994	14.9	1999	2002
1992	17.4		2004+
1990	15.5	1995	1998

VINTAGE PORT

NE Victoria $$$

1992	18.0		2004+
1991	17.8		2003+
1988	16.5	2000	2005
1987	16.5		2007+
1986	18.5		2016+
1985	17.0		2005+
1984	15.0	1996	2001
1983	17.0		2003+
1982	16.5		2002+
1981	16.0		2001+
1980	18.5		2010+

Region: NE Victoria Winemaker: Colin Campbell
Viticulturist: Malcolm Campbell Chief Executives: Colin & Malcolm Campbell

With its two regional specials in The Barkly Durif and the Bobbie Burns Shiraz, Campbells is helping to return the red table wines of Rutherglen to their former popularity and status. While its chardonnay is ripe and approachable, Campbells also boasts one of the most extensive range of premium fortified wines in Australia.

BARKLY DURIF

NE Victoria $$$$

1995	16.7	2000	2003
1994	18.1	2002	2006
1993	16.6	2001	2005
1992	18.3		2004+
1991	17.0	1999	2003
1990	17.5		2002+

Campbells

**Murray Valley Hwy
Rutherglen Vic 3685
Tel: (02) 6032 9458
Fax: (02) 6032 9870**

BOBBIE BURNS SHIRAZ

NE Victoria $$$

1997	16.8	2002	2005
1996	18.2	2004	2008
1995	16.7	2000	2003
1994	17.5	2002	2006
1993	16.7	2001	2005
1992	18.3	2000	2004
1991	14.5	1996	1999
1990	17.5	1995	1998

CABERNET MERLOT

NE Victoria $$

1994	15.8	1999	2002
1993	16.4	2001	2005
1992	15.7	1994	1997
1991	16.0	1993	1996
1990	16.0	1992	1995

CHARDONNAY

NE Victoria $$

1998	16.5	2000	2003+
1997	17.0	1999	2002
1996	16.8	1998	2001
1995	16.1	1997	2000
1994	14.8	1996	1999
1993	16.3	1998	2001
1992	17.4	1997	2000

RIESLING

NE Victoria $$

1998	16.5	2003	2006
1997	15.2	2002	2005
1996	16.5	2001	2004
1994	15.2	1996	1999
1993	16.8	2001	2005
1992	15.3	1994	1997
1991	16.5	1999	2003
1990	15.8	1995	1998
1988	16.5	1993	1996

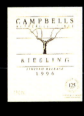

THE ONWINE AUSTRALIAN WINE ANNUAL **2000**

Cape Clairault

**Henry Road
Willyabrup WA 6280
Tel: (08) 9755 6225
Fax: (08) 9755 6229**

VINTAGE PORT

NE Victoria $$$

1993	17.8		2005+
1991	16.2	1999	2003
1990	18.2		2002+
1988	17.5	2000	2005
1986	18.4	1998	2003
1983	18.3	1995	2000

Region: Margaret River Winemaker: Peter Stark
Chief Executive: William Martin

Cape Clairault has long been a justifiable favourite amongst those who prefer their cabernet blends fine, elegant and restrained. The vineyard also produces some of the smartest blends of sauvignon blanc and semillon around. Time alone will tell if its new owners pursue a different tack with viticulture and marketing, but retained winemaker Peter Stark should ensure consistency in wine style.

SEMILLON SAUVIGNON BLANC

Margaret River $$$

1998	17.1	2000	2003
1997	18.5	1999	2002+
1996	18.2	1998	2001
1995	16.9	1997	2000
1994	18.3	1999	2002
1993	17.6	1995	1998
1992	17.5	1994	1997

THE CLAIRAULT (FORMERLY CABERNET SAUVIGNON)

Margaret River $$$$

1996	16.3	2001	2004+
1995	18.5	2003	2007
1994	18.3		2006+
1993	16.4	2001	2005
1993	17.5	2001	2005
1991	18.7		2003+
1990	18.1		2002+
1989	17.4	1997	2001
1988	17.6	1996	2000
1987	16.2	1995	1999
1986	18.0	1998	2006

THE CLAIRAULT SAUVIGNON BLANC

Margaret River $$$

1998	16.7	1999	2000
1997	17.9	1999	2002
1996	18.6	1998	2001
1995	18.3	2000	2003
1994	18.5	1996	1999
1993	18.2	1995	1998
1992	17.8	1994	1997

Region: Margaret River Winemaker: John Durham
Viticulturist: Brenton Air Chief Executive: David Hohnen

David Hohnen's vision and John Durham's expertise continue to reinforce Cape Mentelle as a leading maker of firm, dry reds from a number of grape varieties, but most importantly of all, from cabernet sauvignon. I find recent vintages of shiraz a little meaty.

Cape Mentelle

Lot 722 Wallcliffe Road
Margaret River WA 6285
Tel: (08) 9757 3266
Fax: (08) 9757 3233

CABERNET MERLOT (TRINDERS)

Margaret River $$$

1997	15.2	1999	2002+
1996	17.0	2004	2008
1995	17.3	2003	2007
1994	17.2	1999	2002
1993	17.1	2001	2005
1992	18.0	1997	2000
1991	17.3	1999	2003

CABERNET SAUVIGNON

Margaret River $$$$$

1995	18.3	2003	2007+
1994	17.5	2006	2014
1993	18.3	2005	2013
1992	18.4		2004+
1991	16.0	2003	2011
1990	18.4	1998	2002
1989	18.3	1997	2001
1988	17.8	2000	2008
1987	18.5		2007+
1986	17.5	1998	2006
1985	17.0	1993	1997
1984	18.0	1996	2001
1983	17.2	1995	2003
1982	18.0	1994	1999

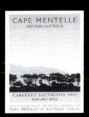

CHARDONNAY
Margaret River $$$$

1998	16.0	2003	2006
1997	18.2	2002	2005
1996	18.6	2001	2004
1995	18.4	2000	2003
1994	18.5	2002	2006
1993	18.5	1998	2001
1992	17.2	1997	2000
1991	17.8	1996	1999
1990	18.4	1995	1998

SEMILLON SAUVIGNON
Margaret River $$$

1998	18.6	2000	2003
1997	18.1	1997	1998
1996	18.3	1997	1998
1995	17.2	1997	2000
1994	16.6	1996	1999
1993	18.2	1995	1998
1992	18.0	1994	1997

SHIRAZ
Margaret River $$$

1997	16.7	2005	2009
1996	17.9		2008+
1995	17.5	2000	2003
1994	18.6	2002	2006
1993	16.8	2001	2005
1992	18.2	2000	2004
1991	18.4		2003+
1990	18.2	1998	2002
1989	16.9	1994	1997
1988	18.6	2000	2005
1987	16.6	1992	1995

ZINFANDEL

Margaret River $$$

1997	18.5	2005	2009+
1996	16.0	2001	2004
1995	18.3	2003	2007
1994	16.8	2002	2006
1993	16.5	1998	2001
1992	18.0	1997	2000
1991	18.0		2003+
1990	18.2	1998	2002
1989	17.0	1997	2001
1988	18.3	1996	2000
1987	17.0	1995	1999
1986	17.0	1994	1998
1985	14.5	1993	1997
1984	16.5	1992	1996
1983	18.0		2003+
1982	17.0	1990	1994
1981	18.2		2001+

Region: Geographe Winemaker: Krister Jonsson
Viticulturist: Peter Pratten Chief Executive: Peter Pratten

With a new winery at his disposal, Krister Jonsson should be able to do more with Capel Vale's smartly-presented but underachieving 'reserve' labels. Although it's more likely a vineyard thing, recent red releases have been too green and skinny, while the dry whites show clear evidence of excessive botrytis.

Capel Vale

**Lot 5 Capel
North West Road
Stirling Estate
Capel WA 6271
Tel: (08) 9727 1986
Fax: (08) 9791 2452**

CABERNET SAUVIGNON

Various, WA $$$

1997	14.8	1999	2002
1996	16.1	1998	2001
1995	18.0	2003	2007
1994	17.8	2002	2006
1993	14.4	1995	1998
1991	17.5	1999	2003
1990	16.8	1998	2002
1989	17.5	1997	2001
1988	17.7	1996	2000

FREDERICK CHARDONNAY

Various, WA $$$$

1997	15.0	1999	2002
1996	18.5	1998	2001
1995	17.6	1997	2000
1994	18.5	1999	2002
1993	16.6	1995	1998
1992	18.2	1997	2000

RIESLING
Various, WA $$

1998	16.0	2000	2003
1997	14.5		1998
1996	16.0	2001	2004
1995	16.9	2003	2007
1994	17.0	1999	2002
1993	18.3	2001	2005
1992	16.1	1997	2000
1991	15.0	1993	1996
1990	15.3	1995	1998
1989	16.8	1997	2001
1988	17.0	1996	2000
1986	18.6	1998	2006
1983	18.8	1995	2003

SHIRAZ
Various, WA $$$

1997	16.4	2002	2005
1996	17.9	2001	2004
1995	18.1	2003	2007
1993	16.3	1998	2001+
1992	16.8	1997	2000
1991	15.0	1999	2003
1990	16.8	1998	2002
1989	18.3	1997	2001
1988	18.0	1996	2000
1987	15.5	1992	1995
1986	18.0	1998	2003

WHISPERING HILL RIESLING
Great Southern $$$

1998	16.0	2000	2003+
1997	18.2	2002	2005
1996	18.5	2004	2008

Region: Hastings River Winemaker: David Barker
Viticulturist: Graham Kaye Chief Executive: Michael Byrne

Cassegrain is effectively operating two separate wineries now that wines like its Reserve Chambourcin are made in biodynamic fashion. Cassegrain has pioneered the use of this hybrid variety in Australia and their efforts are now paying off with some distinctive wines which you will either enjoy or find not to your taste at all.

Cassegrain
764 Fernbank Creek Rd
Port Macquarie
NSW 2444
Tel: (02) 6583 7777
Fax: (02) 6584 0354

CHAMBOURCIN
Hastings River $$

1998	15.7	2000	2003
1997	14.8	1999	2002
1996	17.0	1998	2001
1995	15.7	1996	1997
1994	14.8	1996	1999
1993	15.2	1995	1998
1992	16.1	1994	1997
1991	15.5	1993	1996
1990	16.0	1992	1995

CHARDONNAY
Hastings River $$$

1997	16.7	1999	2002
1996	16.2	1998	2001
1995	16.0	1997	2000
1994	17.6	1999	2002
1993	17.8	1998	2001
1992	18.1	1997	2000
1991	17.7	1996	1999
1990	16.5	1992	1995

FROMENTEAU VINEYARD CHARDONNAY
Hastings River $$$$

1996	16.6	1998	2001
1995	17.6	2000	2003
1993	16.5	1998	2001
1991	18.4	1996	1999
1990	16.2	1995	1998

THE ONWINE AUSTRALIAN WINE ANNUAL

RESERVE CHAMBOURCIN

Hastings Valley $$$

1996	16.0	1998	2001
1995	15.2	1997	2000
1994	16.8	1999	2002

SEMILLON

Hastings River $$$

1998	16.9	2000	2003
1997	16.0	2002	2005
1996	16.5	2001	2004
1993	17.2	2001	2005
1992	16.3	1997	2000
1991	18.0	1999	2003
1990	16.0	1992	1995
1989	15.0	1994	1997

SHIRAZ

Hastings River $$$

1998	16.5	2003	2006
1997	15.2	1999	2002
1996	14.6	1998	2001

Castle Rock Estate

**Porongorup Rd
Porongorup WA 6324
Tel: (08) 9853 1035
Fax: (08) 9853 1010**

Region: Great Southern Winemaker: Michael Staniford
Viticulturist: Angelo Diletti Chief Executive: Angelo Diletti

Castle Rock is a small vineyard in the Porongorup Ranges found within WA's Great Southern region which first came to prominence for the freshness and limey aromaticity of its riesling, of which the 1998 wine is a fragrant and spotlessly clean, steely cellaring style.

CHARDONNAY

Great Southern $$$$

1997	15.2	1998	1999
1995	15.3	1996	1997
1994	16.6	1996	1999

Region: McLaren Vale Winemakers: Pamela Dunsford, Angela Meaney
Viticulturist: Richard Schultz Chief Executive: Robert Gerard

Chapel Hill's excellent performance with red wines from the difficult 1997 vintage, well above the mean in McLaren Vale, reinforces its place amongst the leading lights in this rejuvenated wine area. The Shiraz is lighter than Pam Dunsford would usually release, but is beautifully balanced, dark and harmonious.

Chapel Hill

Chapel Hill Rd
McLaren Vale SA 5171
Tel: (08) 8323 8429
Fax: (08) 8323 9245

CABERNET SAUVIGNON
McLaren Vale, Coonawarra $$$

1997	18.1	2005	2009
1996	18.1	2004	2008+
1995	16.7	2000	2003
1994	17.8	2002	2006
1993	18.0	2001	2005
1992	17.7	1997	2000
1991	17.7	1999	2003
1990	18.5	2002	2010
1989	18.0	1997	2001

McLAREN VALE SHIRAZ
McLaren Vale $$$

1997	18.5	2005	2009
1995	17.7	2000	2003
1994	18.1	1999	2002
1993	18.5	2001	2005
1992	18.0	2000	2004
1991	18.3	1999	2003
1990	17.5	2002	2010
1989	17.5	1997	2001

RESERVE CHARDONNAY
McLaren Vale $$$$

1997	16.7	1999	2002
1996	18.2	2001	2004
1995	17.8	2000	2003
1994	18.7	2002	2006
1993	18.6	1998	2001
1992	18.2	1997	2000
1991	17.6	1996	1999
1990	18.0	1998	2002

Chateau Leamon

**140 km post
Calder Highway
Bendigo Vic 3550
Tel: (03) 5447 7995
Fax: (03) 5447 0855**

THE VICAR
McLaren Vale $$$

1996	18.3	2004	2008+
1994	17.9	2002	2006
1993	16.8	1998	2001

UNWOODED CHARDONNAY
Padthaway $$

1998	16.3	1999	2000
1997	15.7	1998	1999
1996	16.0	1997	1998
1995	15.5	1996	1997
1994	16.2	1996	1999

Region: Bendigo Winemaker: Ian Leamon
Viticulturist: Ian Leamon Chief Executive: Alma Leamon

Two recent vintages of Reserve Shiraz mark a turning point in the development of Chateau Leamon, whose red wines have tended to lack the polish that quality new oak can provide. The 1997 Reserve Shiraz presents fragrant, spicy and concentrated brambly berry fruit with plush, smooth oak, a real step forward in class.

CABERNET MERLOT
Bendigo $$$

1995	16.2	2003	2007
1994	17.2	2002	2006
1993	15.4	1998	2001
1992	17.5	2000	2004
1991	17.4		2003+
1990	16.4		2002+
1989	16.5	1997	2001
1988	17.6	2000	2005
1987	17.0	1999	2004
1986	17.5	1998	2003

SHIRAZ
Bendigo $$$

1997	15.3	2002	2005
1996	13.8	1997	1998
1995	15.7	2000	2003
1994	17.0	2002	2006
1992	17.3		2004+
1990	17.2		2002+

Chateau Reynella

Reynell Road
Reynella SA 5161
Tel: (08) 8392 2222
Fax: (08) 8392 2202

Region: McLaren Vale Winemakers: Stephen Pannell, Tom Newton
Viticulturist: Brenton Baker Chief Executive: Stephen Millar

It may lack the oomph and richness of the best vintages, but Chateau Reynella's 1996 release is a typical example of the style considered by many to define what Australians mean by Vintage Port. Dark, brambly, smooth and spicy, it's crammed with fennel, bitumen and concentrated dark berry fruits, and fortified with the sort of mature spirit you could easily take by itself.

VINTAGE PORT

NE Victoria $$

1996	18.1	2008	2016
1994	18.9		2014+
1993	18.3		2013+
1990	18.6		2010+
1987	18.9		2007+
1983	18.1		2003+
1982	17.0		2002+
1981	18.0		2001+
1980	17.3	2000	2005
1979	18.2		2009+
1978	18.0	1998	2003
1977	16.7	1997	2002
1976	17.8	1996	2001
1975	19.3		2005+
1972	18.3		2002+

Chateau Tahbilk

Off Goulburn Valley Highway
Tabilk Vic 3608
Tel: (03) 5794 2555
Fax: (03) 5794 2360

Region: Goulburn Valley
Winemakers: Alister Purbrick, Neil Larson, Tony Carapetis
Viticulturist: Ian Hendy Chief Executive: Alister Purbrick

Alister Purbrick is determined that Chateau Tahbilk remains true to its generations of winemaking traditions, choosing to use the large old oak casks which have resided in Tahbilk's cellars for many decades ahead of the small oak preferred by most contemporary makers and indeed by Purbrick himself for his Dalfarras brand. My favourite Tahbilk wine remains its Marsanne, which acquires delicious honeysuckle-like complexity after about eight years in the bottle. It's best to keep the reds for even longer, much longer!

1860 VINES SHIRAZ (FORMERLY CLARET)

Goulburn Valley $$$$$

1994	16.1	2006	2014
1993	17.2		2013+
1992	18.3		2012+
1991	16.8		2003+
1990	17.3		2010+
1989	15.0	2001	2011
1988	16.4	2000	2010
1987	17.8		2007+
1986	18.5		2006+

CABERNET SAUVIGNON

Goulburn Valley $$

1996	15.2	2001	2004
1995	17.9		2015+
1994	17.3		2006+
1993	17.6		2005+
1992	18.0		2004+
1991	18.2		2011+
1990	18.1		2010+
1989	15.3	1997	2001
1988	18.4	2000	2005
1987	16.5	1995	1999
1986	18.5		2006+
1985	18.3		2005+
1984	18.2		2004+
1983	18.2		2013+
1982	17.0		2012+
1981	17.6		2001+
1980	17.3		2000+
1979	16.5	1999	2009
1978	17.0	1990	1998
1977	16.0	1989	1994
1976	16.5	1988	1996

CHARDONNAY

Goulburn Valley $$

1997	15.6	1999	2002
1996	15.8	1998	2001
1995	16.6	2000	2003
1994	16.2	1999	2002
1993	16.8	1998	2001
1992	16.6	1994	1997

MARSANNE

Goulburn Valley $$

1998	17.1	2006	2010
1997	18.0	2005	2009
1996	18.0	2004	2008
1995	17.0		2007+
1994	17.8		2006+
1993	16.0	1998	2001
1992	16.8	1997	2000+
1991	17.0	1999	2003
1990	17.0	1998	2002
1989	17.5	1994	1997
1988	18.1		2000+
1987	17.1	1999	2007
1986	17.0	1998	2002

RESERVE RED (FORMERLY SPECIAL BIN)

Goulburn Valley $$$$

1992	16.7		2004+
1991	17.3		2011+
1986	18.1	1998	2003
1985	17.5		2005+
1984	16.4	1996	2001
1983	17.0		2003+
1982	17.3		2002+
1981	18.3		2001+
1980	17.9	1992	1997
1979	16.0	1999	2009
1978	17.4		2008+
1977	16.6	1989	1994
1976	17.0		2006+
1975	17.3		2005+
1974	16.5	1986	1992
1973	18.2	1993	2003
1972	18.0	1984	1990
1971	18.2	1991	1996

RIESLING

Goulburn Valley $$

1998	15.0	2003	2006+
1997	18.1	2005	2009
1996	17.7	2004	2008
1995	17.0	2003	2007
1994	17.6	2002	2006
1993	17.2	2001	2005
1992	17.7	1997	2000
1991	17.9		2003+
1990	17.5	1998	2002

SHIRAZ

Goulburn Valley $$

1996	15.0	2001	2004
1995	16.9		2007+
1994	17.3		2014+
1993	15.8	1998	2001
1992	18.0		2004+
1991	17.7		2011+
1990	16.8		2002+
1989	16.5		2001+
1988	18.0	2000	2008
1987	16.6	1995	1999
1986	18.4		2006+

Chateau Xanadu

Terry Road
Margaret River WA 6285
Tel: (08) 9757 2581
Fax: (08) 9757 3389

Region: Margaret River Winemaker: Jurg Muggli
Viticulturist: Leonard Russell Chief Executive: Conor Lagan

Chateau Xanadu is a self-confident Margaret River whose wines are uniformly well made, distinctive and full of personality. Recent vintages of Chardonnay and Semillon rival the established high standard of the winery's two excellent cabernet releases. Not just a marketing idea but a good wine as well, The Secession is Chateau Xanadu's popular bistro blend of white grapes.

CABERNET RESERVE

Margaret River $$$$$

1996	17.0	2004	2008
1995	18.0		2007+
1994	18.2	2006	2014
1993	18.2		2005+
1992	18.7		2004+
1991	17.2		2003+
1990	18.3		2006+
1989	16.9	1997	2001

CABERNET SAUVIGNON

Margaret River $$$$

1997	16.3	2002	2005
1996	17.6	2004	2008
1995	18.4	2007	2014
1994	17.6	1999	2002
1993	18.5		2005+
1992	18.4	2000	2004
1991	17.5		2003+
1990	16.0	1992	1995
1989	16.5	1997	2001

CHARDONNAY

Margaret River $$$

1998	18.3	2003	2006
1997	17.2	2002	2005
1996	18.4	2004	2008
1995	17.4	1997	2000
1994	18.4	2002	2006
1993	17.8	1998	2001
1992	16.8	1997	2000
1991	16.8	1996	1999
1990	16.5	1992	1995

SECESSION
Margaret River $$

1998	17.0	1999	2000
1997	18.2	1998	1999
1996	17.3	1997	1998
1995	15.0	1996	1997
1994	16.8	1996	1999

SEMILLON
Margaret River $$$

1998	18.0	2003	2006
1997	18.0	2002	2005
1996	18.5	2001	2004
1995	16.3	1996	1997
1994	17.2	2002	2006
1993	17.1	1995	1998
1992	18.4	1997	2000
1991	18.0	1996	1999
1990	16.0	1995	1998
1989	15.0	1994	1997

Region: Great Southern Winemaker: Steven Pester
Viticulturist: Mike Harvey Chief Executive: Ken Lynch

Chatsfield's best wine is its floral, musky Riesling, while its Cabernet Franc is a deliciously spicy early-drinking soft red. Chatsfield has recently moved its winemaking to the Porongorup winery which it owns equally with Jingalla, Montgomery's Hill and Ironwood Estate.

Chatsfield

O'Neill Rd
Mount Barker WA 6324
Tel: (08) 9851 1704
Fax: (08) 9851 1704

CABERNET FRANC
Great Southern $$

1998	16.5	1999	2000
1997	16.9	1997	1998
1996	16.0	1997	1998
1995	16.6	1997	2000
1994	16.8	1996	1999
1992	15.5	1994	1997

CHARDONNAY
Great Southern $$$

1997	15.8	1999	2002
1996	16.2	1997	1998
1995	16.0	1996	1997
1994	18.0	1999	2002
1993	18.2	1998	2001

Clarendon Hills

**Brookmans Road
Blewitt Springs SA 5171
Tel: (08) 8364 1484
Fax: (08) 8364 1484**

GEWURZTRAMINER
Great Southern $$

1998	15.0	2000	2003
1997	16.5	1999	2002
1996	16.0	1997	1998
1995	15.0	1996	1997
1994	18.2	1999	2002
1993	18.5	1998	2001
1992	18.5	1994	1997

RIESLING
Great Southern $$

1998	17.2	2003	2006+
1997	16.5	1999	2002
1996	17.5	1998	2001
1995	16.4	2000	2003
1994	18.4	2002	2006
1993	18.6	1998	2001
1992	17.4	1997	2000
1990	17.5	1992	1995

SHIRAZ
Great Southern $$

1997	15.8	1999	2002
1996	17.2	2001	2004
1995	15.0	1997	2000
1994	18.3	2002	2006
1993	17.4	1998	2001
1992	16.5	1997	2000
1991	17.6	1999	2003
1990	18.0	1998	2002

**Region: McLaren Vale Winemaker: Roman Bratasiuk
Viticulturist: Various Chief Executive: Roman Bratasiuk**

Roman Bratasiuk has chosen to keep separate the wines from the various vineyards he sources fruit from, a European-styled decision which has led to an immediate plethora of Clarendon Hills labels, especially from shiraz, grenache and chardonnay. The sought-after Liandra Shiraz 1997, actually from two vineyards, is a deeply flavoured, brooding wine with assertive new oak, made in true Clarendon Hills style.

ASTRALIS
McLaren Vale $$$$$

1997	18.2	2009	2017
1996	18.6	2008	2016
1995	18.9	2007	2015
1994	18.4	2006	2014

MERLOT

McLaren Vale $$$$

1997	15.3	2002	2005+
1996	17.0	2004	2008
1995	18.0	2003	2007
1994	18.2	2002	2006
1993	17.9	2001	2005

OLD VINES GRENACHE BLEWITT SPRINGS

McLaren Vale $$$$

1997	17.0	2002	2005
1995	18.6	2003	2007+
1994	17.5	2002	2006
1993	17.3	1998	2001

SHIRAZ

McLaren Vale $$$$$

1996	18.7	2004	2008+
1995	18.7	2003	2007
1994	18.4	2002	2006
1993	16.6	1998	2001

**Region: Macedon Winemakers: Keith & Lynette Brien
Viticulturists: Keith & Lynette Brien Chief Executives: Keith & Lynette Brien**

Keith Brien delights in the process of informing wine writers like me that his wines are about as far from typical Australian styles as could be imagined. While this is patently obvious to anyone who has tasted them, it's also quite clear that vineyards located in as cool a site as Cleveland need plenty of sunshine to achieve full physiological ripeness. Not unsurprisingly, Cleveland's best wine is a sparkling one, and its best still wines come from warm to hot years like 1997 and 1998. The 1998 Chardonnay is a pleasing expression of a Chablis-like style, with a tangy mineral quality.

CHARDONNAY

Macedon

1998	17.0	2003	2006
1996	14.2	1998	2001
1994	15.0	1995	1996
1993	17.4	1998	2001
1992	15.2	1994	1997

Cleveland

**Shannon's Rd
Lancefield Vic 3435
Tel: (03) 5429 1449
Fax: (03) 5429 2017**

Clonakilla

Crisps Lane
Murrumbateman
NSW 2582
Tel: (02) 6227 5877
Fax: (02) 6227 5871

MACEDON
Macedon $$$$

96er	15.8	1998	2001
95er	17.0	1997	2000
94er	16.9	1996	1999
93er	15.5	1995	1996
92er	18.2	1994	1997
91er	17.4	1993	1996

PINOT NOIR
Macedon $$$$

1997	16.0	1999	2002+
1996	14.0	2001	2004
1994	17.4	1999	2002
1993	15.3	1998	2001
1992	18.2	1997	2000
1991	16.6	1996	1999
1990	16.5	1992	1995

Region: Canberra Winemaker: Tim Kirk
Viticulturist: Michael Lahiff Chief Executive: John Kirk

Clonakilla has followed the 1994 vintage of its ground-breaking Shiraz, which Tim Kirk blends with viognier and pinot noir, with an absolute stunner from 1997 and a wine nearly as promising from 1998. This vineyard has also strung together an excellent run of riesling releases and a sumptuous, spicy 1998 Viognier.

CABERNET MERLOT
Canberra $$$

1997	16.5	2005	2009+
1996	15.4	1998	2001
1995	16.5	2003	2007
1994	17.8	2002	2006
1993	15.7	1998	2001
1992	16.4	1997	2000

RIESLING
Canberra $$

1999	18.6	2004	2007+
1998	18.3	2003	2006+
1997	18.6	2005	2009
1996	18.4	2001	2004
1995	17.8	2003	2007
1994	15.0	1996	1999
1993	18.4	2001	2005

THE ONWINE AUSTRALIAN WINE ANNUAL

SHIRAZ
Canberra $$$$

1998	18.7	2006	2010+
1997	19.1	2005	2009
1996	16.6	2001	2004
1995	18.2	2003	2007+
1994	18.9	2006	2014+
1993	16.8	1998	2001
1992	18.3	2000	2004
1991	16.5	1999	2003

Region: Pipers River Winemaker:s Shane Clohesy, Philippe Bru
Viticulturist: Chris Smith Chief Executive: Chris Markell

Taltarni's sparkling wine project is one of the most popular premium Australian fizzes, although I find some releases just that little bit too herbal for my taste. It's a creamy, crackly wine with bright, almost tropical fruit and typically bracing Tasmanian acidity.

METHODE CHAMPENOISE
Pipers Brook $$$$

1996	17.8	2001	2004
1995	17.5	1997	2000
1994	18.3	1999	2002
1993	18.2	1998	2901
1992	17.0	1997	2000
1991	15.0	1996	1999

Region: Geelong Winemaker: Roland Kaval
Viticulturist: Lee Evans Chief Executive: Terry Jongebloed

Recent releases from this significant vineyard have been well down on expectations and on the quality levels set and maintained by its founder, Bannockburn winemaker Gary Farr, during his period of tenure. Roland Kaval should quickly turn things around.

CHARDONNAY
Geelong $$$

1998	14.4	2000	2003
1997	14.2	1999	2002
1996	14.8	1998	2001
1995	17.9	2000	2003
1994	18.6	1999	2002
1993	18.3		2001+
1992	18.5		2000+
1991	18.5	1999	2003

Clover Hill
60 Clover Hill Road
Lebrina Tas 7254
Tel: (03) 6395 6115
Fax: (03) 6395 6257

Clyde Park
Midland Hwy
Bannockburn Vic 3331
Tel: (03) 5281 7274
Fax: (03) 5281 7274

Cockfighter's Ghost

Harbridge Fine Wines
10/56 O'Riordan Street
Alexandria NSW 2015
Tel: (02) 9667 1622
Fax: (02) 9667 1442

PINOT NOIR
Geelong $$$

1998	16.0	2003	2006
1997	15.8	2002	2005
1994	16.2	1996	1999
1993	16.1	2001	2005
1992	16.8	1997	2000
1991	17.8	1996	1999
1990	17.5	1998	2002
1989	17.0	1994	1997

Region: Various Winemakers: Neil McGuigan, Phil Ryan
Viticulturist: Evan Powell Chief Executive: David Clarke

Cockfighter's Ghost is one of the most successful of all Australia bistro wine labels and it's easy to see why. Its wines are typically clean and well made, and ready to drink at time of release.

CHARDONNAY
Hunter Valley $$

1998	16.8	2000	2003
1997	15.1	1998	1999
1996	14.8	1997	1998

SEMILLON
Hunter Valley $$

1998	16.2	2000	2003+
1997	16.0	1999	2002
1996	16.5	1998	2001+

SHIRAZ
Hunter Valley $$

1997	14.9	1999	2002
1996	16.0	1998	2001
1995	15.4	1997	2000

Coldstream Hills

**31 Maddens Lane
Coldstream Vic 3770
Tel: (03) 5964 9388
Fax: (03) 5964 9389**

Region: Yarra Valley Winemakers: James Halliday, Paul Lapsley
Viticulturist: Nicky Harris Chief Executive: Bruce Kemp

Coldstream Hills operates at both ends of the Yarra Valley scale, with fresh, lively varietal wines from chardonnay, pinot noir, plus the early-drinking Briarston blend at one extreme, with the limited runs of Reserve labels at the other. Recent vintages of Reserve Chardonnay and Reserve Pinot Noir have been exceptional, while the recent release of 1997 Merlot hints at how good the Reserve Merlot from that year might yet become.

BRIARSTON (FORMERLY CABERNET MERLOT)

Yarra Valley $$$

1997	15.2	1998	1999
1996	16.0	1998	2001
1995	15.4	1997	2000
1994	16.5	1999	2002
1993	15.6	1998	2001
1992	18.3	1997	2000
1991	16.7	1996	1999

CHARDONNAY

Yarra Valley $$$

1998	16.8	2000	2003
1997	17.6	1999	2002
1996	17.5	1998	2001
1995	17.4	1997	2000
1994	17.6	1996	1999

PINOT NOIR

Yarra Valley $$$

1998	16.9	2000	2003
1997	17.5	2002	2005
1996	17.8	1998	2001
1995	15.0	1996	1997
1994	17.0	1999	2002
1993	17.3	1995	1998
1992	16.7	1994	1997
1991	16.5	1993	1996

RESERVE CABERNET SAUVIGNON

Yarra Valley $$$$

1995	17.0	2000	2003
1994	17.5	2002	2006
1993	18.0	1998	2002
1992	19.0	2004	2012+
1991	18.2	1999	2003
1990	18.0	1995	1998

RESERVE CHARDONNAY

RESERVE CHARDONNAY
Yarra Valley $$$$

1997	18.7	2002	2005+
1996	18.7	2001	2004
1995	18.5	2000	2003
1994	18.7	1999	2002
1993	17.0	1995	1998
1992	19.0	2000	2004
1991	18.2	1993	1996
1990	18.3	1995	1998

RESERVE PINOT NOIR

RESERVE PINOT NOIR
Yarra Valley $$$$

1997	18.5	2004	2008
1996	18.8	2001	2004
1995	17.3	1997	2000
1994	18.5	1999	2002
1993	16.5	1995	1998
1992	18.5	1997	2000
1991	16.5	1993	1996
1990	16.0	1991	1992

Cope-Williams

**Romsey Vineyards
Glenfern Rd
Romsey Vic 3434
Tel: (03) 5429 5428
Fax: (03) 5429 5655**

Region: Macedon Winemaker: Michael Cope-Williams
Viticulturist: Angelo Gosetti Chief Executive: Gordon Cope-Williams

Specialising in a first class Romsey Brut (distinct from the 'Macedon' of other local makers), Cope-Williams also releases a tangy, flinty Chardonnay with Coteaux Champenois pretensions and some rather leafy, autumnal dry reds, of which the Pinot Noir is best. The property also hosts a picturesque cricket ground, a Royal Tennis court, a restaurant and a small conference centre.

CHARDONNAY
Macedon $$$

1998	17.4	2003	2006
1997	17.3	2003	2006
1996	15.0	1998	2001
1995	16.8	2000	2003
1994	16.8	1999	2002
1992	17.9	1997	2000
1991	18.0	1993	1996

ROMSEY BRUT
Macedon $$$$

1995	17.8	1997	2000+
1994	17.4	1999	2002
1993	18.5	1998	2001
1992	18.0	1994	1997
1991	18.2	1993	1996

Region: McLaren Vale Winemaker: Grant Harrison
Viticulturist: Trevor Williams Chief Executive: Mark Lloyd

Coriole is well known for both its spicy, earthy Shiraz and sumptuous Lloyd Reserve Shiraz, but is making wonderful progress with its Sangiovese, a wine acquiring fine, drying astringency to partner its sour-edged fruit. Coriole's range of white wines includes one of the nation's more attractive and drinkable examples of Chenin Blanc.

Coriole

**Chaffeys Road
McLaren Vale SA 5171
Tel: (08) 8323 8305
Fax: (08) 8323 9136**

CABERNET SAUVIGNON
McLaren Vale $$$

1994	18.0	2006	2014
1993	16.5	1998	2001
1992	15.6	1997	2000
1991	17.3	1999	2003
1990	16.0	1998	2002
1989	16.5	1994	1997

CHARDONNAY
McLaren Vale $$$

1996	16.8	1998	2001
1995	14.0	1996	1997
1994	15.0	1996	1999
1993	16.3	1995	1998
1992	18.0	1997	2000

CHENIN BLANC
McLaren Vale $$

1998	16.0	1999	2000
1997	16.6	1999	2002
1996	16.7	1998	2001
1995	15.5	1996	1997
1994	17.2	1999	2002
1993	16.0	1998	2001

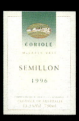

LLOYD RESERVE SHIRAZ

McLaren Vale $$$$

1995	17.0	2003	2007
1994	18.4	2002	2006
1993	18.4	2001	2005
1992	18.2	2000	2004
1991	18.2	1999	2003
1990	18.0		2002+
1989	18.3		2001+

MARY KATHLEEN

McLaren Vale $$$$

1995	17.1	2003	2007
1994	16.7	2002	2006
1992	15.7	1994	1997

REDSTONE SHIRAZ CABERNET GRENACHE

McLaren Vale $$

1997	16.3	2002	2005
1996	16.0	2004	2008
1995	16.8	2001	2004
1994	17.6	2002	2006
1993	15.9	1998	2001
1992	16.7	2000	2004

SANGIOVESE

McLaren Vale $$

1997	17.2	2002	2005
1996	17.0	2001	2004
1995	17.2	2003	2007
1993	16.5	2001	2005
1992	15.3	1997	2000

SEMILLON

McLaren Vale $$$

1996	17.5	1998	2001
1995	17.0	1997	2000
1994	16.0	1996	1999
1993	16.7	1998	2001
1992	15.8	1994	1997

THE ONWINE AUSTRALIAN WINE ANNUAL

SHIRAZ
McLaren Vale $$$

1997	16.7	2002	2005
1996	17.7	2001	2004
1995	18.2	2002	2007
1994	16.8	2002	2006
1993	17.5	2001	2005
1992	18.2	1997	2000
1990	18.0	1995	1998
1989	17.5	1994	1997

Region: Macedon **Winemaker:** Patrick Carmody
Viticulturist: Patrick Carmody **Chief Executive:** Patrick Carmody

Against the modern trend, Pat Carmody chooses not to use a high percentage of new oak to mature his Craiglee shiraz, which he crafts into an elegant, spicy wine with sweet cherry/plum flavours and fine tannins. It's a proven cellar style and acquires even more spiciness with age. Craiglee's Chardonnay is typically long, savoury and mineral.

Craiglee
Sunbury Road
Sunbury Vic 3429
Tel: (03) 9744 4489
Fax: (03) 9744 7905

CHARDONNAY
Macedon $$$

1997	17.0	2002	2005
1996	17.5	2001	2004
1995	17.5	2000	2003
1994	18.2	1999	2002
1993	17.7	1998	2001
1992	18.0	1997	2000
1991	18.5	1993	1996
1990	18.0	1995	1998
1989	16.0	1990	1991

SHIRAZ
Macedon $$$

1996	17.8	2004	2008
1995	17.6	2003	2007
1994	17.6	1999	2002
1993	18.6	2001	2005
1992	16.8	1997	2000
1991	17.5	1999	2003
1990	18.2	1998	2002
1989	17.5	1991	1994
1988	18.5	1996	2000

Craigmoor

**Craigmoor Rd
Mudgee NSW 2850
Tel: (02) 6372 2208
Fax: (02) 6372 4464**

Region: Mudgee Winemaker: Brett McKinnon
Viticulturist: Stephen Guilbaud-Oulton Chief Executive: Andre Boucard

Craigmoor is one of Orlando Wyndham's successful Mudgee-based wineries whose wines constantly amaze me with their intensity, flavour and value. Each is a very reliable bet from year to year and will usually drink very well when young or after a few years' age.

CABERNET SAUVIGNON
Mudgee $$ 5

1996	17.7	2004	2008
1995	16.2	2000	2003
1994	15.8	1996	1999
1993	16.0	1995	1998
1992	17.0	2000	2004

CHARDONNAY
Mudgee $$ 4

1998	16.5	2000	2003
1997	16.8	1999	2002
1996	18.2	2001	2004
1995	17.0	1997	2000
1994	17.0	1996	1999
1993	17.3	1995	1998

SEMILLON
Mudgee $$ 4

1998	17.5	2003	2006+
1997	16.8	2002	2005
1996	18.3	2004	2008
1995	18.0	2003	2007
1994	16.6	1999	2002
1993	16.8	1997	2001

SHIRAZ
Mudgee $$ 5

1996	16.5	2001	2004
1995	16.9	2000	2003
1994	16.6	1996	1999
1993	17.0	2001	2005
1991	17.3	1999	2003
1990	17.8	1998	2002

Region: Riverina Winemaker: Ian Hongell
Viticulturist: Andrew Schulz Chief Executive: Graham Cranswick Smith

Cranswick Estate's Autumn Gold is a first-class dessert wine made using late-harvest semillon from Griffith. Picked earlier than the De Bortoli Noble One with a lesser degree of botrytis infection, it is clearly less luscious, but reveals intense honeycomb and citrusy flavours.

AUTUMN GOLD
Riverina $$$$$

1996	18.6	2001	2004
1995	18.3	2000	2003
1994	18.3	1996	1999
1993	18.5	2001	2005

Region: WA, Winemaker: Larry Cherubino
Viticulturist: Ron Page Chief Executive: Stephen Millar

BRL Hardy's Crofters label is simply one of the hottest prospects around for value. The Cabernet Merlot, which has a habit of doing very well in wine shows, is a terrifically good Western Australian red based around ripe small berry fruit and some pretty smart oak.

CABERNET MERLOT
Various, WA $$$

1997	18.0	2002	2005+
1996	17.2	2001	2004
1995	17.3	2000	2003
1994	16.7	1999	2002

Cranswick Estate

**Walla Avenue
Griffith NSW 2680
Tel: (02) 6962 4133
Fax: (02) 6962 2888**

Crofters

**Houghton Wines Dale Road
Middle Swan WA 6056
Tel: (08) 8392 2222
Fax: (08) 8392 2202**

Cullen

**Caves Road
Willyabrup via Cowaramup
WA 6284
Tel: (08) 9755 5277
Fax: (08) 9755 5550**

Region: Margaret River Winemakers: Vanya Cullen, Trevor Kent
Viticulturist: Dick Marcus Chief Executive: Diana Cullen

Buffeted around by the storms and high winds of 1996/97 growing season, the Cullens only made a hatful of 1997 Chardonnay, which they only released in magnums. One of Australia's most important vineyards, Cullen's Cabernet Sauvignon Merlot is arguably the most sought-after Australian cabernet blend of the moment. It's unbelievably consistent and its longevity is only threatened by a single factor: that it is so darned easy to enjoy while young!

CABERNET SAUVIGNON MERLOT

Margaret River $$$$$

1997	18.6	2005	2009+
1996	18.7		2008+
1995	19.3		2007+
1994	18.7		2006+
1993	17.9	2001	2005
1992	18.7		2004+
1991	18.2		2003+
1990	18.5		2002+
1989	15.0		2001+
1988	17.0	2000	2005
1987	16.5		2007+
1986	19.0	1998	2003
1985	17.0	1997	2002
1984	17.7	1996	2001
1983	16.5		2003+
1982	17.5	1994	1999
1981	16.5		2001+
1980	18.0	2000	2005

CHARDONNAY

Margaret River $$$$

1998	16.7	2002	2005+
1997	18.6	2002	2005
1996	18.9	2001	2004
1995	18.3	2000	2003
1994	17.5	1996	1999
1993	18.4	1998	2001
1992	18.6	1997	2000
1990	18.6	1995	1998
1989	16.0	1994	1997

PINOT NOIR
Margaret River $$$$

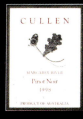

1998	17.0	2000	2003
1997	16.0	1999	2002
1996	16.8	1998	2001
1995	15.8	1997	2000
1994	16.5	1999	2003
1993	18.0	2001	2005
1992	16.6	2000	2004
1991	16.5	1999	2003

SAUVIGNON BLANC (SEMILLON)
Margaret River $$$$

1998	16.8	2000	2003
1997	17.5	1999	2002
1995	17.6	2000	2003
1994	18.2	1996	1999
1993	18.7	1998	2001
1992	16.8	2000	2004
1991	17.0	1996	1999

Region: McLaren Vale, Fleurieu Peninsula
Winemakers: Chester Osborn, Philip Dean
Viticulturists: Phil Williams, Mark Needle Chief Executive: d'Arry Osborn

d'Arenberg
Osborn Road
McLaren Vale SA 5171
Tel: (08) 8323 8206
Fax: (08) 8323 8423

Like most McLaren Vale vineyards, d'Arenberg had a tougher time during the stop-start 1997 vintage, but thanks to the maturity of its vineyards has nevertheless produced a fine range of regional red wines, albeit a slightly earlier-maturing collection. Unlike many of their neighbours, d'Arenberg's reds are modest in their use of oak.

d'ARRY'S ORIGINAL SHIRAZ GRENACHE
McLaren Vale $$

1997	16.8	2002	2005+
1996	16.8	2004	2008
1995	17.7	2003	2007
1994	17.8	2002	2006
1993	16.8	2001	2005
1992	17.4	2000	2004
1991	16.5	1999	2003
1990	17.4	1998	2002
1989	16.0	1997	2001
1988	18.0		2000+
1987	16.4	1997	1999
1986	17.0	1996	1998

IRONSTONE PRESSINGS

McLaren Vale $$$$

1997	17.5	2005	2009
1996	18.4		2008+
1995	18.1		2007+
1994	16.8		2006+
1993	17.6		2005+
1992	18.6	2000	2004
1991	17.6		2003+
1990	17.0		2002+
1989	16.8		2001+

PEPPERMINT PADDOCK CHAMBOURCIN

McLaren Vale $$$

1996	16.9	2001	2004
1995	16.4	2000	2003
1994	16.0	1999	2002
1993	16.6	1998	2001

THE CUSTODIAN GRENACHE

McLaren Vale $$$

1997	17.8	2002	2005
1996	17.6	2004	2008
1995	18.2	2003	2007
1994	16.8	1999	2002

THE DEAD ARM SHIRAZ

McLaren Vale $$$$$

1997	17.8	2005	2009
1996	18.8		2008+
1995	18.5		2007+
1994	18.2		2006+
1993	16.8	2001	2005

THE DRY DAM RIESLING

McLaren Vale $$

1997	16.2	2002	2005
1996	16.0	2001	2004
1995	17.8	2003	2007
1994	17.6	2002	2006
1993	16.8	1998	2001
1992	16.0	2000	2004
1990	17.0	1998	2002

THE ONWINE AUSTRALIAN WINE ANNUAL

THE FOOTBOLT OLD VINE SHIRAZ

McLaren Vale $$$

1997	16.2	2002	2005+
1996	17.2	2004	2008
1995	17.3	2003	2007
1994	17.5		2006+
1993	17.0	2001	2005
1992	17.0		2004+
1991	18.0		2003+
1990	17.0	1998	2002
1989	16.9	1997	2001
1988	17.0	1996	2000
1987	16.0	1995	1999

THE HIGH TRELLIS CABERNET SAUVIGNON

McLaren Vale $$$

1997	16.5	2002	2005+
1995	17.8	2003	2007
1994	16.6	1999	2002
1993	16.3	2001	2005
1992	16.3	1997	2000
1991	17.7	2003	2011
1990	17.9	2002	2010

THE NOBLE RIESLING

McLaren Vale $$$$$

1997	17.0	2002	2005
1996	16.1	1998	2001
1995	17.1	2000	2003
1994	18.2	2002	2006
1993	16.8	1995	1998
1992	18.4	1997	2000
1991	17.0	1996	1999

THE OLIVE GROVE CHARDONNAY

McLaren Vale $$

1998	17.8	2003	2006
1997	16.6	1999	2002
1996	16.1	1997	1998
1995	16.7	1997	2000
1994	16.8	1996	1999
1993	17.0	1998	2001
1992	16.0	1997	2000
1991	14.0	1996	1999
1990	17.5	1998	2002

THE TWENTYEIGHTH ROAD MOURVEDRE

McLaren Vale $$$

1997	16.3	2002	2005
1996	17.9	2004	2008+
1995	16.8	2003	2007

VINTAGE FORTIFIED SHIRAZ

NE Victoria $$$

1997	18.1	2005	2009+
1995	18.3		2007+
1993	18.2		2005+
1987	18.5		2007+
1978	17.0	1998	2008
1976	18.0	1996	2006
1975	18.2	1995	2005
1973	18.6	1993	2003

Dalfarras

**Goulburn Valley Highway
Nagambie Vic 3608
Tel: (03) 5794 2637
Fax: (03) 5794 2360**

Regions: Goulburn Valley, Coonawarra, McLaren Vale Winemaker: Alister Purbrick
Viticulturist: Ian Hendy Chief Executive: Alister Purbrick

With a brand new winery complex the other side of Nagambie, Dalfarras now has a new home outside its parent, Chateau Tahbilk. These wines give Alister Purbrick and his team more of a chance to try their hand with contemporary styles, although the reds will take just as long to approach their best as do their Tahbilk counterparts.

CABERNET SAUVIGNON

Coonawarra (Formerly Goulburn River) $$

1997	16.8	2005	2009+
1996	15.6		2008+
1995	16.6	2003	2007
1993	15.0	2001	2005
1992	16.2		2004+
1991	17.8		2011+
1990	16.0	2002	2010

MARSANNE

Goulburn Valley $$

1997	16.0	1999	2002
1996	15.2	1998	2001
1995	15.0	1997	2000
1994	14.5	1995	1996

SAUVIGNON BLANC
Goulburn Valley, McLaren Vale $$

1998	16.8	1999	2000
1997	14.0		1998
1996	15.5	1997	1998
1995	15.0	1996	1997

SHIRAZ
Goulburn Valley $$

1997	16.2	2002	2005
1996	17.6	2004	2008+
1995	17.8	2003	2007+
1994	16.8	2006	2014
1993	15.3	2001	2005
1992	16.6	2000	2004
1991	17.8	1999	2003
1990	16.4	1998	2002

Region: Pyrenees Winemaker: David Jones
Viticulturist: David Jones Chief Executive: David Jones

Its premier wines of Shiraz and Chardonnay continue to enhance the reputation of Dalwhinnie's 18 ha vineyard near Moonambel. The Shiraz is simply a wonderful wine - a black, often peppery and usually spicy expression with great concentration and brooding power. The sumptuous Chardonnay is one of Victoria's finest.

CHARDONNAY
Pyrenees $$$$

1997	18.3	2002	2005
1996	18.4	2004	2008
1995	18.3	2000	2003
1994	18.5	2002	2006
1993	18.6	1998	2001
1992	18.2	2000	2004
1991	18.0	1999	2003
1990	18.5	1998	2002

MOONAMBEL CABERNET
Pyrenees $$$$

1997	17.1		2009+
1996	17.8		2008+
1995	18.3	2003	2007
1994	16.2	1999	2002
1993	17.5		2005+
1992	17.3		2004+
1991	17.8		2003+
1990	16.5	1998	2002

Dalwhinnie
**RMB 4378 Taltarni Road
Moonambel Vic 3478
Tel: (03) 5467 2388
Fax: (03) 5467 2237**

MOONAMBEL SHIRAZ

Pyrenees $$$$

1997	19.1	2005	2009+
1996	18.4	2008	2016
1995	18.1		2007+
1994	17.7		2006+
1993	18.2	2001	2005
1992	19.0		2004+
1991	18.4		2011+
1990	18.2		2002+
1989	16.0	1997	2001
1988	18.5		2000+
1987	16.5	1995	1999
1986	17.0	1994	1998
1985	16.5	1993	1997

David Traeger

139 High St
Nagambie Vic 3608
Tel: (03) 5794 2514
Fax: (03) 5794 1776

Region: Goulburn Valley Winemaker: David Traeger
Viticulturist: David Traeger Chief Executive: David Traeger

With more mature vines now to draw from, David Traeger can look forward to making wines of even more concentration and complexity. Aside from the spicy and often quite floral Verdelho, he's a red wine specialist with access to an ever-increasing resource of mature central Victorian vineyards.

CABERNET

Goulburn Valley $$$

1997	15.7	2005	2009
1996	16.8	2004	2008
1995	16.5	2003	2007
1993	17.6	2001	2005
1992	18.4		2004+
1990	18.2		2002+
1989	17.8	1997	2001
1988	16.5	1996	2000

SHIRAZ

Goulburn Valley $$$

1997	18.0	2005	2009+
1996	17.8	2004	2008
1995	17.0	2003	2007
1993	15.5	1998	2001
1992	16.4	2000	2004
1990	16.8	1998	2002
1988	18.1	1996	2000

VERDELHO
Goulburn Valley $$

1998	17.5	2003	2006
1997	17.6	1999	2002
1996	17.5	1998	2001
1995	18.0	2000	2003

Region: Eden Valley Winemakers: Adam Wynn, Andrew Ewart
Viticulturist: Adam Wynn Chief Executive: Adam Wynn

David Wynn is generally a brand of easy, early-drinking table wines of no great complexity or claim to attention, but the Patriarch Shiraz is made into a more sumptuous, firmly structured and often statuesque wine of considerable merit. 1997 was a lighter year.

PATRIARCH SHIRAZ
Eden Valley $$$$

1997	16.2	2002	2005
1996	18.7	2003	2008
1995	18.4	2003	2007
1994	17.8	1999	2002
1993	17.8	2001	2005
1992	17.6	2002	2004
1991	18.4	1999	2003
1990	17.9	1998	2002

Region: Riverina Winemaker: Darren De Bortoli
Viticulturist: Kevin De Bortoli Chief Executive: Deen De Bortoli

Australia's premier dessert wine is this luscious, complex and concentrated wine from De Bortoli in Griffith. These wines mature beautifully for a decade and more.

NOBLE ONE
Riverina $$$$$

1997	18.6	2005	2009
1996	17.3	2001	2004
1995	18.6	2003	2007
1994	19.0	2002	2006
1993	18.2	1998	2001
1992	18.4	1997	2000
1991	18.7		2003+
1990	18.7	1998	2002
1988	17.8	1996	2000
1987	18.0	1995	1999
1986	16.0	1991	1994
1985	17.7	1993	1997
1984	18.2	1992	1996
1983	16.5	1995	2000
1982	18.3	1990	1994

David Wynn
High Eden Ridge
Eden Valley SA 5235
Tel: (08) 8564 1101
Fax: (08) 8361 3400

De Bortoli
De Bortoli Road
Bilbul NSW 2680
Tel: (02) 6964 9444
Fax: (02) 6964 9400

De Bortoli Yarra Valley

Pinnacle Lane
Dixon's Creek Vic 3775
Tel: (03) 5965 2271
Fax: (03) 5965 2442

Region: Yarra Valley Winemakers: Stephen Webber, David Slingsby-Smith, David Bicknell Viticulturist: Philip Lobley Chief Executive: Darren De Bortoli

Its excellent recent string of vintages confirms De Bortoli's arrival amongst the best of the Yarra Valley's wineries. It boasts some of the Valley's more consistent cabernet vineyards, while its Chardonnay and Pinot Noir are developing more finesse and power.

CABERNET SAUVIGNON
Yarra Valley $$$$

1996	17.5	2001	2004
1995	18.8		2007+
1994	16.7	1999	2002
1993	17.2	2001	2005
1992	18.2	2000	2004
1991	16.8	1999	2003
1990	17.4	1995	1998

CHARDONNAY
Yarra Valley $$$

1998	18.0	2003	2006
1997	17.8	2002	2005
1996	18.5	2001	2004+
1995	16.8	1997	2000
1994	16.0	1996	1999
1993	16.0	1995	1998
1992	17.6	1997	2000
1991	18.1	1996	1999
1990	18.2	1995	1998

PINOT NOIR
Yarra Valley $$$$

1997	18.3	2002	2005
1996	18.6	2001	2004
1995	15.0	1996	1997
1994	17.5	1999	2002
1992	16.7	1994	1997
1991	17.3	1993	1996

SHIRAZ
Yarra Valley $$$$

1997	18.5	2002	2005+
1996	18.1	2001	2004
1995	18.2	2003	2007
1994	18.1	1999	2002
1993	17.2	1998	2001
1992	18.0	2000	2004

Region: Mansfield Winemaker: Rosalind Ritchie
Viticulturist: David Ritchie Chief Executives: Robert & Vivienne Ritchie

Delatite is a high-altitude cool-climate vineyard near the Victorian ski town of Mansfield which consistently produces fine, aromatic and steely white wines whose bracing acids perfectly counter their attractive fruit intensity. The pick are from riesling and gewürztraminer. A late, drought-affected vintage in 1999 has produced some exceptional parcels of riesling, but in very low yields.

Delatite

cnr Stoney's &
Pollard's Rds
Mansfield Vic 3722
Tel: (03) 5775 2922
Fax: (03) 5775 2911

CHARDONNAY

Mansfield $$$

1996	17.2	2001	2004
1995	16.2	1997	2000
1994	18.2	1999	2002
1993	18.3	1998	2001
1992	17.4	2000	2004
1991	16.8	1996	1999
1990	16.5	1995	1998
1989	16.0	1994	1997

DEAD MAN'S HILL GEWURZTRAMINER

Mansfield $$$

1999	18.0	2004	2009
1998	16.5	2003	2006
1997	18.4	2005	2009
1996	18.5	2004	2008
1995	18.0	2000	2003
1994	18.0	2002	2006
1992	18.2	2000	2004
1991	18.0	1996	1999
1990	16.5	1992	1995
1989	17.5	1994	1997

DEMELZA

Mansfield $$$$

1994-95	18.2	1999	2002+
1987/88	16.2	1995	1997
1991	15.3	1996	1999

THE ONWINE AUSTRALIAN WINE ANNUAL 2000

DEVIL'S RIVER

Mansfield $$$

1997	15.1	2002	2005
1996	15.4	2001	2004
1995	16.7	2000	2003
1994	16.5		2006+
1993	17.6		2005+
1992	18.0	2000	2004
1991	17.0	1999	2003
1990	17.0	1998	2002

MERLOT

Mansfield $$$$

1997	15.0	1998	1999
1996	16.0	2001	2005
1994	17.5	2002	2006
1993	15.3	1995	2000

PINOT NOIR

Mansfield $$$

1998	14.0		1998
1997	17.6	2002	2005
1996	16.7	2001	2004
1995	15.5	2000	2003
1994	15.4	1999	2003
1992	16.8	1997	2000
1990	17.0	1998	2002
1989	17.5	1994	1997

RIESLING

Mansfield $$$

1998	18.5	2006	2010
1997	16.5	2005	2009
1996	18.2	2004	2008
1995	18.0	2000	2003
1994	18.5	2002	2005
1993	18.8	2001	2005
1992	18.6	2000	2004
1991	18.0	1999	2003
1990	18.5	1998	2002
1989	17.5	1997	2001
1988	17.0		2008
1987	17.5	1995	1999
1986	18.5	1994	1998

THE ONWINE AUSTRALIAN WINE ANNUAL

SAUVIGNON BLANC

Mansfield $$$

1998	16.5	1999	2002+
1997	17.8	1999	2002
1996	16.0	1997	1998
1995	18.5	1996	1997

SHIRAZ

Mansfield $$$

1997	16.8	2002	2005+
1996	15.7	1998	2001
1994	15.0	1996	1999
1993	15.2	1998	2001
1992	16.7	1997	2000
1991	15.0	1996	1999
1990	17.6	1998	2002

Region: Margaret River Winemaker: Janice McDonald
Viticulturist: Simon Robertson Chief Executive: Bruce Kemp

The Margaret River outpost of Australia's largest wine company, Southcorp Wines, Devil's Lair has become a chardonnay and cabernet blend specialist after a wise recent decision to remove its pinot noir. When you taste the seductive 1997 Chardonnay and very smart, sophisticated 1996 Devil's Lair (red) it's easy to see why.

Devil's Lair

Rocky Rd
via Margaret River
WA 6285
Tel: (08) 9757 7573
Fax: (08) 9757 7533

CHARDONNAY

Margaret River $$$$

1998	16.9	2000	2003+
1997	18.6	2002	2005
1996	18.2	2001	2004
1995	10.0	2000	2003
1994	18.4	1996	1999
1993	18.5	1998	2001
1992	17.5	1994	1997

RED (FORMERLY CABERNET SAUVIGNON)

Margaret River $$$$

1997	16.7	2002	2005+
1996	18.7	2004	2008
1995	18.3	2003	2007
1994	18.2	2002	2006
1993	18.4	2001	2005
1992	18.0		2004+
1991	17.4	1999	2003
1990	18.4		2002+

Diamond Valley

2130 Kinglake Road
St Andrews Vic 3761
Tel: (03) 9710 1484
Fax: (03) 9710 1369

Region: Yarra Valley Winemakers: David Lance, James Lance
Viticulturist: David Lance Chief Executive: David Lance

A simply brilliant pinot noir vintage in 1997 has put Diamond Valley right back in the lead group of Australian pinot noir makers. The Estate (white) label is a sumptuous, yet superbly restrained wine of considerable style, while the Close-Planted Pinot Noir reveals a wilder, spicier expression of the variety.

BLUE LABEL CHARDONNAY

Yarra Valley $$$

1998	16.5	2000	2003
1997	17.5	1999	2000
1996	16.8	1998	2001
1995	16.0	1996	1997
1994	15.6	1996	1999
1993	16.8	1993	1998
1992	17.9	1997	2000

BLUE LABEL PINOT NOIR

Yarra Valley $$$

1998	17.0	2000	2003
1997	18.3	1998	2001
1996	17.5	1998	2001
1994	15.6	1996	1999
1993	15.0	1998	2001
1992	15.6	1994	1997
1991	18.0	1993	1996

CLOSE-PLANTED PINOT NOIR

Yarra Valley $$$$

1997	18.4	1999	2002
1996	18.5	2001	2004
1995	18.1	1997	2000

ESTATE CABERNET

Yarra Valley $$$

1996	16.6	2001	2004+
1994	17.2	2002	2006+
1992	15.6	2000	2004
1991	15.6	1999	2003
1990	18.1	1998	2002
1989	16.3	1997	2001
1988	17.0	1996	2000

ESTATE CHARDONNAY

Yarra Valley $$$$

1997	16.6	1999	2002
1996	16.3	1998	2001
1995	17.8	2000	2003
1994	18.2	2002	2006
1993	16.6	1998	2001
1992	18.1	1997	2000
1991	16.3	1996	1999
1990	18.0	1995	1998

ESTATE PINOT NOIR

Yarra Valley $$$$

1997	19.0	2002	2005+
1996	16.8	2001	2004
1995	17.1	2000	2003
1994	16.4	1996	1999
1993	17.6	1998	2001
1992	16.4	1994	1997
1991	18.0	1996	1999
1990	16.8	1992	1995

Region: Coal Creek Valley Winemaker: Peter Althaus
Viticulturist: Peter Althaus Chief Executive: Peter Althaus

A recent vertical tasting of Domaine A red wines turned my views of Tasmanian viticulture on their head. The points below are real, very real. In lesser years the wines are sold as 'Stoney Vineyard'.

CABERNET SAUVIGNON

Coal Creek Valley $$$$$

1995	18.4	2007	2015
1994	18.0	2006	2014
1993	16.8	2005	2013
1992	17.3	2004	2012
1991	18.8	2003	2011
1990	16.3	1995	1998

PINOT NOIR

Coal Creek Valley $$$$$

1997	18.3	2005	2009
1995	16.8	1997	2000
1994	18.7	1999	2002+
1992	18.3	1997	2000+
1991	18.0	1996	1999
1990	16.6	1995	1998

Domaine A
105 Tea Tree Road
Campania Tas 7026
Tel: (03) 6260 4174
Fax: (03) 6260 4390

Domaine Chandon

Greenpoint
Maroondah Highway
Coldstream Vic 3770
Tel: (03) 9739 1110
Fax: (03) 9739 1095

Region: Yarra Valley Winemakers: Wayne Donaldson, Neville Rowe, James Gosper
Viticulturist: Bernie Wood Chief Executive: Chris Lynch

Having redefined the premium Australian sparkling wine market over the last decade, Domaine Chandon must think it's running out of challenges. Based in Victoria's Yarra Valley, it sources fruit from a significant number of vineyards in the cooler and more southerly regions from several states. My favourite Domaine Chandon wines are the punchy, uncompromising Blanc de Blancs, which has an uncanny ability to improve after an extra three years on the cork, plus the long, clean and austere Blanc de Noirs. Domaine Chandon's first Non Vintage wine is shortly due for release.

VINTAGE BLANC DE BLANCS

Southern Australia $$$$

1995	18.5	1997	2000+
1993	18.4	1998	2001
1992	18.8	2000	2004
1991	18.7	1999	2003
1990	18.1	1995	1998
1989	17.7	1994	1997
1986	18.6	1994	1998

VINTAGE BLANC DE NOIRS

Southern Australia $$$$

1994	18.5	1996	1999
1993	18.4	1998	2001
1992	18.7	1997	2000
1991	17.8	1996	1999
1990	18.3	1992	1995

VINTAGE BRUT

Southern Australia $$$$

1996	17.9	1998	2001
1995	17.5	1997	2000
1994	18.5	1996	1999
1993	18.6	1995	1998
1992	18.5	1994	1997
1991	18.7	1996	1999
1990	18.4	1992	1995

VINTAGE BRUT ROSÉ

Southern Australia $$$$

1995	18.1	1997	2000
1994	18.3	1996	1999
1993	18.3	1998	2001
1992	17.4	1994	1997
1989	18.3	1994	1997

Dromana Estate

**Harrison's Road
Dromana Vic 3936
Tel: (03) 5987 3800
Fax: (03) 5981 0714**

Region: Mornington Peninsula Winemaker: Garry Crittenden
Viticulturist: Garry Crittenden Chief Executive: Garry Crittenden

The excellent 1997 vintages of the Reserve Chardonnay and Reserve Pinot Noir have done much to enhance Dromana Estate's currency amongst serious drinkers of the Burgundian varieties. They're each something of a walk on the wild side of winemaking, but the results are simply delicious. Dromana Estate is also home to Garry Crittenden's ground-breaking 'i' series of wines made with Italian varieties.

CABERNET MERLOT

Mornington Peninsula $$$$

1997	17.0	2002	2005+
1996	16.0	1998	2001
1995	16.4	2000	2003
1994	17.8	2002	2006
1993	17.6	2001	2005
1992	17.2	2000	2004
1991	16.8	1996	1999
1990	18.0	1998	2002

CHARDONNAY

Mornington Peninsula $$$$

1998	17.2	2000	2003
1997	16.1	1999	2002
1996	16.5	1998	2001
1995	17.0	1997	2000
1994	18.6	1999	2002
1993	18.0	1998	2001
1992	18.0	1997	2000
1991	18.5	1996	1999
1990	17.0	1995	1998

Elderton

3 Tanunda Road
Nuriootpa SA 5355
Tel: (08) 8562 1058
Fax: (08) 8562 2844

PINOT NOIR

Mornington Peninsula $$$$

1998	16.5	1999	2000
1997	17.6	2002	2005
1996	18.0	2001	2004
1995	18.2	1997	2000
1994	18.1	1999	2002
1993	18.0	1998	2001

RESERVE CHARDONNAY

Mornington Peninsula $$$$

1997	18.7	2002	2005
1996	17.6	2001	2004
1995	17.9	1997	2000
1994	18.4	1996	1999

RESERVE PINOT NOIR

Mornington Peninsula $$$$

1997	18.8	2002	2005+
1996	18.3	2001	2005+
1995	18.0	2000	2003+
1994	15.0	1996	1999

Region: Barossa Valley Winemaker: James Irvine
Viticulturist: David Young Chief Executive: Lorraine Ashmead

With the exception of the Command Shiraz, a more powerfully structured wine matured in oak for more than two years, Elderton's collection of red wines presents an early-drinking smorgasbord of ripe Barossa flavours, creamy oaky textures and supple, soft tannins. It's little wonder they're so popular.

CABERNET SAUVIGNON/MERLOT

Barossa Valley $$$

1997	16.0	1999	2002+
1996	16.8	2001	2004
1995	16.5	2000	2003
1994	18.0	1999	2002
1993	17.4	1998	2001
1992	16.6	1997	2000
1991	17.5	1996	1999
1990	17.3	1995	1998
1989	15.5	1994	1997
1988	17.0	1990	1993

COMMAND SHIRAZ
Barossa Valley $$$$$

1995	17.6	2003	2007
1994	18.4	2002	2006
1993	16.8	2001	2005
1992	18.6		2004+
1990	17.8	1995	1998
1988	18.3	1996	2001
1987	18.5	1999	2004
1986	17.7	1998	2003

RIESLING
Barossa Valley $$

1997	13.5	1998	1999
1994	16.7	1999	2002
1993	18.2	1998	2001
1992	16.3	1994	1997
1991	18.0	1999	2003

SHIRAZ
Barossa Valley $$$

1996	16.2	1998	2003+
1995	17.2	2000	2003
1994	16.8	1999	2002
1993	17.0	1995	1998
1992	16.4	2000	2004
1991	17.0	1999	2003
1990	16.8	1998	2002

Region: Mornington Peninsula
Winemakers: Tod Dexter, Kevin McCarthy, Michael Cope-Williams
Viticulturist: Lawrence Tedesco Chief Executive: Baillieu Myer

Elgee Park releases some delicious wines from riesling, chardonnay and the northern Rhône white variety of viognier, which it typically fashions into a citrusy, chalky wine.

CUVÉE BRUT
Mornington Peninsula $$$$

1995	16.5	1997	2000
1994	17.2	1999	2002
1993	16.0	1995	1998
1992	17.6	1994	1997

Elgee Park

**RMB 5560 Junction Road
Merricks North Vic 3926
Tel: (03) 5989 7338
Fax: (03) 5989 7424**

Evans Family

**Loggerheads Palmers Lane
Pokolbin NSW 2321
Tel: (02) 4998 7333
Fax: (02) 4998 7798**

FAMILY RESERVE CHARDONNAY

Mornington Peninsula $$$

1997	15.3	1999	2002
1995	16.5	1996	1997
1994	16.1	1996	1999
1993	18.7	1998	2001
1992	18.3	1997	2000
1991	17.4	1996	1999
1990	17.5	1995	1998

FAMILY RESERVE PINOT NOIR

Mornington Peninsula $$$$

1997	16.7	1999	2002
1996	16.2	1998	2001+
1995	15.6	1997	2000

FAMILY RESERVE VIOGNIER

Mornington Peninsula $$

1997	17.0	1999	2002
1996	17.2	1998	2001
1995	17.2	1997	2000
1994	15.0	1996	1999
1992	15.2	1993	1994

**Region: Lower Hunter Valley Winemaker: Keith Tulloch
Viticulturist: Alan Townley Chief Executive: Len Evans**

Len Evans' own chardonnay is a boots-and-all affair dished up with considerable pomp, style and circumstance - a little like lunch with the man himself. Typical of most Hunter chardonnays, it drinks best after around five years of age.

CHARDONNAY

Lower Hunter Valley $$$$

1998	17.6	2003	2006
1997	15.6	2002	2005
1996	18.6	2001	2004
1995	18.5	2003	2007
1994	16.8	1999	2002
1993	18.1	1998	2001
1990	17.5	1992	1995

Region: Margaret River Winemaker: Brian Fletcher
Viticulturist: Murray Edmonds Chief Executive: Franklin Tate

While its wines are generally capable enough and interesting to open up, I can't help the feeling that Evans & Tate aren't keeping up with either their own expectations or the performance of several of their neighbours, many of which are admittedly much smaller. There's a hardness about several recent red releases, while some of the whites are atypically greenish. The Margaret River Semillon maintains a high standard.

Evans & Tate

cnr Caves & Metricup Rds
Willyabrup WA 6280
Tel: (08) 9755 6244
Fax: (08) 9755 6346

BARRIQUE 61 CABERNET MERLOT

Margaret River $$$

1997	15.9	2002	2005
1996	14.8	1997	1998
1995	15.0	1997	2000
1994	17.2	1999	2002
1993	15.0	1998	2001

GNANGARA SHIRAZ

Swan Valley $$

1996	16.7	1998	2001
1995	16.9	1997	2000
1994	15.0	1996	1999
1993	16.7	1998	2001
1992	15.6	1994	1997
1991	16.8	1993	1996
1990	16.7	1992	1995

MARGARET RIVER CABERNET SAUVIGNON

Margaret River $$$$

1997	17.6	2005	2009
1996	17.0	2004	2008
1995	15.9	2003	2007
1994	18.3	2002	2006
1993	18.2	2001	2005
1992	18.4	2000	2004
1991	18.0	1999	2003
1990	15.0	1995	1998
1989	15.0	1991	1994

MARGARET RIVER CHARDONNAY

Margaret River $$$$

1996	16.0	2001	2004
1995	15.3	1996	1997
1994	16.5	1999	2002
1993	18.1	1995	1998
1991	14.8	1992	1993
1990	16.2	1995	1998

MARGARET RIVER CLASSIC

Margaret River $$$

1998	17.5	1998	1999
1997	16.8	1997	1998
1996	16.5	1996	1997
1995	18.0	1996	1997
1994	18.0	1996	1999

MARGARET RIVER MERLOT

Margaret River $$$$

1996	16.8	2001	2004
1995	16.8	2000	2003
1994	16.7	1999	2002
1993	17.0	2001	2005
1992	17.3	1997	2000
1991	18.3	1999	2003
1990	18.0	1998	2002
1989	17.8	1994	1997
1988	16.5	1993	1996

MARGARET RIVER SAUVIGNON BLANC

Margaret River $$$

1997	16.2	1998	1999
1996	17.6	1997	1998
1995	15.0	1995	1996

MARGARET RIVER SEMILLON

Margaret River $$$

1997	18.0	2002	2005
1996	17.5	1998	2001
1995	18.5	2000	2003
1994	18.2	1999	2002
1993	18.5	1998	2001
1991	17.5	1996	1999
1990	16.0	1998	2002
1989	18.0	1994	1997
1988	16.5	1996	2000

MARGARET RIVER SHIRAZ

Margaret River $$$$

1996	17.2	2004	2008
1995	17.8		2007+
1994	18.3	2002	2006
1993	15.8	2001	2005
1992	18.0	2000	2004
1991	18.0	1999	2003
1990	18.4	1995	1998
1989	15.5	1991	1994

TWO VINEYARDS CHARDONNAY

Swan Valley and Margaret River $$$

1998	16.8	2000	2003
1997	15.0	1998	1999
1996	17.1	1998	2001
1995	16.7	1997	2000
1994	17.6	1996	1999
1993	15.3	1994	1995

THE ONWINE AUSTRALIAN WINE ANNUAL 2000

Fergusson

Wills Road
Yarra Glen Vic 3775
Tel: (03) 5965 2237
Fax: (03) 5965 2405

Fox Creek

Malpas Rd
Willunga SA 5171
Tel: (08) 8556 2403
Fax: (08) 8556 2104

Region: Yarra Valley Winemaker: Chris Keyes
Viticulturist: Chris Keyes Chief Executive: Peter Fergusson

Fergusson's is a small Yarra Valley maker whose vineyard is found in a picturesque small valley near Dixon's Creek. Its Chardonnay is flavoursome and generously structured, while its red wines are typically earthy and spicy, especially the 'Jeremy' Shiraz.

'JEREMY' SHIRAZ

Yarra Valley $$$

1997	16.7	2002	2005
1996	14.3	2001	2004
1995	17.0	2003	2007
1994	16.5	1996	1999
1993	16.0	2001	2005
1991	18.0	1999	2003

'VICTORIA' CHARDONNAY

Yarra Valley $$$

1997	16.3	1998	2002
1996	16.0	1998	2001
1995	16.8	1997	2000
1994	17.8	1999	2002
1993	16.9	1995	1998
1992	17.7	1997	2000

Region: McLaren Vale Winemaker: Sparky Marquis
Viticulturists: Sparky and Sarah Marquis
Chief Executives: Jim and Helen Watts

Fox Creek is an energetic new McLaren Vale vineyard which burst onto the scene with its sumptuous 1994 Reserve Shiraz, a wine quick to join the ranks of the serious 'Grange Pretenders'. Since then it has constantly repeated its good form with shiraz and has launched a rich, sumptuous Reserve Cabernet Sauvignon label, plus a flinty, mineral Verdelho.

RESERVE CABERNET SAUVIGNON

McLaren Vale $$$$

1997	17.0	2005	2009+
1996	17.9	2004	2008+
1995	16.5	2000	2003

THE ONWINE AUSTRALIAN WINE ANNUAL

RESERVE SHIRAZ

McLaren Vale $$$$

1997	18.4	2005	2009
1996	18.6		2008+
1995	18.1	2003	2005
1994	18.4		2006+

VERDELHO

McLaren Vale $$

1998	16.7	2000	2003
1997	15.2	1998	1999
1996	16.6	1998	2001

Region: Great Southern Winemakers: Barrie Smith, Judy Cullam
Viticulturist: Barrie Smith Chief Executives: Barrie Smith, Judy Cullam

It's been a little erratic in recent vintages, but Frankland Estate has undoubted potential as a maker of fine wine from both shiraz and the red Bordeaux varieties, plus riesling. It's found well towards the north of the large Great Southern region and can list amongst its achievements the excellent Olmo's Reward blend of 1995.

Frankland Estate

Frankland Rd
Frankland WA 6396
Tel: (08) 9855 1555
Fax: (08) 9855 1583

CABERNET SAUVIGNON

Great Southern $$$

1997	16.3	2002	2005
1996	17.5		2008+
1995	16.2		2007+
1994	16.0	1999	2002
1993	17.6		2005+
1992	16.6	1997	2000
1991	16.6	1996	1999

CHARDONNAY

Great Southern $$$

1997	15.3	1999	2002
1996	16.0	2001	2004
1994	18.5	1992	2002
1993	15.5	1998	2001
1992	16.4	1994	1997

ISOLATION RIDGE RIESLING

Great Southern $$

1998	15.6	2000	2003
1997	16.5	2002	2005
1996	17.4	2001	2004
1995	17.6	2000	2003
1994	16.6	1999	2002
1993	16.0	1995	1998
1992	16.7	1997	2000
1991	17.2	1993	1996

ISOLATION RIDGE SHIRAZ

Great Southern $$

1997	15.2	1999	2002
1996	16.9	2001	2004
1995	17.1	2000	2003
1994	17.4	1999	2002
1993	16.3	2001	2005
1992	16.5	2000	2004

OLMO'S REWARD

Great Southern $$$

1996	17.0	2001	2004
1995	18.7		2007+
1994	16.5	2002	2006
1993	17.5	1998	2001
1992	17.3	1997	2000

Freycinet

15919 Tasman Highway
Bicheno Tas 7215
Tel: (03) 6257 8384
Fax: (03) 6257 8454

Region: East Coastal Tasmania Winemakers: Claude Radenti & Lindy Bull
Viticulturist: Geoff Bull Chief Executive: Geoff Bull

Freycinet's heat trap-like site on Tasmania's east coast gives it a brilliant advantage when it comes to ripening grapes and a real headstart with its best varieties of pinot noir and chardonnay. Freycinet's Chardonnay is its most consistent effort, a surprisingly generous and spicy wine with great depth and intensity.

CABERNET SAUVIGNON

East Coastal Tasmania $$$$

1995	16.2	2000	2003
1994	18.3	2002	2006
1992	15.8	2000	2004
1991	18.0	2003	2011
1990	16.0	1998	2002

CHARDONNAY

East Coastal Tasmania $$$$

1996	16.7	1998	2001
1995	18.6	2003	2007
1994	18.2	2002	2006
1992	16.6	1994	1999
1991	16.3	1993	1996

PINOT NOIR

East Coastal Tasmania $$$$

1997	16.0	1999	2002
1996	17.0	2001	2004
1995	18.5	2000	2003
1994	16.0	1996	1999
1993	14.9	1998	2001
1992	15.7	1997	2000
1991	18.7	1996	1999
1990	16.2	1995	1998

Region: Clare Valley Winemaker: Stephen George
Viticulturist: Chief Executive: Stephen George

Stephen George makes a blockbusting, dark, peppery shiraz from old-vine Clare Valley fruit with an astringent, savoury finish for genuinely long term cellaring. He also creates his own version of the traditional cabernet-malbec Clare blend, a wine of similar dimensions, power and longevity.

Galah

**Tregarthen Rd
Ashton SA 5137
Tel: (08) 8390 1243
Fax: (08) 8390 1243**

SHIRAZ

Clare Valley $$$

1997	17.8		2009+
1996	16.2	2001	2004
1995	18.0		2007+
1994	18.1	2002	2006
1993	15.6	1998	2001
1992	17.9		2004+
1991	17.5	1999	2003
1990	17.6		2002+
1989	16.0	1997	2001

THE ONWINE AUSTRALIAN WINE ANNUAL 2000

Gembrook Hill

Launching Place Road
Gembrook Vic 3783
Tel: (03) 5968 1622
Fax: (03) 5968 1699

Region: Yarra Valley Winemakers: David Lance, Dr Ian Marks
Viticulturist: Dr Ian Marks Chief Executive: Dr Ian Marks

It's located in a cooler, higher portion of the Yarra Valley, so its wines, Pinot Noir and Chardonnay especially, may lack the richness and weight of those grown on the Valley floor. Gembrook Hill's does grow one of our most enticing and racy Sauvignon Blancs.

CHARDONNAY
Yarra Valley $$$$

1997	15.6	1999	2002
1995	17.6	2000	2003
1994	16.9	1999	2002
1993	17.9	1998	2001

PINOT NOIR
Yarra Valley $$$$

1997	16.8	1999	2002
1996	15.8	1997	1998
1995	16.0	1996	1997
1994	16.0	1996	1999
1993	17.9	1998	2001
1992	16.8	1994	1997

SAUVIGNON BLANC
Yarra Valley $$$$

1998	18.5	2000	2003
1997	18.0	1998	1999
1996	17.0	1998	2001
1994	16.0	1996	1999

Geoff Merrill

291 Pimpala Road
Reynella SA 5161
Tel: (08) 8381 6877
Fax: (08) 8322 2244

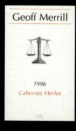

Region: McLaren Vale Winemaker: Geoff Merrill
Viticulturist: Goe DiFabio Chief Executive: Geoff Merrill

The best of Geoff Merrill's present wines is the Reserve Cabernet Sauvignon 1995, which recently made the grade on Qantas First Class. Generally, Merrill's style remains fine and relatively light.

CABERNET MERLOT (FORMERLY MOUNT HURTLE)

McLaren Vale, Goulburn Valley, Coonawarra $$$

1996	15.8	1998	2001
1995	16.7	2003	2007
1994	16.5	1996	1999
1993	16.6	1995	1998
1992	16.2	1997	2000
1991	16.7	1996	1999
1990	17.9	1998	2002

CABERNET SAUVIGNON RESERVE (FORMERLY CABERNET SAUVIGNON)

Coonawarra, McLaren Vale, Goulburn Valley $$$$

1995	17.2	2003	2007
1994	16.6	1999	2002
1993	17.0		2005+
1992	16.3	2000	2004
1991	15.0	1999	2003
1990	16.6	1998	2002
1989	18.0	1997	2001
1988	17.5	1996	2000
1987	17.0	1995	1999
1986	17.5	1994	1998

CHARDONNAY RESERVE

South-Eastern Australia $$$$

1996	15.5	1997	1998
1995	15.8	1997	2000
1994	16.4	1996	1999
1993	15.2	1995	1998
1992	16.5	1997	2000
1991	17.9	1996	1999
1990	18.0	1998	2002

SAUVIGNON BLANC (FORMERLY MOUNT HURTLE)

McLaren Vale $$

1997	14.6		1998
1996	16.7	1996	1997
1995	16.8	1996	1997
1994	17.9	1998	1999

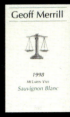

SHIRAZ (FORMERLY MOUNT HURTLE)

McLaren Vale $$$$

1995	16.1	2000	2003
1994	17.0	1999	2002
1992	16.7	1998	2001
1991	16.4	1997	2000

THE ONWINE AUSTRALIAN WINE ANNUAL 2000

Geoff Weaver

2 Gilpin Lane
Mitcham SA 5062
Tel: (08) 8272 2105
Fax: (08) 8271 0177

Region: Adelaide Hills Winemaker: Geoff Weaver
Viticulturist: Geoff Weaver Chief Executive: Geoff Weaver

Each of Geoff Weaver's quartet of table wines from Lenswood in the Adelaide Hills reflects his preference for restrained, elegant and complex wine that gradually unravels itself in a glass before you. His Riesling, Sauvignon Blanc and Chardonnay are each pristine and spotless, while the suppleness and tightness of the Cabernet Merlot unashamedly flies directly against the modern trend in Australian red wine.

CABERNET MERLOT
Adelaide Hills $$$$

1994	17.9	2002	2006
1993	18.1	2001	2005
1991	16.2	1999	2003
1990	18.3	1998	2002
1988	15.0	1993	1996

CHARDONNAY
Adelaide Hills $$$

1997	18.5	2002	2005+
1996	17.8	1998	2001
1995	18.4	2000	2003+
1994	17.0	1999	2002
1993	18.3	2001	2005
1992	17.3	1997	2000
1991	18.5	1996	1999
1990	16.5	1995	1998

RIESLING
Adelaide Hills $$

1998	18.1	2003	2006
1997	18.5	2005	2009
1996	16.0	1998	2001
1995	17.8	2003	2007
1994	14.0	1995	1996
1993	18.4	2001	2005
1991	18.4	1999	2003
1990	17.2	1995	1998

SAUVIGNON BLANC
Adelaide Hills $$$

1998	18.5	2000	2003
1997	18.3	1999	2002
1996	18.1	1998	2001
1995	16.6	1997	2000
1994	18.6	1996	1999
1993	18.8	1995	1998
1992	18.5	1994	1999

Region: NE Victoria   Winemaker: Rick Kinzbrunner
Viticulturist: Rick Kinzbrunner   Chief Executive: Rick Kinzbrunner

Rick Kinzbrunner's distinctive south-facing site on eroded gravel soils produces Australia's finest Chardonnay plus some pretty handy but lesser-known cabernet blends. But he really turned the heat on the pinot debate with the 1997 wine, a masterfully crafted pinot and a clear stylistic successor to the stellar 1992 vintage.

CABERNET SAUVIGNON/MERLOT/ CABERNET FRANC
NE Victoria $$$$

1996	18.3	2004	2008+
1995	18.3	2003	2007
1994	18.1	2002	2006
1993	18.0	1998	2001
1992	18.6		2004+
1991	18.9	1999	2003
1990	17.9	1998	2002
1988	18.4	1996	2000
1987	15.0	1995	1999
1986	16.7	1994	1998

Giaconda

**Cnr Wangaratta
& McClay Rds
Beechworth Vic 3747
Tel: (03) 5727 0246
Fax: (03) 5727 0246**

CHARDONNAY
NE Victoria $$$$$

1997	19.2	2005	2009
1996	19.2	2001	2004+
1995	18.4	2000	2003+
1994	18.8	2002	2006
1993	18.8	2001	2005
1992	19.0	1997	2000
1991	18.4	1995	1999
1990	18.6	1998	2002
1989	17.8	1991	1994

Goona Warra

**Sunbury Road
Sunbury Vic 3429
Tel: (03) 9740 7766
Fax: (03) 9744 7648**

PINOT NOIR
NE Victoria $$$$$

1997	18.8	2002	2005+
1996	18.0	2001	2004+
1995	18.3	2000	2003
1994	18.2	1999	2002
1993	17.9	1998	2001
1992	19.0	1997	2000
1991	18.5	1996	1999
1990	17.5	1995	1998
1989	18.7	1994	1997
1988	18.6	1993	1996

Region: Macedon Winemaker: John Barnier
Viticulturist: John Barnier Chief Executive: John Barnier

In almost complete contrast to the scale and magnificence of its century-old bluestone winery in Sunbury, Goona Warra's output is restricted to small amounts of Chardonnay, Semillon, Cabernet Franc and Pinot Noir, of which the semillon is the most consistent and reliable. In warmer years the Cabernet Franc produces ripe fleshy wines of spiciness and charm.

CABERNET FRANC
Macedon $$$

1996	17.8	2001	2004
1995	15.0	1997	2000
1994	16.0	1996	1999
1993	17.3	1998	2001
1992	17.3	1997	2000
1991	16.5	1993	1996

SEMILLON
Macedon $$$

1997	17.9	2002	2005
1996	17.6	2001	2004
1995	18.2	2000	2003
1994	17.7	1999	2002
1993	17.2	1998	2001
1992	16.5	1997	2000
1991	18.0	1996	1999

Region: Great Southern Winemaker: Keith Bown
Viticulturist: Cate Finlay Chief Executive: Ted Avery

Goundrey

Muir Highway
Mount Barker WA 6324
Tel: (08) 9851 1777
Fax: (08) 9851 1997

Goundrey's future looks bright under its new ownership and the efforts presently being made to fulfill the potential of its excellent large vineyard. While there's little doubt that the company's best wines are still ahead of it, present releases continue to disappoint perhaps rather more than they should. A fine exception is the ripe, almost jammy 1996 Reserve Cabernet Sauvignon.

RESERVE CABERNET SAUVIGNON

Great Southern $$$

1996	17.0	2002	2008
1993	16.0	2001	2005
1992	15.6	1997	2000
1991	18.1		2003+
1990	15.5	1998	2002
1989	17.0	1997	2001
1988	15.5	1996	2000
1987	16.0	1995	1999
1986	14.5	1994	1998
1985	17.6	1993	1997

RESERVE CHARDONNAY

Great Southern $$$

1998	15.6	2000	2003
1997	16.4	1999	2002
1995	16.2	1997	2000
1994	18.0	1999	2002
1993	16.3	1995	1998
1992	17.4	1997	2000
1991	18.0	1996	1999

RESERVE RIESLING

Great Southern $$

1998	16.5	2000	2003
1997	17.0	2002	2005
1996	18.1	2004	2008
1995	16.0	2003	2007
1994	18.4	2002	2006
1993	18.7	1998	2001
1991	17.5	1996	1999
1990	17.0	1995	1998
1989	16.5	1994	1997

Gramp's

**Barossa Valley Way
Rowland Flat SA 5352
Tel: (08) 8521 3111
Fax: (08) 8521 3100**

RESERVE SHIRAZ
Great Southern $$$

1997	16.2	2002	2005+
1996	15.6	1998	2001
1994	18.1	2002	2006
1993	17.4	2001	2005
1992	18.5	2000	2004

Region: Barossa Valley Winemaker: Philip Laffer
Viticulturist: Joy Dick Chief Executive: Andre Boucard

Gramp's is an exclusively Barossa region label of Orlando Wyndham whose wines are generous, ripe and relatively early to mature and easy to understand. The Botrytis Semillon often makes a pleasant surprise.

BOTRYTIS SEMILLON
Barossa Valley $$$$

1997	16.7	1999	2002
1996	16.8	1998	2001
1994	15.0	1995	1996

CABERNET MERLOT
Barossa Valley $$

1996	15.8	1998	2001
1995	15.6	1997	2000
1994	15.0	1999	2002
1993	13.5	1995	1998
1992	16.6	1994	1997
1991	17.5	1996	1999
1990	17.6	1995	1998
1989	15.5	1991	1994

CHARDONNAY
Barossa Valley $$

1998	15.0	1999	2000
1997	16.7	1999	2002
1996	16.0	1998	2001
1995	14.5	1996	1997

GRENACHE
Barossa Valley $$

1997	16.6	1999	2002
1996	16.4	1998	2001
1995	15.9	1997	2000
1994	15.3	1996	1999

Region: Barossa Valley Winemaker: Grant Burge
Viticulturist: Michael Schrapel Chief Executive: Grant Burge

While the Meshach continues to attract the headlines, I actually prefer to open the Filsell Shiraz, whose expression of intense, ripe Barossa fruit is usually dealt with rather more sensitively in terms of cooperage. As a group, the Grant Burge wines are consistent, honest and suit the needs of those with and those without a cellar.

Grant Burge
**Barossa Valley Way
Jacob's Creek
Tanunda SA 5352
Tel: (08) 8563 3700
Fax: (08) 8563 2807**

CAMERON VALE CABERNET SAUVIGNON
Barossa Valley $$$

1997	16.0	2002	2005
1996	17.6	2004	2008
1995	17.4	2003	2007
1994	16.7	2002	2006
1993	16.6	2001	2005

FILSELL SHIRAZ
Barossa Valley $$$$

1997	18.3	2005	2009
1996	18.6	2008	2016
1995	18.5	2007	2015
1994	18.2	2002	2006
1993	16.8	2001	2005
1992	16.0	2000	2004
1991	18.5	2003	2011
1990	18.2	2002	2010

HILLCOT MERLOT
Barossa Valley $$$$

1997	15.8	1999	2002
1996	16.3	1998	2001
1995	16.5	2000	2003
1994	16.8	1999	2002

MESHACH
Barossa Valley $$$$$

1995	18.6	2003	2007+
1994	18.0	2006	2014
1993	18.0	2001	2005
1992	18.4	2004	2012
1991	19.1	2003	2011
1990	18.3		2010+
1988	18.3	2000	2008

THORN RIESLING
Eden Valley $$

1998	18.0	2003	2006
1997	16.1	1999	2002
1996	16.8	1998	2001+
1995	15.1	1996	1997

ZERK SEMILLON
Barossa Valley $$$

1998	16.6	2000	2003
1997	16.8	2002	2005
1996	15.0	1997	1998
1995	16.0	1996	1997

Green Point
Maroondah Highway
Coldstream Vic 3770
Tel: (03) 9739 1110
Fax: (03) 9739 1095

Region: Yarra Valley Winemakers: Wayne Donaldson, Tony Jordan
Viticulturist: Michael Murtagh Chief Executive: Tony Jordan

Domaine Chandon markets its still table wines under the same label it sells its sparkling wine overseas: Green Point. The Reserve Chardonnay is a rich, complex and heavily worked wine with genuine potential, while releases to date of Reserve Pinot Noir have yet to develop comparable sweetness of fruit and intensity.

YARRA VALLEY CHARDONNAY
Yarra Valley $$$

1998	16.9	2003	2006
1996	15.0	1996	1997
1995	18.2	2000	2003
1994	17.8	1999	2002
1993	16.7	1998	2001
1992	17.9	1997	2000

Region: Clare Valley Winemaker: Jeffrey Grosset
Viticulturist: Jeffrey Grosset Chief Executive: Jeffrey Grosset

Grosset

King Street
Auburn SA 5451
Tel: (08) 8849 2175
Fax: (08) 8849 2292

Named Riesling Winemaker of the Year (in Hamburg) in 1998 and The Wine Magazine's Winemaker of the Year to boot, Jeffrey Grosset is on a roll. With the benchmark modern Clare riesling in the Polish Hill, an outstanding chardonnay and a hugely promising pinot noir from the Adelaide Hills, plus a first-rate Bordeaux blend and several other wines approaching that class including one of the country's best dessert wines, Grosset has dealt himself a full hand.

GAIA (CABERNET SAUVIGNON BASED)

Clare Valley $$$$

1996	17.5	2004	2008
1995	18.0		2007+
1994	18.5		2006+
1993	18.3		2005+
1992	18.6		2004+
1991	16.6	1996	1999
1990	16.8	2002	2010
1989	16.6	1994	1997
1988	15.6	1990	1993
1987	16.5	1992	1995
1986	18.0	1994	1998

NOBLE RIESLING

Clare Valley $$$$

1998	16.7	2000	2003
1997	18.7	2002	2005
1996	18.2	1998	2001
1995	18.5	2000	2003
1994	18.5	1999	2002
1993	17.2	1995	1998
1992	17.6	1994	1997

PICCADILLY (CHARDONNAY)

Piccadilly Valley (Largely Clare until 1993) $$$$

1998	17.3	2003	2006
1997	18.3	2002	2005
1996	18.7	2001	2004
1995	18.4	2000	2003
1994	18.4	2002	2006
1993	18.1	1998	2001
1992	16.8	1997	2000
1991	17.7	1996	1999

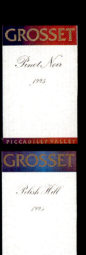

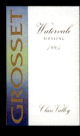

PINOT NOIR
Adelaide Hills $$$$

1998	18.2	2003	2006
1997	18.6	2002	2005+
1996	18.5	2004	2008
1995	17.5	1997	2000
1994	18.1	1999	2002
1993	17.0	1998	2001

POLISH HILL
Clare Valley $$$

1998	18.2	2006	2010
1997	19.0	2005	2009
1996	18.5	2004	2008
1995	19.0		2007+
1994	18.6	2002	2006
1993	18.7	2001	2005
1992	18.3	2000	2004
1991	16.5	1996	1999
1990	18.4		2002+
1989	15.0	1991	1994
1988	17.5	1993	1996
1987	18.0	1999	2004
1986	17.7	1994	1998

SEMILLON SAUVIGNON BLANC
Clare Valley (with Adelaide Hills from 1992) $$$

1998	18.0	2003	2006
1997	17.0	1998	1999
1996	18.1	1998	2001
1995	18.3	1997	2000
1994	18.5	1999	2003
1993	18.3	2001	2005
1992	17.5	1997	2000
1991	18.0	1996	1999
1990	17.5	1998	2002

WATERVALE RIESLING
Clare Valley $$

1998	18.5	2003	2006
1997	18.3	2002	2005
1996	17.2	2001	2004
1995	18.5	2000	2003
1994	18.4	2002	2006
1993	18.5	2001	2005
1992	17.8	1997	2000
1991	17.7	1996	1999
1990	18.5		2002+

Region: Yarra Valley Winemakers: Stephen Webber, David Slingsby-Smith, David Bicknell
Viticulturist: Philip Lobley Chief Executive: Darren De Bortoli

Gulf Station is a fast-growing De Bortoli brand of attractive early-drinking white wines made from Yarra Valley fruit. The Chardonnay is deliberately made with modest oak treatment, but presents generous, vibrant ripe grapefruit and peachy flavours.

CHARDONNAY
Yarra Valley $$

1998	17.3	1999	2002
1997	16.9	1999	2002
1996	16.5	1997	1998
1995	17.0	1996	1997

RIESLING
Yarra Valley $$

1998	17.6	2003	2006
1997	16.0	2002	2005
1996	15.0	1998	2001
1994	15.8	1994	1999

Region: McLaren Vale Winemaker: Phillipa Treadwell
Viticulturist: Adam Jacobs Chief Executive: Dr Richard Hamilton

Hamilton, which was Richard Hamilton in a former but recent incarnation, is a McLaren Vale brand whose white wines are more restrained and elegant than most from this region and whose reds have a distinctive tightness and herbal spiciness.

ALMOND GROVE CHARDONNAY
McLaren Vale $$

1998	16.0	2000	2003
1997	16.0	1999	2000
1996	16.7	1998	2001
1995	16.5	1997	2000
1994	16.8	1996	1999
1993	16.8	1995	1998
1992	16.0	1994	1997

BURTON'S VINEYARD
McLaren Vale $$

1996	16.9	2001	2004
1995	18.1	2003	2007
1994	16.6	1999	2002
1992	15.7	1998	2001

Gulf Station
Pinnacle Lane
Dixon's Creek Vic 3775
Tel: (03) 5965 2271
Fax: (03) 5965 2442

Hamilton
Main Road
Willunga SA 5172
Tel: (08) 8556 2288
Fax: (08) 8556 2868

Hanging Rock

**Jim Road
Newham Vic 3442
Tel: (03) 5427 0542
Fax: (03) 5427 0310**

HUT BLOCK CABERNETS
McLaren Vale $$

1996	15.4	2004	2008
1995	17.6	2003	2007
1994	16.8	1999	2002
1993	16.3	1998	2001
1992	17.1	2000	2004
1991	18.5	1999	2003

OLD VINES SHIRAZ
McLaren Vale $$$

1996	16.4	2001	2004+
1995	18.3	2003	2007
1994	17.5	2002	2006
1992	16.0	2000	2004

Region: Macedon Winemaker: John Ellis
Viticulturist: John Ellis Chief Executive: John Ellis

John Ellis must be delighted again to have access to premium shiraz fruit from Heathcote, enabling him to resurrect his most important red wine label. He's also done very well with the latest Cuvée of his Macedon sparkling wine, a typically rich, crackly and mouthfilling effort of great flavour and complexity.

HEATHCOTE SHIRAZ
Heathcote $$$$$

1997	17.0	2002	2005+
1992	18.4		2004+
1991	18.0		2011+
1990	18.7		2002+
1989	16.0	1997	2001
1988	16.8	1993	1996
1987	18.4		2007+

MACEDON
Macedon $$$$

Cuvee VI	18.6	2000	2002
Cuvee V	16.0	1997	2000
Cuvee IV	18.4	1996	1999
Cuvee III	17.6	1995	1996
Cuvee II	18.8	1994	1997
Cuvee I	18.5	1993	1996

"THE JIM JIM" (SAUVIGNON BLANC)

Macedon $$$

1998	16.6	1999	2000
1997	16.6		1998
1996	15.1	1997	1998
1995	18.3	1997	2000
1994	16.2	1995	1996

VICTORIA CABERNET SAUVIGNON & MERLOT

Victoria $$$

1997	15.3	2002	2005+
1996	16.4	2001	2004
1995	16.6	2003	2007
1994	15.7	2002	2006

VICTORIA CHARDONNAY

Victoria $$$

1997	16.6	2002	2005
1996	14.5	1998	2001
1995	14.6	1996	1997
1994	16.0	1995	1996
1993	17.4	1998	2001

VICTORIA SHIRAZ

Victoria $$$

1997	17.5	2002	2005
1996	16.8	2001	2004
1995	15.1	2000	2003

Hardys

Reynell Rd
Reynella SA 5161
Tel: (08) 8392 2222
Fax: (08) 8392 2202

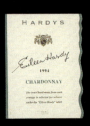

Region: McLaren Vale Winemakers: Peter Dawson, Stephen Pannell (red),
Tom Newton (white), Ed Carr (sparkling).
Viticulturist: Brenton Baker Chief Executive: Stephen Millar

It's a tribute to all those involved that BRL Hardy is now seen as a worthy rival to Southcorp's domination of Australia's red wine industry. In this respect, the Eileen Hardy Shiraz is perhaps the greatest success of all, and its auction prices now reflect the consistently high quality of the last seven vintages. The Tintara Shiraz remains a personal favourite for sheer quality and value.

EILEEN HARDY CHARDONNAY

Padthaway, McLaren Vale $$$$

1997	18.3	2002	2005
1996	18.5	2001	2004
1995	18.1	2000	2003
1994	17.4	1996	1999
1993	17.2	1998	2001
1992	15.6	1997	2000
1991	17.8	1996	1999
1990	18.1	1995	1998

EILEEN HARDY SHIRAZ

McLaren Vale, Padthaway $$$$$

1996	18.8	2001	2004+
1995	18.8	2007	2015
1994	18.0	2002	2006
1993	18.0		2005+
1992	18.0	2000	2004
1991	17.9		2003+
1990	18.5		2002+
1989	17.0	1997	2001
1988	17.0	1996	2000
1987	17.5	1995	1999
1986	16.5	1994	1998
1976	18.2	1988	1996
1970	18.9	1990	1995

NOTTAGE HILL CABERNET SHIRAZ

South Australia $

1998	16.4	2000	2003+
1996	15.0	2001	2004
1995	15.2	1997	2000
1994	15.5	1996	1999

SIEGERSDORF RHINE RIESLING

Padthaway $

1998	16.7	2003	2006+
1997	16.7	2002	2005
1996	16.5	2001	2004
1995	15.8	1996	1997
1994	17.2	2002	2006
1993	16.1	1995	1998
1992	18.2	2000	2004
1991	17.9	1996	1999
1990	17.0	1995	1998
1989	15.0	1991	1994
1988	18.0	1996	2000
1987	17.0	1992	1998
1986	16.5	1991	1994

THOMAS HARDY CABERNET SAUVIGNON

McLaren Vale, Coonawarra $$$$

1995	17.7	2003	2007+
1994	18.0		2006+
1993	17.3	2001	2005
1992	18.2	2000	2004
1991	18.5		2003+
1990	18.6		2002+
1989	18.3		2001+

TINTARA GRENACHE

McLaren Vale $$$$

1997	17.4	2002	2005+
1996	18.2	2001	2004+
1995	18.1	2000	2003

TINTARA SHIRAZ

McLaren Vale $$$$

1997	18.6	2005	2009
1996	18.3	2004	2008
1995	18.7	2000	2003+

Heathcote Winery

183 High St
Heathcote Vic 3523
Tel: (03) 5433 2595
Fax: (03) 5433 3081

Region: Heathcote Winemaker: Mark Kelly
Viticulturist: Lee Haselgrove Chief Executive: Steve Wilkins

Under new ownership, The Heathcote Winery looks set to cement a place amongst the leading makers of shiraz in this emerging region, whose only real limit to growth appears to be its water supply. I'm very impressed by the concentration and Rhône-ish expression of the 1997 Mail Coach Shiraz.

CHARDONNAY
Heathcote $$$

1998	16.6	2000	2003+
1997	14.7	1998	1999
1996	16.8	1998	2001
1994	14.5	1995	1996

MAIL COACH SHIRAZ
Heathcote $$$

1997	18.0	2002	2005+
1995	15.6	1997	2000
1994	17.6	1999	2002

Heggies Vineyard

Heggies Range Rd
Eden Valley SA 5353
Tel: (08) 8561 3200
Fax: (08) 8561 3393

Region: Eden Valley Winemakers: Simon Adams, Kevin Glastonbury, Louisa Rose
Viticulturist: Robin Nettelbeck Chief Executive: Robert Hill Smith

Merlot and viognier are playing more of a role at this traditional Eden Valley vineyard whose riesling has made classic wines for so long in both dry and dessert styles. Louisa Rose has had much to do with the viognier, which has become the country's benchmark expression of this variety. The Merlot is also evolving into a very elegant, tight-knit wine of true varietal definition.

BOTRYTIS RIESLING
Eden Valley $$$$

1998	18.0	2002	2006
1997	17.1	2002	2005
1996	18.0	2001	2004
1995	16.0	1997	2000
1994	17.7	1999	2002
1992	18.4	1997	2000
1991	18.0	1996	1999
1990	17.5	1992	1995

CHARDONNAY
Eden Valley $$$

1997	16.0	1999	2002
1996	16.3	1998	2001
1995	17.5	2000	2003
1994	16.5	1996	1999
1993	16.7	1995	1998
1992	17.0	1994	1997
1991	18.0	1996	1999

MERLOT (FORMERLY CABERNET BLEND)
Eden Valley $$$$

1995	18.0	2000	2003+
1994	18.2	2002	2006
1993	18.3	2001	2005
1992	16.0	2000	2004
1991	16.6	1996	1999
1990	17.4	1998	2002
1989	16.6	1994	1997
1988	17.5	1996	2000
1987	16.1	1989	1992

PINOT NOIR
Eden Valley $$$$

1997	17.8	2002	2005
1996	16.0	2001	2004
1994	14.5	1995	1996
1993	14.0	1994	1995

RIESLING
Eden Valley $$

1998	19.0	2006	2010+
1997	16.9	2002	2005
1996	16.5	2003	2007
1995	18.3	2003	2007
1994	14.0	1996	1999
1993	18.5		2005+
1992	18.2	1997	2000
1991	15.2	1993	1996
1990	15.5	1995	1998
1989	15.0	1991	1994
1988	18.5	1993	1996
1987	15.0	1989	1992
1986	17.5	1991	1994

Henschke

**Moculta Road
Keyneton SA 5353
Tel: (08) 8564 8223
Fax: (08) 8564 8294**

VIOGNIER
Eden Valley $$

1998	18.0	2000	2003
1997	17.9	1999	2002
1996	15.7	1997	1998
1995	14.5	1996	1997
1994	17.0	1999	2002
1993	17.5	1998	2001
1992	16.5	1997	2000

Region: Eden Valley Winemaker: Stephen Henschke
Viticulturist: Prue Henschke Chief Executive: Stephen Henschke

While a recent tasting of every vintage of Hill of Grace clearly justifies this wine's exalted status, it's exciting also to witness the continued improvement of the other important Henschke reds: the Mount Edelstone, the Abbotts Prayer and the Keyneton Estate. It's also worth noting the excellent quality of Henschke's 1998 white wines, just to show that there's more than a single trick in Steve Henschke's winemaking hand.

ABBOTTS PRAYER
Adelaide Hills $$$$$

1996	18.3	2004	2008+
1995	18.5	2003	2007
1994	18.7		2006+
1993	18.5		2005+
1992	17.7	2000	2004
1991	18.0		2003+
1990	19.0	2002	2010
1989	16.9	1994	1997

CRANES EDEN VALLEY CHARDONNAY (FORMERLY BAROSSA RANGES CHARDONNAY)
Eden Valley $$$

1998	17.9	2003	2006
1997	17.0	2002	2005
1996	18.2	2001	2004
1995	17.3	1997	2000
1994	18.2	1999	2002
1993	17.5	1995	1998
1992	17.7	1997	2000
1991	18.5	1996	1999
1990	18.7	1998	2002

CROFT CHARDONNAY

Adelaide Hills $$$$

1998	18.3	2003	2006+
1997	16.0	2002	2005
1996	18.4	2001	2004
1995	17.3	1997	2000
1994	18.4	1999	2003
1993	16.8	1995	1998
1990	18.3	1995	1998

CYRIL HENSCHKE CABERNET SAUVIGNON

Eden Valley $$$$$

1996	18.4		2008+
1995	17.6	2003	2007
1994	18.8		2006+
1993	18.7		2005+
1992	18.3		2004+
1991	18.7		2003+
1990	18.8		2002+
1989	17.4		2001+
1988	19.0	1996	2000
1987	16.0	1992	1995
1986	17.8	1998	2003
1985	18.1	1997	2002
1984	18.8	1992	1996
1983	17.0	1995	2000
1982	16.0	1987	1990
1981	18.5	1993	1998
1980	17.3	1992	1997
1979	16.0	1987	1991
1978	17.6	1990	2000

GILES PINOT NOIR

Adelaide Hills $$$$

1997	17.3	2002	2005
1996	17.3	2001	2004
1994	16.8	1999	2002
1993	17.0	1998	2002
1992	15.3	1994	1997
1991	18.3	1996	1999
1989	17.3	1994	1997

GREEN'S HILL RIESLING
Adelaide Hills $$

1998	18.1	2003	2006+
1997	18.3	2005	2009
1996	18.6	2004	2008
1995	18.0	2003	2007
1994	18.0	2002	2006
1993	18.3	1998	2001

HILL OF GRACE
Eden Valley $$$$$

1997	18.7		2017+
1996	19.0	2008	2016
1995	18.2		2015+
1994	18.7		2014+
1993	17.8		2013+
1992	18.8		2012+
1991	18.6		2011+
1990	19.0		2010+
1989	16.0	1994	1997
1988	18.9		2008+
1987	16.6	1999	2007+
1986	19.2		2006+
1985	17.4	2005	2015
1984	16.6	1996	2004
1983	15.4	1991	1995
1982	16.8	1994	2002
1981	15.3	1986	1989
1980	16.7	1992	2000
1979	17.3	1991	1999
1978	18.8	1998	2008
1977	17.2	1989	1997+
1976	18.4		1996+
1975	16.0	1983	1987
1973	18.6		1993+
1971	18.3		1991+
1970	18.2		1990+
1969	15.7	1981	1989
1968	19.0		1988+
1967	18.2		1987+
1966	19.0	1986	1996+
1965	16.5	1973	1979+
1964	16.7	1976	1984+
1963	16.4	1975	1983
1962	19.5	1982	1992+
1961	18.8	1973	1981+
1959	18.0	1979	1989
1958	18.8	1978	1988+

JULIUS RIESLING
Eden Valley $$

1998	17.5	2006	2010
1997	18.5	2005	2009
1996	18.5	2004	2008
1995	17.5	1997	2000
1994	18.6		2006+
1993	18.6	2000	2005
1992	18.4	2000	2004
1991	17.0	1999	2003
1990	18.7	1995	1998
1989	16.0	1994	1997
1988	16.5	1993	1996
1987	18.5	1999	2004
1986	17.0	1991	1994

KEYNETON ESTATE
Eden Valley $$$$

1996	18.2	2004	2008+
1994	18.1	2002	2006
1993	18.3		2005+
1992	18.0	1997	2000
1991	17.8	1999	2003
1990	16.5	1995	1998
1989	16.0	1994	1997
1988	18.1	1996	2000
1987	15.5	1992	1995
1986	18.5	1998	2003
1985	16.0	1997	2002
1984	18.2	1992	1996
1983	14.5	1991	1995
1982	17.0	1994	1999

LOUIS EDEN VALLEY SEMILLON
Eden Valley $$$

1998	16.6	2003	2006
1997	17.0	2002	2005
1996	15.8	1998	2003
1995	18.3	2000	2003
1994	18.0	2002	2006
1993	18.7	1998	2001
1992	17.9	1997	2000
1991	18.4	1996	1999
1990	18.0	1998	2002
1989	16.7	1994	1997

MOUNT EDELSTONE
Eden Valley $$$$$

1996	18.6	2004	2008+
1995	18.1		2007+
1994	18.9		2006+
1993	18.6		2005+
1992	18.5		2004+
1991	18.8		2003+
1990	18.6		2002+
1989	16.8	1997	2003
1988	18.5	2000	2005
1987	16.0	1995	2001
1986	18.2	1998	2003
1985	16.0		2005+
1984	16.5	1996	2001
1983	17.0	1995	2000
1982	17.0	1994	1999
1981	15.0	1993	1998
1980	17.0	2000	2005
1979	15.0	1991	1996
1978	18.0	1990	1995
1977	16.0	1989	1994
1976	15.0	1988	1993
1975	16.0	1987	1992
1974	14.0	1982	1986
1973	15.0	1985	1990
1972	18.8	1992	1997

Hickinbotham

cnr Wallace's Rd
& Nepean Hwy
Dromana Vic 3936
Tel: (03) 5981 0355
Fax: (03) 5981 0355

Region: Mornington Peninsula Winemaker: Andrew Hickinbotham
Viticulturist: Andrew Hickinbotham Chief Executive: Ian Hickinbotham

The modern Hickinbotham wines are made with refreshing disregard to winemaking risks, a path that has led to the creation of some complex, unique wines, perhaps at the expense of consistency. The family's vineyard at Dromana is capable of producing arrestingly intense and ripe flavours in pinot noir and merlot.

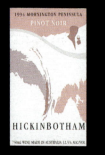

PINOT NOIR
Mornington Peninsula $$$

1997	15.4	2002	2005
1994	17.7	1999	2002
1993	16.7	1995	1998
1992	16.9	1997	2000
1991	16.5	1996	1999

Highbank Vineyards

Riddoch Highway
Coonawarra SA 5263
Tel: 1 800 643 311
Fax: (08) 8736 3122

Region: Coonawarra Winemakers: Dennis Vice, Trevor Mast
Viticulturist: Dennis Vice Chief Executive: Dennis Vice

Highbank is an exciting new entrant in the famous Coonawarra region which has adopted a totally organic vineyard system under the energetic and enthusiastic management of Dennis Vice. The vineyard's principal wine is a joyous blend of Bordeaux varieties made at Mount Langi Ghiran with another proponent of organic viticulture, Trevor Mast.

COONAWARRA
Coonawarra $$$$

1997	18.7	2005	2009
1994	18.6	2002	2006
1993	18.1	1998	2001
1992	18.4	2000	2004

Hill-Smith Estate

Flaxman's Valley Rd
Eden Valley SA 5353
Tel: (08) 8561 3200
Fax: (08) 8561 3393

Region: Eden Valley Winemaker: Hugh Reimers
Viticulturist: Robin Nettlebeck Chief Executive: Robert Hill Smith

The Hill-Smith Estate's Chardonnay and Sauvignon Blanc are consistently generous, flavoursome, well made and true to type. The Chardonnay is more forward and brassy, while the Sauvignon Blanc will suit those who enjoy the herbaceous aspect of this variety's character.

CHARDONNAY
Eden Valley $$

1998	16.6	2000	2003+
1997	16.2	1999	2002
1996	16.5	1998	2001
1995	17.4	2000	2003
1994	14.3	1996	1999
1993	17.0	1995	1998
1992	17.0	1994	1997

SAUVIGNON BLANC
Eden Valley $$

1998	18.2	1999	2000
1997	16.5	1998	1999
1996	17.2	1998	2001
1995	17.2	1996	1997
1994	17.3	1996	1999

Hollick

Riddoch Highway
Coonawarra SA 5263
Tel: (08) 8737 2318
Fax: (08) 8737 2952

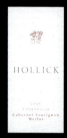

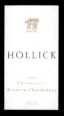

Region: Coonawarra Winemakers: Ian Hollick, Matt Pellew
Viticulturist: Ian Hollick Chief Executive: Ian Hollick

Recent vintages of Hollick wines don't capture the magic of the early 1990s, but offer easy-drinking, lighter expressions of Coonawarra reds and whites which aren't going to need long in the cellar to look at their best.

CABERNET SAUVIGNON MERLOT

Coonawarra $$$

1997	15.0	1999	2002
1996	14.5	1997	1998
1995	16.1	1997	2000
1994	17.5	1999	2002
1993	17.0	1998	2001
1992	16.7	1997	2000
1991	17.4	1996	1999
1990	18.0	1995	1998

RAVENSWOOD (CABERNET SAUVIGNON)

Coonawarra $$$$$

1996	16.0	2001	2004
1994	16.9	2002	2006+
1993	17.8	2001	2005
1992	18.0	2000	2004
1991	18.7		2003+
1990	18.4		2002+
1989	17.9		2001+
1988	18.2	2000	2005

RESERVE CHARDONNAY

Coonawarra $$$

1997	15.0	1998	1999
1996	16.0	1998	2001
1995	15.2	2000	2003
1994	17.7	1999	2002
1993	17.1	1995	1998
1992	16.8	1994	1997
1991	18.0	1996	1999
1990	17.0	1995	1998

RIESLING
Coonawarra $$

1998	15.5	2000	2003
1997	15.1	1999	2002
1995	16.5	2000	2003
1994	16.6	1999	2002
1992	18.4	1997	2000
1991	17.5	1993	1996

WILGHA SHIRAZ
Coonawarra $$$$

1996	15.0	1998	2001
1994	17.5	1996	1999
1993	17.3	1998	2001
1992	16.8	1997	2000
1991	17.8	1996	1999
1990	17.5	1995	1998
1989	16.5	1991	1994
1988	17.0	1993	1996

Houghton

Dale Road
Middle Swan WA 6055
Tel: (08) 9274 5100
Fax: (08) 9274 5372

Region: Various WA   Winemaker: Larry Cherubino
Viticulturist: Ron Page   Chief Executive: Stephen Millar

While I can't help thinking that the benchmark White Burgundy has rather gone off the boil in recent years, Houghton's red wines are moving from strength to strength. The premium Jack Mann wine has set a very high standard with its first three vintages, the sumptuous, concentrated 1996 wine especially.

JACK MANN RED
Great Southern $$$$$

1996	18.7	2004	2008+
1995	18.2	2003	2007+
1994	17.8	2002	2005

WHITE BURGUNDY
Swan Valley $

1998	16.0	2000	2003
1997	16.0	1999	2002
1996	15.7	1998	2001
1995	15.5	1997	2000
1994	16.0	1999	2002
1993	16.8	1998	2001

Howard Park

Lot 11 Scotsdale Road
Denmark WA 6333
Tel: (08) 9848 2345
Fax: (08) 9848 2064

Region: Great Southern Winemaker: Michael Kerrigan
Chief Executive: Geoff Burch

Now that its founder and visionary John Wade is no longer part of the equation at Howard Park, its challenge will be to maintain the quality and dedication to style that he achieved so consistently from his very first vintage in WA. Howard Park is set for major expansion plans under owner Geoff Burch, including the development of a winery at Margaret River, far away from the Great Southern region it has championed so well.

CABERNET SAUVIGNON MERLOT

Great Southern $$$$$

1996	19.0		2008+
1995	15.0	2000	2003
1994	19.2		2006+
1993	18.1	2001	2005
1992	19.4		2004+
1991	18.4		2003+
1990	18.7		2002+
1989	18.7		2001+
1988	19.0		2000+
1987	18.4	1999	2004
1986	18.5		2006+

CHARDONNAY

Great Southern $$$$

1998	18.7	2003	2006+
1997	16.0	1999	2002
1996	17.5	1998	2001
1995	18.5	2000	2003
1994	18.5	1999	2002
1993	18.0	1998	2001

RIESLING

Great Southern $$$

1998	18.1	2006	2010
1997	17.7	2002	2005
1996	18.4		2008+
1995	18.7		2007+
1994	18.5		2006+
1993	18.4	2001	2005
1992	18.2	2000	2004
1991	18.5		2003+
1990	18.0	1998	2002
1989	17.8	1994	1997
1988	18.5	2000	2005
1987	16.2	1995	1999
1986	18.8	1998	2003

Region: McLaren Vale Winemaker: John Hugo
Viticulturist: John Hugo Chief Executive: John Hugo

A small McLaren Vale maker with a lower profile than its quality warrants, Hugo is as reliable a brand as you can find. Although the 1997 vintage was unusually difficult, John Hugo's richly flavoured reds tend to develop superbly in the bottle.

Hugo

Elliott Road
McLaren Flat SA 5171
Tel: (08) 8383 0098
Fax: (08) 8383 0446

CABERNET SAUVIGNON
McLaren Vale $$$

1997	15.0	2002	2005+
1996	17.0	2001	2004
1995	16.8	2000	2003
1994	16.5	1992	2002
1993	17.5	2001	2005
1992	18.2	1997	2000

CHARDONNAY
McLaren Vale $$

1998	15.8	1999	2000
1997	17.2	2002	2005
1996	16.0	1999	2001
1994	17.3	1999	2002
1993	18.0	2001	2005
1992	16.6	1994	1997

SHIRAZ
McLaren Vale $$$

1997	16.2	1999	2002+
1996	17.6	2001	2004
1995	17.3	2000	2003
1994	17.2	1999	2002
1993	17.2	2001	2005
1992	17.7	1997	2000
1991	17.0	1996	1999
1990	18.3	1995	1998

Huntington Estate

**Cassilis Road
Mudgee NSW 2850
Tel: (02) 6373 3825
Fax: (02) 6373 3730**

Region: Mudgee Winemaker: Susan Roberts
Viticulturist: Robert Welch Chief Executive: Bob Roberts

It's a constant source of amazement that more people are not familiar with the exceptional value presented by Huntington Estate's richly textured cellaring styles of red wine, which include a creamy Shiraz, a sumptuously firm Cabernet Merlot and generously flavoured Cabernet Sauvignon.

CABERNET SAUVIGNON
Mudgee $$

1995	16.4	2003	2007
1994	16.6	2002	2006
1993	16.8	2001	2005
1992	18.2	2004	2012
1991	17.0	1996	1999
1990	16.5	1995	1998
1989	18.0	1994	1997
1988	15.0	1993	1996

SEMILLON
Mudgee $$

1998	15.7	2000	2003
1997	17.0	2002	2005
1996	18.1	2001	2004
1995	17.7	2000	2003
1994	16.0	1999	2003
1993	16.7	1998	2001
1992	15.0	1994	1997
1991	17.5	1996	1999

SHIRAZ
Mudgee $$

1995	16.7	2003	2007+
1994	15.7	1999	2002
1993	18.6		2005+
1992	16.7	1997	2000
1991	17.6	1999	2003
1990	16.7	1998	2002
1989	16.5	1994	1997
1988	16.5	1993	1996

Region: Geelong Winemaker: Daryl Sefton
Viticulturist: Daryl Sefton Chief Executive: Nini Sefton

Idyll is one of the earliest of the recent small vineyard and winery developments in the Geelong region in Victoria. Its rich fertile soils encourage fleshy soft reds with wild spicy flavours. Even more spicy is Idyll's very individual interpretation of gewürztraminer; a broad, mouthfilling style which shows some variation from year to year, but can hit the high notes as the 1994 vintage revealed.

Idyll

265 Ballan Road
Moorabool Vic 3221
Tel: (03) 5276 1280
Fax: (03) 5276 1537

CABERNET SAUVIGNON SHIRAZ

Geelong $$

1997	15.7	2005	2009
1996	15.0	2001	2004
1995	16.0	2003	2007
1994	16.3	2002	2006
1993	18.0	2001	2005
1992	17.0	1997	2000
1991	17.2	1999	2003
1990	16.9	1998	2002
1989	16.5		2001+
1988	16.5	2000	2005
1987	16.0	1995	1999
1986	17.5	1994	1998

CLASSIC DRY GEWURZTRAMINER

Geelong $$

1997	14.5	1999	2000
1996	15.0	1996	1997
1995	16.5	1996	1997
1994	17.5	1999	2002
1992	16.8	1994	1997
1991	16.0	1996	1999

SHIRAZ

Geelong $$

1997	15.3	2005	2009
1996	15.0	1998	2001
1995	17.8	2002	2006
1994	18.3	2002	2006
1993	17.6	2001	2005
1992	15.1	1994	1997
1991	15.4	1999	2003

Ingoldby

Kangarilla Road
McLaren Vale SA 5171
Tel: (08) 8323 8853
Fax: (08) 8323 8271

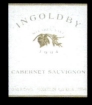

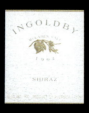

Region: McLaren Vale Winemaker: Phillip Reschke
Viticulturist: Guy Rayner Chief Executive: Ray King

It's a bit of a shame that Ingoldby wines are fading from their richness and structure of yesteryear. Now part of the Mildara Blass group, this label still provides wines which if indeed flavoursome and competent, just lack the punch and penetration of others doing similar things at McLaren Vale.

CABERNET SAUVIGNON
McLaren Vale $$

1997	14.9	1999	2002+
1996	15.0	1998	2001
1995	16.9	2000	2003
1994	17.0	1999	2002
1993	16.8	2000	2005
1992	18.1	2000	2004
1991	18.7		2003+
1990	17.0		2002+

SHIRAZ
McLaren Vale $$

1997	16.4	2002	2005
1996	16.0	1998	2001
1995	17.2	2000	2003
1994	16.1	1996	1999
1993	17.5	1999	2001
1991	18.6	1999	2003
1990	18.0	1998	2002

James Irvine

Roeslers Rd
Eden Valley SA 5235
Tel: (08) 8564 1046
Fax: (08) 8546 1046

Region: Eden Valley Winemaker: James Irvine
Viticulturist: James Irvine Chief Executive: Marjorie Irvine

Sure it's contentious, sure it's occasionally old-fashioned, ripe and porty, and sure it's seen rather a lot of oak, but Jim Irvine's rather gawdily packaged Grand Merlot never lets you down for flavour or longevity. The best vintages need at least eight years to settle and I'm confident that wines like the 1994 will pass the test.

GRAND MERLOT
Eden Valley $$$$$

1995	17.8	2003	2007
1994	18.8		2006+
1993	18.6		2005+
1992	16.8	2000	2004
1991	18.4	1999	2003
1990	18.2		2002+
1989	17.2	1994	1997
1988	18.2	1996	2000
1987	16.2	1992	1995
1986	18.1	1994	1998

Jamiesons Run

**Riddoch Highway
Coonawarra SA 5263
Tel: (08) 8736 3380
Fax: (08) 8736 3307**

Region: Coonawarra Winemaker: David O'Leary
Viticulturist: Vic Patrick Chief Executive: Ray King

It's a brand created by Mildara Blass around a popular wine, but as far as I'm concerned, I'd only order the 'original' red, based on what I've had to taste. And why not? It stands the test of time and also drinks very well at time of release.

CHARDONNAY
Coonawarra $$

1998	15.0		1999
1997	15.7	1998	1999
1996	16.8	1998	2001
1995	16.8	1996	1997

RED
Coonawarra $$

1996	16.4	2001	2004
1995	17.0	2000	2003
1994	18.2	2002	2006
1993	17.9	2001	2005
1992	16.5	2000	2004
1991	16.4	1999	2003
1990	16.6	1998	2002
1989	16.7	1993	1996
1988	17.9	1996	2000

Region: Pipers River Winemaker: Tony Davis
Viticulturist: Ben Wagner Chief Executive: Robert Hill Smith

Jansz began its short life as the much-awaited Heemskerk brand of methode champenoise originally developed in conjunction with Champagne Louis Roederer. Roederer stepped backwards, then did Heemskerk, which was recently acquired by Pipers Brook, themselves working studiously on the Pirie sparkling wine. They didn't need Jansz, so S. Smith & Son (owners of Yalumba), who may or may not have developed their own 'D' label in conjunction with Champage Deutz, snapped it up. And on it goes...

Jansz

**1216 Pipers Brook Rd
Pipers Brook Tas 7254
Tel: (03) 6382 7122
Fax: (03) 6382 7225**

BRUT CUVEE
Pipers River $$$$

95	16.7	1997	2000+
94	17.6	1999	2002
93	18.5	1998	2001
92	18.5	1997	2000
91	16.8	1993	1996

Jasper Hill

**Drummonds Lane
Heathcote Vic 3523
Tel: (03) 5433 2528
Fax: (03) 5433 3143**

Region: Heathcote Winemaker: Ron Laughton
Viticulturist: Ron Laughton Chief Executive: Ron Laughton

Something rather unexpected happened at a recent historic tasting of virtually every Jasper Hill wine ever made. I came out feeling much happier about the purity, intensity and vitality of the Georgia's Paddock Shiraz than the Emily's Paddock, some recent vintages of which looked rather exaggerated, over-ripe and porty by comparison. Either way, there's no doubting Jasper Hill's place amongst our most important shiraz vineyards.

EMILY'S PADDOCK SHIRAZ /CABERNET FRANC

Heathcote $$$$$

1997	18.5		2009+
1996	16.9	2004	2008
1995	16.2	2000	2003
1994	18.4	2002	2006
1993	15.9		2005+
1992	18.7		2004+
1991	18.6		2011+
1990	18.4		2002+
1989	14.8	1994	1997
1988	18.7	2000	2008+

GEORGIA'S PADDOCK RIESLING

Heathcote $$$

1998	17.2	2003	2006
1997	18.0	2005	2009
1996	16.0	1998	2001
1994	17.2	1999	2002
1993	14.5	1994	1995
1992	16.8	1997	2000
1991	18.5	1999	2003
1990	16.7	1998	2002
1989	17.0	1994	1997+
1988	18.3	1996	2000
1987	15.6	1992	1995
1986	15.2	1991	1994
1985	17.8	1993	1997

GEORGIA'S PADDOCK SHIRAZ

Heathcote $$$$$

1997	18.0		2008+
1996	18.5		2008+
1995	18.9		2007+
1994	18.7	2002	2006+
1993	19.0		2005+
1992	18.8		2004+
1991	18.7	1999	2003+
1990	18.5		2002+
1989	15.7	1997	2001
1988	18.6		2008+
1987	15.8	1999	2007
1986	18.1		2006+
1985	18.7		2005+

Region: Clare Valley Winemaker: Mark Barry
Viticulturist: Peter Barry Chief Executive: Peter Barry

Jim Barry's leading red wine, The Armagh, is aimed both stylistically and fiscally at those who'd like to buy Grange but can only afford half a bottle. The 1996 wine again justifies the wine's lofty reputation, while the 1996 McCrae Wood presents some of The Armagh's style and quality at around a third of its price.

CABERNET BLEND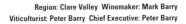

Clare Valley $$

1997	15.1	1999	2002
1996	15.4	1997	1998
1995	15.9	2000	2003
1994	16.8	1996	1999
1993	17.0	1998	2001
1992	16.8	1997	2000

Jim Barry
Main North Road
Clare SA 5453
Tel: (08) 8842 2261
Fax: (08) 8842 3752

CABERNET SAUVIGNON

Clare Valley $$

1997	15.3	2002	2005
1996	15.4	2001	2004
1995	17.9	2003	2007
1994	16.4	1999	2002
1993	16.5	1998	2001
1992	17.4	2000	2004
1990	16.5	1995	1998
1989	16.7	1994	1997
1988	18.5	1996	2000

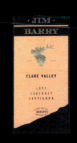

McCRAE WOOD SHIRAZ

Clare Valley $$$

1996	18.0	2004	2008
1995	17.5	2000	2003
1994	18.3	2002	2006
1993	16.2	1995	1998
1992	18.1	2000	2004

THE ARMAGH SHIRAZ

Clare Valley $$$$$

1996	19.1	2004	2008
1995	18.6	2003	2007+
1994	18.0	2002	2006
1993	18.7		2005+
1992	18.8		2004+
1991	18.0		2003+
1990	18.6		2010+
1989	18.3		2009+
1988	18.2	2000	2005
1987	18.1		2007+
1985	16.0	1997	2002

WATERVALE RIESLING

Clare Valley $$

1998	18.1	2003	2006+
1997	18.0	2005	2009
1996	16.7	2004	2008
1995	17.5	2003	2007+
1994	16.4	1999	2002
1993	17.5	2001	2005

Region: Great Southern Winemaker: Stephen Pester
Viticulturists: Geoff Clarke & Barry Coad Chief Executive: Shelley Coad

Jingalla is a small vineyard in the Porongorup Ranges of WA's Great Southern district which produces supple, restrained and occasionally leafy red wines, plus spicy, aromatic whites.

Jingalla

RMB 1316 Bolganup Dam Rd
Porongorup WA 6324
Tel: (08) 9853 1023
Fax: (08) 9853 1023

CABERNET SAUVIGNON

Great Southern $$$

1996	16.8	2004	2008
1995	15.0	2000	2003+
1994	16.5	1999	2002
1993	14.2	1998	2001
1991	16.7	1999	2003
1989	17.0	1994	1997
1988	17.0	1996	2000
1987	16.5	1999	2004
1986	15.0	1991	1994

RIESLING
Great Southern $$

1998	15.5	1999	2000
1996	17.5	2001	2004
1995	16.0	1997	2000
1994	17.6	1999	2002
1993	18.0	1998	2001
1990	17.2	1992	1995

VERDELHO
Great Southern $$

1998	14.7	1999	2000
1997	16.0	1999	2002
1996	18.3	2001	2004
1995	17.6	2000	2003
1994	16.8	1996	1999
1993	15.8	1994	1995

Region: Eden Valley Winemakers: Karl Seppelt, Petaluma
Viticulturist: Karl Seppelt Chief Executive: Karl Seppelt

Karl Seppelt makes a range of red and white still and sparkling wines of which the highlights are a very fruit-driven and forward Chardonnay and ephemeral appearances of Chardonnay Brut and Sparkling Shiraz.

Karl Seppelt
**Ross Dewell's Rd
Springton SA 5235
Tel: (08) 8568 2378
Fax: (08) 8568 2799**

CHARDONNAY
Adelaide Hills $$

1996	15.0	1998	2001
1995	16.2	2000	2003
1994	13.8	1996	1999
1992	15.0	1993	1994

SHIRAZ
Langhorne Creek $$

1996	16.3	2001	2004+
1988	15.8	1993	1996
1986	15.2	1991	1994

SPARKLING SHIRAZ
Adelaide Hills $$$

1994	15.3	1999	2002
1992	16.8	1997	2000
1991	17.8	1996	1999
1989	18.0	1991	1994

Katnook Estate

Riddoch Highway
Coonawarra SA 5263
Tel: (08) 8737 2394
Fax: (08) 8737 2397

Region: Coonawarra Winemaker: Wayne Stehbens
Viticulturist: Leon Oborne Chief Executive: David Yunghanns

Of all the wineries based in Coonawarra, Katnook Estate has arguably enjoyed the best decade in the 1990s. The Cabernet Sauvignon seems to acquire more elegance and complexity with successive vintages, while the reserve 'Odyssey' label is a more opulent, plush expression of riper fruit and assertive new oak. Katnook is also winning new friends for its supple, fleshy Merlot and can't have lost too many over its rich and sumptuous Chardonnay.

CABERNET SAUVIGNON
Coonawarra $$$$

1997	18.7		2009+
1996	18.6	2008	2016
1995	16.5	2000	2003
1994	18.5	2002	2006
1993	18.4		2005+
1992	18.3	2000	2004
1991	18.6		2003+
1990	17.8		2002+
1988	17.5	1993	1996
1987	16.5	1991	1995
1986	18.3	1998	2003
1985	16.5	1993	1997
1984	16.5	1988	1992
1983	16.0	1991	1995
1982	16.0	1990	1994
1981	17.0	1989	1993
1980	18.0	1992	1997

CHARDONNAY
Coonawarra $$$$

1996	18.2	2001	2004
1995	18.4	2000	2003
1994	18.3	1999	2002
1993	18.4	1998	2001
1992	18.2	1997	2000
1991	16.8	1996	1999
1990	17.8	1998	2002
1989	18.2	1997	2001

CHARDONNAY BRUT
Coonawarra $$$

1995	17.2	2000	2003
1994	15.0	1996	1999
1993	17.1	1995	1998
1990	18.4	1995	1998

MERLOT
Coonawarra $$$$

1997	18.2	2002	2005+
1996	18.5	2004	2008
1995	16.0	1997	2000
1994	18.3	1999	2002
1993	18.3	1998	2001
1992	18.2	1997	2000
1991	16.0	1996	1999
1990	17.8	1995	1998

ODYSSEY
Coonawarra $$$$$

1994	18.7	2002	2006+
1992	16.9	1997	2000
1991	18.7	2003	2011

RIESLING
Coonawarra $$

1998	17.6	2003	2006+
1997	17.0	2002	2005
1996	16.0	2001	2004
1995	15.0	2000	2003
1994	16.8	1999	2002

SAUVIGNON BLANC
Coonawarra $$$

1998	16.6		1999
1997	17.6	1999	2002
1996	18.3	1998	2001
1995	18.5	1997	2000
1994	17.5	1995	1996

Kay's Amery

**Kays Road
McLaren Vale SA 5171
Tel: (08) 8323 8211
Fax: (08) 8323 9199**

Region: McLaren Vale Winemaker: Colin Kay
Viticulturist: Colin Kay Chief Executive: Colin Kay

Kays' red wines are reaping the rewards of a renewed emphasis on the vineyard and quality of oak. The Block 6 is, for the time being at least, one of the true bargains in premium Australian red wine, while the Shiraz, Cabernet Sauvignon and Grenache are simply fine, honest reds whose prices are almost bashfully modest.

BLOCK 6 SHIRAZ
McLaren Vale $$$$

1996	18.7	2004	2008+
1995	18.2	2003	2007+
1994	18.4		2005+
1993	18.2		2005+
1992	18.5		2004+
1991	18.2	1999	2003
1990	18.1		2002+
1989	17.2	1994	1997
1988	15.6	1993	1996
1987	14.5	1989	1992

CABERNET SAUVIGNON
McLaren Vale $$$

1997	17.2	2005	2009
1996	17.8	2004	2008
1995	16.8	2003	2007
1994	17.0		2006+
1993	16.0	2001	2005
1992	16.7	2000	2004
1989	16.7	1995	1997
1985	16.0	1990	1993

SHIRAZ
McLaren Vale $$$

1997	16.5	2002	2005+
1996	18.4	2004	2008
1995	17.5		2006+
1994	17.1		2006+
1993	16.2	2001	2005
1992	16.7	2000	2004

Region: Geographe Winemaker: Paul Boulden
Viticulturist: Paul Boulden Chief Executive: Ben Killerby

Killerby is an energetic wine company established in 1973 by Dr Barry Killerby. It's made a number of very Rhône-ish Shirazes, firm, fleshy Cabernet Sauvignons and tight-knit Chardonnays, but recent vintages have seen it go a little off the boil. Hopefully it's only a temporary thing.

Killerby

**Lakes Road
Capel WA 6230
Tel: 1-800 655 722
Fax: 1-800 679 578**

CABERNET SAUVIGNON

Geographe $$$ 5

Year	Score		
1997	15.8	2002	2005
1996	15.2	2004	2008
1995	16.0	2003	2007
1994	15.0	1999	2002
1993	18.2		2005+
1992	18.5	2000	2004
1991	16.0		2003+
1989	18.5		2001+

CHARDONNAY

Geographe $$$ 4

Year	Score		
1998	15.8	2000	2003+
1997	16.0	1998	1999
1996	18.1	2001	2004
1995	18.0	2000	2003
1994	18.2	1999	2002
1993	17.9	1998	2001
1992	18.2	1994	1997
1991	18.5	1999	2003
1990	16.8	1995	1998
1989	17.5	1997	2001

SEMILLON

Geographe $$$ 3

Year	Score		
1998	15.3	2000	2003
1997	17.0	2002	2005
1996	18.2	2001	2004
1995	18.3	2000	2003
1994	17.6	2002	2006
1993	17.0	1998	2001
1992	17.5	1997	2000
1991	17.5	1999	2003
1990	16.0	1995	1998
1989	17.5	1997	2001
1988	16.5	1993	1996

Kings Creek

237 Myers Road
Bittern Vic 3918
Tel: (03) 5983 2102
Fax: (03) 5983 5153

SHIRAZ
Geographe $$$

1997	15.7	2002	2005
1996	16.7	2001	2004
1995	18.3	2003	2007
1994	18.3	2002	2006
1993	18.1	2001	2005
1992	15.0	1997	2000
1991	18.4	1999	2003
1989	16.8	1997	2001

Region: Mornington Peninsula **Winemaker:** Brian Cole
Viticulturist: Brian Cole **Chief Executive:** Jim Phillips

Some poorly finished recent vintages of Pinot Noir have taken the gloss from Kings Creek's steady development as a major player in Victoria's Mornington Peninsula region. The 1998 Chardonnay is heavily worked and marginally green, but reveals more of the vineyard's inherent potential.

CHARDONNAY
Mornington Peninsula $$$

1998	17.4	2003	2006
1997	16.0	1998	1999
1996	18.2	2001	2004
1995	18.2	2000	2003
1994	16.6	1999	2002
1993	18.6	1998	2001
1992	17.8	1994	1997

PINOT NOIR
Mornington Peninsula $$$

1998	15.0	2000	2003
1997	15.0	1999	2002
1996	18.2	2001	2004
1995	18.4	2000	2003
1994	18.3	1999	2002
1993	16.6	1998	2001
1992	18.5	1997	2000
1991	16.5	1993	1996

THE ONWINE AUSTRALIAN WINE ANNUAL

Kingston Estate

**Sturt Highway
Kingston on Murray
SA 5331
Tel: (08) 8583 0244
Fax: (08) 8583 0304**

Region: Riverlands Winemaker: Rod Chapman
Viticulturist: John Petch Chief Executive: Bill Moularadellis

Kingston Estate has come from nowhere over the last three or four years to become a major player in the Riverlands, making Merlot, Shiraz, Cabernet Sauvignon and Chardonnay which stack up time and again as simply excellent value for money.

MERLOT
Riverlands $$

1998	15.3	2000	2003
1997	15.7	1999	2002
1996	15.0	1997	1998

Knappstein

**2 Pioneer Avenue
Clare SA 5453
Tel: (08) 8842 2600
Fax: (08) 8842 3831**

Region: Clare Valley Winemaker: Andrew Hardy
Viticulturist: Ray Klavins Chief Executive: Brian Croser

With one of the Clare Valley's best 1998 Rieslings in its stable, a deliciously spicy 1998 Gewürztraminer, plus two skillfully crafted 1996 reds in the very rich, robust Enterprise Shiraz and Enterprise Cabernet Sauvignon, this is a winery going places fast. Knappstein's consistency and quality under Andrew Hardy has been exceptional.

CABERNET MERLOT
Clare Valley $$$

1997	16.8	2002	2005
1996	17.4	2002	2006
1995	16.8	2000	2003
1994	16.8	2002	2006
1993	16.0	1998	2001
1992	16.5	1997	2000
1991	17.5	1999	2003
1990	17.0	1992	1995

CABERNET SAUVIGNON
Clare Valley $$$$

1994	18.3	2002	2006
1993	17.6	2001	2005
1990	18.5	1998	2002
1989	18.0	1997	2001
1988	17.8	1993	1996
1987	16.4	1989	1992
1986	18.0	1994	1998

CHARDONNAY

Clare Valley, Lenswood $$$

1996	16.4	1998	2001
1995	17.0	2000	2003
1994	15.0	1996	1999
1993	18.2	1995	1998
1992	18.0	1997	2000
1991	18.0	1993	1996
1990	17.0	1995	1998

GEWURZTRAMINER

Clare Valley $$

1998	18.2	2003	2006
1997	18.4	2002	2005
1996	18.2	2001	2004
1995	16.8	2000	2003
1994	17.5	2002	2006
1993	18.5	1998	2001
1992	17.0	1994	1997
1991	18.0	1993	1996

RIESLING

Clare Valley $$

1998	18.7	2006	2010
1997	18.5	2005	2009
1996	18.3	2004	2008
1995	17.8	2003	2007
1994	18.3		2006+
1993	18.6	2001	2005
1992	17.5	1997	2000
1991	17.0	1996	1999
1990	18.0	1998	2002
1989	17.0	1991	1994

SEMILLON SAUVIGNON BLANC (FORMERLY FUME BLANC)

Clare Valley $$$

1998	15.9	2000	2003
1997	16.0	1999	2002
1996	17.7	2001	2004
1995	18.0	1997	2000
1994	16.8	1999	2002
1993	18.4	1995	1998
1992	18.0	1997	2000
1991	17.0	1993	1996

Region: Macedon Winemaker: Llew Knight
Viticulturist: Llew Knight Chief Executive: Llew Knight

It's hardly a surprise that one of mainland Australia's latest vineyards to ripen tends to perform best and most consistently with its Riesling, its Chardonnay coming a close second. Llew Knight has yet to release his red wines from the recent run of warmer vintages and they're already widely anticipated.

Knights Granite Hills

**Burke & Wills Tk
Baynton RSD 391
Kyneton Vic 3444
Tel: (03) 5423 7264
Fax: (03) 5423 7288**

CABERNET SAUVIGNON

Macedon $$$

1995	16.8	2003	2007
1992	15.8	1997	2000
1991	16.2		2003+
1989	15.8	1991	1994
1988	15.0	1996	2000

CHARDONNAY

Macedon $$$

1996	17.2	2001	2004
1995	18.0	2003	2007
1994	15.2	1996	1999
1993	17.8	1998	2001
1992	18.0	2000	2004
1991	18.0	1996	1999
1990	18.5	1995	1998
1989	16.0	1991	1994

RIESLING

Macedon $$$

1998	17.6	2003	2006+
1997	18.5		2009+
1995	18.0	2003	2007
1994	16.8	2002	2006
1993	15.6	1998	2001
1992	18.4	2000	2004
1991	16.5	1996	1999
1990	18.0	1995	1998
1989	15.0	1991	1994

SHIRAZ

Macedon $$$

1996	14.5	1998	2003
1995	15.2	2000	2003
1992	15.7	1997	2000
1991	15.0	1993	1996
1989	15.0	1991	1994
1988	16.2	1996	2000

Krondorf

Krondorf Road
Tanunda SA 5352
Tel: (08) 8563 2145
Fax: (08) 8562 3055

Lake's Folly

Broke Road
Pokolbin NSW 2320
Tel: (02) 4998 7507
Fax: (02) 4998 7322

Region: Barossa Valley Winemaker: Nick Walker
Viticulturist: Syd Kyloh Chief Executive: Ray King

Krondorf, formerly one of the most energetic and dynamic of all Australian wine companies, has become something of a quiet backwater in the Mildara Blass stable. The wines are ok, the prices are realistic, but where's all the excitement gone? And who's the family in 'Family Reserve'?

FAMILY RESERVE CABERNET SAUVIGNON

South Australia $$

1996	15.8	2001	2004
1995	17.0	2003	2007
1994	17.1	2002	2006
1993	16.8	1995	1998
1990	17.6	1995	1998
1989	16.4	1997	2001
1988	16.7	1996	2000

FAMILY RESERVE CHARDONNAY

South Australia $$

1997	14.6	1998	1999
1996	16.1	1998	2001
1995	17.0	2000	2003
1994	14.7	1995	1996

Region: Lower Hunter Valley Winemaker: Stephen Lake
Viticulturist: Bob Davies Chief Executive: Stephen Lake

I'm constantly amazed by successive red wine releases from Lake's Folly for the ability of its vineyard and Stephen Lake to defy logic and season. The 1997 edition is tight-knit and fine-grained, with dark berry/plum fruit and touches of Hunter earthiness.

CABERNETS

Lower Hunter Valley $$$$

1997	18.4	2005	2009
1996	18.4		2008+
1995	17.2		2007+
1994	18.7		2006+
1993	18.8		2005+
1992	17.6	2000	2004
1991	17.5		2003+
1990	16.0	1998	2002
1989	17.8		2001+
1988	16.0	1996	2000
1987	17.0	1995	1999
1986	16.0	1994	1998
1985	17.4	1997	2005

CHARDONNAY
Lower Hunter Valley $$$$

1997	15.6	1999	2002
1996	18.6	2001	2004
1995	18.7	2003	2007
1994	17.8	2002	2006
1993	18.7	2001	2005
1992	17.8	2000	2004
1991	17.8	1999	2003
1990	16.5	1995	1998
1989	18.0	1997	2001
1988	16.5	1993	1996
1987	18.0	1992	1995
1986	18.2	1998	2003

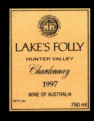

**Region: Clare Valley Winemakers: Kerri Thompson, Belinda Kleinig
Viticulturist: Ian Smith Chief Executive: Stephen Millar**

From its Classic Clare range downwards, if you can call it that, to the excellent traditionally labelled Bin series of wines, Leasingham offers exceptional value and regional flavour in virtually all its wines. The Classic Clare Shiraz is another of the top-notch BRL Hardy reds which owe their existence to the parent company's entirely refocussed approach towards all aspects of red wine production from the vineyard upwards.

Leasingham
7 Dominic Street
Clare SA 5453
Tel: (08) 8842 2555
Fax: (08) 8842 3293

BIN 7 RIESLING
Clare Valley $$

1998	17.8	2006	2010
1997	15.6	2002	2005
1996	17.0	2001	2004+

BIN 37 CHARDONNAY
Clare Valley $$

1998	16.6	1999	2000
1997	15.2	1999	2002
1996	16.8	1998	2001
1994	14.5	1995	1996
1993	16.5	1995	1998
1991	16.5	1993	1996
1990	18.0	1995	1998
1989	17.0	1994	1997

BIN 56 CABERNET MALBEC

Clare Valley $$

1997	15.8	2002	2005+
1996	17.0	2004	2008
1995	17.0	2000	2003
1994	17.1	1999	2002
1993	16.7	2001	2005
1992	18.0	2000	2004
1991	16.0	1997	2000
1990	17.0	1998	2002
1989	15.8	1994	1997
1988	17.0	1993	1996

BIN 61 SHIRAZ

Clare Valley $$

1997	17.6	2005	2009
1996	17.2	2001	2004
1995	18.0	2003	2007
1994	18.2	1999	2002
1993	16.8	2001	2005
1992	16.3	1997	2000

CLASSIC CLARE CABERNET SAUVIGNON

Clare Valley $$$$

1996	17.5	2004	2008
1995	16.0	2000	2003
1994	17.5	2002	2006
1993	18.0	2001	2005
1992	18.5		2004+
1991	18.4	1996	1999

CLASSIC CLARE RIESLING

Clare Valley $$

1996	18.2	2004	2008
1995	18.4	2003	2007
1994	18.6	2002	2006+

CLASSIC CLARE SHIRAZ

Clare Valley $$$$

1996	18.7	2001	2004+
1995	17.9	2003	2007
1994	18.5	1999	2002
1993	18.3	2001	2005
1992	16.5	1997	2000
1991	18.5		2003+

Region: Coonawarra Winemaker: Phillipa Treadwell
Viticulturist: Adam Jacobs Chief Executive: Dr Richard Hamilton

Leconfield

Riddoch Highway
Coonawarra SA 5263
Tel: (08) 8737 2326
Fax: (08) 8737 2285

There's no denying the current popularity of Leconfield's wines, especially its reds, but I would enthuse more wildly over them if I didn't usually encounter an underlying thread of greenness and hard, tough tannins. Of them all, Merlot included, I prefer the rather wild, brambly and often sneezy expression of the Shiraz.

CABERNET SAUVIGNON

Coonawarra $$$

1997	15.8	1999	2002
1996	15.5	2001	2004
1995	16.3	1997	2000
1994	16.8	1999	2002
1993	14.8	2001	2005
1992	17.3	1997	2000
1991	17.5	1999	2003
1990	17.0	1998	2002

CHARDONNAY

Coonawarra $$$

1998	17.0	2000	2003
1997	14.5	1998	1999
1996	16.4	1998	2001
1995	15.0	1996	1997

OLD VINES RIESLING

Coonawarra $$$

1998	16.9	2003	2006+
1997	17.3	2002	2005
1996	16.0	2001	2004
1995	17.5	2000	2003
1994	10.0	2002	2006
1993	17.7	1998	2001
1992	16.0	1994	1997

SHIRAZ

Coonawarra $$$

1997	17.8	2002	2005
1996	17.8	1998	2001
1995	18.1	2003	2007
1994	17.7	1999	2002
1993	18.2	2001	2005
1992	18.0	1997	2000
1990	18.7	1998	2002

Leeuwin Estate

Stevens Road
Witchcliffe WA 6286
Tel: (08) 9757 6253
Fax: (08) 9757 6364

Region: Margaret River Winemaker: Bob Cartwright
Viticulturist: John Brocksopp Chief Executive: Denis Horgan

I've shown my hand elsewhere in this book by stating my preference for Giaconda Chardonnay, but Leeuwin Estate's Art Series wine runs a very close second. Factor into the equation that this well-established Margaret River producer turns out many times the volume of Giaconda and it's apparent just how unbelievably proficient and how consistent Bob Cartwright, John Brocksopp and team have become with this variety. Leeuwin enthusiasts might keep an eye out for the expected forthcoming release of a premium Shiraz.

CABERNET SAUVIGNON

Margaret River $$$$

1995	14.5	2003	2007
1994	16.8		2006+
1993	16.5	2001	2005
1992	18.7	2000	2004
1991	18.4	2003	2011
1990	18.7	2002	2010
1989	18.6	2001	2009
1988	18.4	1996	2000
1987	16.0	1999	2004
1986	17.8	1994	1998
1985	16.5	1990	1993

CHARDONNAY

Margaret River $$$$$

1996	18.6	2001	2005+
1995	19.4	2004	2008
1994	18.4	2002	2006
1993	18.3	2001	2005
1992	19.2	2000	2004+
1991	18.6	1999	2003
1990	18.0	1998	2002
1989	17.8	1997	2001
1988	17.0	1996	2000
1987	19.0	1995	1999
1986	18.0	1994	1998
1985	18.5	1993	1997
1984	16.1	1992	1996
1983	18.0	1995	2000
1982	18.6	1990	1994
1981	18.4	1993	1998
1980	18.1	1988	1992

PINOT NOIR

Margaret River $$$$

1995	15.0	2000	2003
1994	15.0	1996	1999
1993	16.0	1998	2001
1992	13.0	1994	1997
1991	16.9	1996	1999
1989	17.7	1994	1997
1988	17.0	1993	1996

PRELUDE CABERNET SAUVIGNON

Margaret River $$$

1994	15.7	2002	2006
1993	15.6	1998	2001
1991	16.8	1999	2003
1990	17.3		2002+
1989	18.1		2001+
1988	17.0		2000+

PRELUDE CHARDONNAY

Margaret River $$$

1997	16.0	1999	2002
1996	15.0	1997	1998
1994	17.8	1999	2002
1993	18.2	1998	2001
1992	16.8	1997	2000
1991	17.9	1996	1999
1989	17.5	1994	1997

RIESLING

Margaret River $$

1997	16.0	2002	2005
1996	17.0	2001	2004
1995	16.8	2000	2003
1994	16.0	1999	2002
1993	16.5	1998	2001
1992	16.7	1997	2000
1991	17.5	1999	2003
1990	17.0	1992	1995

Lenswood Vineyards

(Vineyard only) Croft's Rd
Lenswood SA 5240
Tel: (08) 8389 8111
Fax: (08) 8389 8555

SAUVIGNON BLANC

Margaret River $$$$

1997	18.5	1999	2002
1996	18.6	1998	2001
1995	18.3	1997	2000
1994	18.3	1996	1999
1993	18.0	1995	1998
1992	18.1	1994	1997

Region: Lenswood Winemaker: Tim Knappstein
Viticulturists: Tim Knappstein, Paul Smith Chief Executive: Annie Knappstein

Tim Knappstein's story is almost that of a perpetual mid-life winemaking crisis. Beginning in the Clare Valley, where he spent some excellent years making riesling and traditional Clare reds with Leasingham before establishing Knappstein Wines, he then developed Lenswood Vineyards. Now he's known for racy, vital Sauvignon Blanc, complex and richly structured Chardonnay and heady, opulent Pinot Noir. And yes, for the moment, he's satisfied.

CHARDONNAY

Adelaide Hills $$$$

1997	16.7	1999	2002+
1996	18.2	2001	2004
1995	18.6	2000	2003
1994	18.5	1999	2002
1993	17.8	1998	2001
1992	18.4	1997	2000
1991	18.5	1996	1999

PINOT NOIR

Adelaide Hills $$$$

1997	17.8	2002	2005
1996	16.0	2004	2008
1995	18.0	2000	2003+
1994	18.5	1999	2002+
1993	18.5	1998	2001
1992	18.0	2000	2004
1991	17.8	1996	1999

SAUVIGNON BLANC

Adelaide Hills $$$

1998	18.3	1999	2000
1997	17.6	1998	1999
1996	18.0	1997	1998
1995	18.6	1997	2000
1994	17.5	1995	1996

Lenton Brae

**Caves Road
Willyabrup Valley
Margaret River WA 6295
Tel: (08) 9755 6255
Fax: (08) 9755 6268**

Region: Margaret River Winemaker: Edward Tomlinson
Viticulturist: Bruce Tomlinson Chief Executive: Bruce Tomlinson

Lenton Brae is an emerging Margaret River winery of real class. Its leading wines are its Cabernet Sauvignon, while its white wines, featuring a Chardonnay, Sauvignon Blanc and Semillon Sauvignon Blanc, are consistently stylish and flavoursome.

CABERNET MERLOT
Margaret River $$$$

1998	16.1	2000	2003
1997	15.0	1998	1999
1996	16.0	2001	2004
1995	16.8	2000	2003
1993	15.0	1995	1998

CABERNET SAUVIGNON
Margaret River $$$$

1996	18.6	2004	2008+
1995	18.2	2003	2007
1994	17.8	2006	2014
1993	15.0	1995	1998
1992	16.7	2000	2004

CHARDONNAY
Margaret River $$$

1998	17.9	2000	2003
1997	16.8	1999	2002+
1996	16.8	2001	2004
1995	15.7	1996	1997
1994	17.6	1996	1999

SAUVIGNON BLANC
Margaret River $$$

1998	17.4	1999	2000
1997	17.3	1999	2002
1996	18.3	1998	2001
1995	17.3	1997	2000

SEMILLON SAUVIGNON BLANC
Margaret River $$$

1998	15.7	2000	2003
1997	16.4	1999	2002
1996	18.1	2001	2004
1995	17.5	1997	2000

Leo Buring

Tanunda Rd
Nuriootpa SA 5355
Tel: (08) 8560 9389
Fax: (08) 8562 1669

Region: Barossa Valley Winemaker: Geoff Henriks
Viticulturist: John Matz Chief Executive: Bruce Kemp

Still a benchmark in Australian riesling, Leo Buring shows time and again that riesling is one of our best cellaring wines, although the company style has developed considerably since the classic wines made by John Vickery in the 1960s and 1970s. The newly released Leonay Eden Valley Riesling from 1995 is simply awesome. It's a near-perfect essay in the limey, long and steely expression of this grape, with flavours and acids that go on and on.

CLARE VALLEY CHARDONNAY

Clare Valley $$

1997	16.4	1999	2002
1996	14.5	1997	1998
1994	16.3	1996	1999
1993	16.0	1995	1998
1992	16.0	1993	1996

CLARE VALLEY RIESLING DW 33

Clare Valley $$

1998	16.7	2000	2003
1997	17.5	2005	2009
1996	17.5	2004	2008
1995	15.8	2000	2003
1994	18.0	2002	2006
1993	18.5	2001	2005
1992	16.8	1997	2000
1990	16.0	1995	1998

LEONAY WATERVALE RIESLING

Clare Valley $$$

1994	18.4		2006
1994	18.4	2002	2006
1992	18.5	2000	2004
1991	18.6		2003+
1990	18.0	1998	2002
1988	18.2	1996	2000
1981	14.5	1989	1993
1980	16.0	1988	1992
1973	18.4	1981	1985
1972	19.0	1992	1997

Leydens Vale

**Vinoca Rd
Avoca Vic 3467
Tel: (03) 5465 3202
Fax: (03) 5465 3529**

Region: Pyrenees Winemaker: Kim Hart
Viticulturist: Kim Hart Chief Executive: Kim Hart

Leydens Vale is a multi-regional label of Blue Pyrenees Estate. It has featured a delicious and almost sour merlot from time to time, but at present offers a limey, musky Riesling and a spicy, earthy Shiraz.

RIESLING
Southern Australia $$

1998	17.5	2000	2003+
1997	18.0	2002	2005
1995	15.0	1997	2000
1994	16.8	1999	2002

SHIRAZ
Pyrenees $$$

1996	16.2	2001	2004
1995	15.0	2000	2003
1994	16.0	1999	2002

Region: Yarra Valley Winemaker: Jim Brayne
Viticulturist: Alex Van Driel Chief Executive: Kevin McLintock

Lillydale Vineyards offers the keys to wine enjoyment through its approachable varietal wines with their fresh, lively primary fruit flavours, lack of complication and soft, easy-going drinkability. They're not the Yarra Valley at its finest, but they're excellent fun and value. Lillydale Vineyards is now owned by McWilliams Wines, which has wisely chosen to continue making its wonderfully spicy and aromatic Gewürztraminer.

Lillydale Vineyards

**Lot 10 Davross Court
Seville Vic 3139
Tel: (03) 5964 2016
Fax: (03) 5964 3009**

CABERNET MERLOT
Yarra Valley $$

1997	16.8	2002	2005
1996	15.8	1998	2001
1995	15.3	1997	2000
1994	16.9	1999	2002
1992	17.5	1997	2000
1991	17.6	1999	2003
1990	16.5	1995	1998

THE ONWINE AUSTRALIAN WINE ANNUAL 2000

CHARDONNAY
Yarra Valley $$

1998	16.6	1999	2000
1997	17.0	1999	2002
1996	16.2	1998	2001
1995	15.7	1997	2000
1994	15.0	1996	1999
1992	16.8	1994	1997

GEWURZTRAMINER
Yarra Valley $$

1998	16.8	2000	2003
1996	17.0	2001	2004
1995	18.4	2000	2003
1993	15.5	1995	1996

PINOT NOIR
Yarra Valley $$

1998	16.2	1999	2000
1997	16.8	1999	2002
1996	17.2	1998	2001
1995	16.2	1997	2000
1994	16.5	1996	1999
1993	16.3	1995	1998
1991	15.8	1996	1999

Regions: Coonawarra and Padthaway Winemaker: Greg Clayfield
Viticulturist: Max Arney Chief Executive: Bruce Kemp

Lindemans

**Riddoch Highway
Coonawarra SA 5263
Tel: (08) 8736 3205
Fax: (08) 8736 3250**

Lindemans is one of the major classic labels of Southcorp Wines, with major vineyard resources in Padthaway, Coonawarra and the Limestone Coast in the southeast corner of South Australia.

LIMESTONE RIDGE SHIRAZ CABERNET SAUVIGNON
Coonawarra $$$$

1994	18.6		2006+
1993	17.4	2001	2005
1992	16.6	1997	2000
1991	18.4		2003+
1990	16.5	1995	1998
1989	16.8	1991	1994
1987	16.0	1989	1992
1986	16.5	1994	1998
1985	16.0	1990	1993
1984	16.0	1989	1992
1982	17.0	1987	1990
1981	17.0	1989	1993
1980	18.5	1998	1992

PADTHAWAY CABERNET SAUVIGNON/MERLOT

Padthaway $$$

1996	17.0	2001	2004
1995	17.3	2003	2007
1994	16.7	1999	2002
1993	16.7	1998	2001
1992	17.0	1997	2000

PADTHAWAY CHARDONNAY

Padthaway $$

1998	18.0	2003	2006
1997	18.0	2002	2005
1996	16.0	2001	2004
1995	15.5	1997	2000
1994	16.8	1999	2002
1993	17.7	1998	2001
1992	18.2	1997	2000

PYRUS

Coonawarra $$$$

1995	18.1	2003	2007
1994	18.4	2002	2006
1993	16.8	1998	2001
1992	16.5	1997	2000
1991	17.5	1996	1999
1990	17.8	1995	1998
1988	16.5	1993	1996
1987	14.5	1989	1992
1986	16.0	1988	1991
1985	18.0	1987	1990

RESERVE PORPHYRY

Coonawarra and Padthaway $$$

1994	17.3	1999	2002
1993	16.0	1998	2001
1990	16.0	1992	1995
1989	16.0	1994	1997
1988	17.8	1993	1996
1987	17.0	1995	1999
1983	17.0	1991	1995

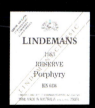

Lindemans Hunter Valley

McDonalds Rd
Pokolbin NSW 2320
Tel: (02) 4998 7503
Fax: (02) 4998 7682

ST. GEORGE CABERNET SAUVIGNON

Coonawarra $$$$

1995	18.5	2003	2007+
1994	18.6	2006	2014
1993	16.8	1998	2001
1992	16.7	2000	2004
1991	17.2	1996	1999
1990	17.6	1995	1998
1989	16.0	1994	1997
1988	18.0	1993	1996
1987	15.0	1989	1992
1986	16.5	1991	1994
1985	17.0	1990	1993
1984	16.0	1986	1989
1982	16.5	1990	1994
1981	16.0	1989	1993
1980	18.0	1992	1997

Region: Lower Hunter Valley Winemaker: Patrick Auld
Viticulturist: Jerome Scarboroug Chief Executive: Bruce Kemp

Lindemans is one of the Hunter Valley's longest established wine makers, with a rich tradition of benchmark semillon and shiraz. Its best wines today are its Hunter Semillon and Steven Vineyard Shiraz. Its chardonnays can be rather perplexing, especially since they represent the first time on record that I prefer a major maker's unwooded variant to its oaked expression. And that's weird.

CHARDONNAY

Lower Hunter Valley $$

1995	15.2	1997	2000
1994	15.2	1996	1999
1993	17.8	2001	2005
1992	16.7	1994	1997
1991	17.5	1999	2003

NON-OAKED CHARDONNAY (FORMERLY CHABLIS)

Lower Hunter Valley, Young $$

1996	16.0	1997	1998
1995	16.0	1996	1997
1994	14.8	1995	1996
1993	15.5	1995	1998

RESERVE CHARDONNAY

Lower Hunter Valley $$$

1996	16.0	1998	2001
1995	17.0	2000	2003
1994	16.0	1996	1999
1992	16.8	1997	2000
1991	18.3	1996	1999

SEMILLON (FORMERLY RIESLING)

Lower Hunter Valley, Young $$

1996	17.4	2001	2004
1995	16.6	2000	2003
1994	17.8	2002	2006
1993	17.2	1998	2001
1992	17.0	2000	2004
1991	18.0	1999	2003
1990	16.5	1995	1998

SHIRAZ

Lower Hunter Valley $$$

1994	18.0	1999	2002
1993	15.3	1995	1998
1991	18.3		2003+
1990	17.5		2002+
1989	14.5	1991	1994
1988	15.0	1993	1996
1987	17.0	1995	1999

STEVEN VINEYARD SHIRAZ

Lower Hunter Valley $$$

1996	16.5	2001	2004+
1995	18.5	2003	2007
1994	18.0	2002	2006
1991	18.6		2003+
1990	18.2		2002+
1989	16.0	1994	1997
1988	16.5	1996	2000
1987	17.0	1999	2004
1986	18.0	1998	2003

Maglieri

**Douglas Gully Road
McLaren Flat SA 5171
Tel: (08) 8383 0177
Fax: (08) 8383 0136**

Main Ridge Estate

**Lot 48 William Road
Red Hill Vic 3937
Tel: (03) 5989 2686
Fax: (03) 5931 0000**

Region: McLaren Vale Winemaker: John Loxton
Viticulturist: Chris Dundon Chief Executive: Ray King

Another successful medium sized brand lured into the Mildara Blass pond, Maglieri has a simply awesome recent track record with its red wines, especially with the McLaren Vale special, shiraz. The Steve Maglieri label is given to reserve parcels of this wine and the 1995 wine is little short of spectacular.

STEVE MAGLIERI SHIRAZ

McLaren Vale $$$$$

1997	18.0	2002	2005+
1995	18.7	2003	2007
1994	18.3	2002	2006
1993	15.0	1995	1998

Region: Mornington Peninsula Winemaker: Nat White
Viticulturist: Nat White Chief Executives: Rosalie & Nat White

Steadily redirecting their vineyard entirely towards chardonnay and pinot noir, Nat and Rosalie White have entered a golden period with their premium red label of Half Acre Pinot Noir. The 1997 wine is perhaps the finest from the Mornington Peninsula in its best year to date, while the 1998 edition looks almost as worthy, in a more reserved, earthy and bony style.

CABERNET MERLOT

Mornington Peninsula $$$

1994	15.2	2002	2006
1993	18.3	2001	2005
1992	17.6	2000	2004
1991	17.1	1996	1999
1990	18.0	1998	2001
1989	16.0	1994	1997
1988	17.6	1993	1996

CHARDONNAY

Mornington Peninsula $$$$

1998	18.0	2003	2006+
1997	17.6	2002	2005
1996	16.0	1998	2001
1995	17.8	1997	2000
1994	19.0	2002	2006
1993	18.4	1998	2001
1992	18.9	2000	2004
1991	18.5	1996	1999
1990	17.6	1995	1998
1989	16.0	1997	2001
1988	16.8	1993	1996

HALF ACRE PINOT NOIR (PREMIUM MAIN RIDGE PINOT NOIR SINCE 1993)

Mornington Peninsula $$$$

1997	18.7	2002	2005+
1996	17.5	2004	2008
1995	18.5	2003	2007
1994	18.3	2002	2006
1993	16.8	1998	2001
1992	18.2	1997	2000
1991	17.0	1996	1999
1990	16.0	1992	1995

Region: Coonawarra Winemaker: Bruce Gregory
Viticulturist: Brian Lynn Chief Executive: Brian Lynn

The small Coonawarra brand of Majella has proven an instant success in the marketplace with its ripe, fleshy and assertive red wines, grown at the Lynns' own mature vineyard on some of Coonawarra's finest ground. The Shiraz is usually concentrated, generous and simply a breeze to enjoy.

SHIRAZ

Coonawarra $$$

1997	16.5	1999	2002+
1996	18.5	2001	2004
1994	18.2	2002	2006

Region: Adelaide Hills Winemaker: Reg Tolley
Viticulturist: Reg Tolley Chief Executive: Reg Tolley

Malcolm Creek's Chardonnay is a soft, reserved and creamy wine with attractive peach and citrus flavours and buttery oak. Warmer vintages of Cabernet Sauvignon tend to produce fine-grained and elegant wines with a pleasing intensity of small berry fruits.

CABERNET SAUVIGNON

Adelaide Hills $$$

1996	17.3	2004	2008+
1995	16.3	2000	2003
1994	14.5	1996	1999
1992	13.5	1997	2000
1991	15.0	1999	2003
1990	16.3	1998	2002
1989	16.8	1997	2001
1988	17.8	1993	1996
1987	16.0	1992	1995
1986	18.0	1994	1998

Majella
Lynn Road
Coonawarra SA 5263
Tel: (08) 8736 3055
Fax: (08) 8736 3057

Malcolm Creek
Bonython Road
Kersbrook SA 5231
Tel: (08) 8389 3235
Fax: (08) 8263 3235

Mamre Brook

**Angaston Road
Angaston SA 5353
Tel: (08) 8564 3355
Fax: (08) 8564 2209**

CHARDONNAY

Adelaide Hills $$$

1997	16.8	2002	2005
1996	15.2	1998	2001
1995	16.8	2000	2003
1993	17.0	1995	1998
1991	14.7	1993	1996
1990	17.9	1998	2002
1989	17.1	1994	1997

**Region: Barossa Valley Winemaker: Nigel Dolan
Viticulturist: Murray Heidenreich Chief Executive: Ray King**

Nigel Dolan is performing great feats with one of the Barossa Valley's most treasured wine labels. Where once there was but a single Mamre Brook red there are now two, since the Cabernet Sauvignon and Shiraz are now made and bottled separately. While I clearly have a soft spot for the Cabernet Sauvignon, I actually prefer the Shiraz, due to enter this book in a year's time once it has completed the required three releases.

CABERNET SAUVIGNON (FORMERLY CABERNET SHIRAZ)

Barossa Valley $$$

1997	18.2	2005	2009
1996	18.3	2004	2008
1995	16.5	1997	2000
1994	17.0	2002	2006
1993	17.5	1998	2001
1988	15.5	1993	1998
1986	18.2		2006+
1985	16.0	1990	1993
1984	18.3	1996	2001

CHARDONNAY

South Australia (Early vint. some Hunter V.) $$$

1998	16.0	2000	2003
1997	15.2	1998	1999
1996	16.7	1998	2001
1995	16.0	1997	2000
1994	18.0	1999	2002
1993	18.4	1998	2001
1990	17.5	1995	1998

Region: Mornington Peninsula Winemakers: Ian Home & Daniel Greene
Viticulturist: David Jordan Chief Executive: Ian Home

Two terrific recent vintages in 1997 and 1998 have given new lustre to Massoni, one of the few genuinely respected Mornington Peninsula wine brands. The Chardonnay is a traditionally rich and opulent expression of the variety, seen at its best in 1997. The 1998 Chardonnay just lacks the depth of fruit of the previous edition, while the 1998 Pinot Noir has an edge in elegance and fineness over the rather chunky, robust 1997 wine.

Massoni

RMB 6580
Mornington-Flinders Rd
Red Hill Vic 3937
Tel: (03) 5989 2352
Fax: (03) 5989 2014

PINOT NOIR
Mornington Peninsula $$$$

1998	18.6	2003	2006+
1997	18.2	2002	2005+
1996	15.2	1997	2000
1995	16.1	1997	2000
1994	18.5	1999	2002
1993	18.2	1998	2001
1992	17.5	2000	2004
1991	16.5	1999	2003

RED HILL CHARDONNAY
Mornington Peninsula $$$$

1998	18.2	2000	2003+
1997	18.6	2002	2005+
1996	16.6	1998	2001
1995	16.2	1997	2000
1994	18.8	2002	2006
1993	18.2	1998	2001+
1992	18.0	1997	2000
1991	18.6	1996	1999
1990	10.6	1995	1998
1989	18.2	1994	1997

Maxwell

**Olivers Road
McLaren Vale SA 5171
Tel: (08) 8323 8200
Fax: (08) 8323 8900**

Region: McLaren Vale Winemaker: Mark Maxwell
Viticulturist: Mark Maxwell Chief Executive: Mark Maxwell

Maxwell's best wines are its traditional red styles: the Ellen St. Shiraz and Lime Cave Cabernet Sauvignon. The shiraz is very ripe and highly spiced with fennel and cloves, while the cabernet sauvignon reveals cassis-like fruit and a robust tannic backbone.

ELLEN STREET SHIRAZ

McLaren Vale $$

1997	15.8	2002	2005
1996	16.4	2001	2004
1994	17.0	1999	2002
1993	16.5		2005+
1992	15.6	1994	1997
1991	16.2	1999	2003

LIME CAVE CABERNET SAUVIGNON

McLaren Vale $$$

1996	16.0	2002	2006
1994	17.6	2002	2006
1993	16.9	2001	2005
1992	16.7	2000	2004
1990	16.8		2002+

SAUVIGNON BLANC

McLaren Vale $$

1998	16.7	1999	2000
1996	15.8	1996	1997
1995	15.6	1996	1997

McAlister Vineyards

RMB 6810 Golden Beach
Longford South-East
Gippsland Vic 3851
Tel: (03) 5149 7229
Fax: (03) 5149 7229

Region: Gippsland Winemaker: Peter Edwards
Viticulturist: Peter Edwards Chief Executive: Peter Edwards

The McAlister is fast becoming a must-have wine for any serious collector of more elegant and sophisticated Australian blends of red Bordeaux vareities. Its 1996 wine is an earlier-drinking expression from one of the coolest years Peter Edwards has yet to deal with. The occasional McAlister Merlot Noirs are highly rated.

THE McALISTER
Gippsland $$$$

1996	15.3	1998	2001
1995	16.3	2000	2003
1994	18.7	2002	2006
1993	17.0	1998	2001
1992	18.1	2000	2004
1991	18.1	1999	2003
1990	18.5		2002+
1989	16.0	1997	2001
1988	18.0	2000	2005
1987	17.8	1999	2004
1986	17.0	1994	1998

Merricks Estate

end of Thompsons Lane
Merricks Vic 3916
Tel: (03) 5989 8416
Fax: (03) 9629 4035

Region: Mornington Peninsula Winemaker: Alex White
Viticulturist: George Kefford Chief Executives: Jacki and George Kefford

Merricks Estate was the first Mornington Peninsula vineyard to make a name for its Shiraz, although today this wine tends to look rather greenish against wines like Paringa Estate's. Merricks Estate's Pinot Noir tends to ripen better than its other red varieties.

CABERNET SAUVIGNON
Mornington Peninsula $$$

1994	16.3	1999	2002
1993	15.0	1998	2001
1992	15.2	1997	2000
1991	17.4	1999	2003
1990	16.8	1995	1998
1989	16.2	1991	1994
1988	18.0	1993	1996

CHARDONNAY
Mornington Peninsula $$$

1998	16.7	2000	2003+
1997	16.3	1998	1999
1996	16.0	1998	2001
1994	18.0	1999	2002
1993	17.8	1998	2001
1992	16.5	1997	2000
1991	16.5	1993	1996
1990	17.5	1995	1998

Metala

**Nuriootpa Road
Angaston SA 5353
Tel: (08) 8564 3355
Fax: (08) 8564 2209**

PINOT NOIR
Mornington Peninsula $$$

1997	16.6	1999	2002
1995	15.2	1997	2000
1994	17.8	1999	2002
1993	17.4	1995	1998

SHIRAZ
Mornington Peninsula $$$

1997	16.3	1999	2002+
1995	13.0	1996	1997
1993	18.3	2001	2005
1992	17.6	1997	2000
1991	16.8	1996	1999
1990	18.5	1995	1998
1989	15.0	1994	1997
1988	18.5	1996	2000

Region: Barossa Valley Winemaker: Nigel Dolan
Viticulturists: Tom and Guy Adams Chief Executive: Ray King

Another brand of Mildara Blass Ltd, the Stonyfell Metala continues to be released under its historic white label. A section of the vineyard's original plantings is used to continue with the Original Vines label which commenced so successfully with the very refined, silky and concentrated 1994 wine, to which the rather de luxe 1996 effort is a very worthy successor indeed.

SHIRAZ CABERNET
Langhorne Creek $$

1997	16.8	2002	2005
1996	17.4	2001	2004
1995	17.0	2000	2003
1994	17.5	2002	2006
1993	17.9	2001	2005
1992	17.5	2000	2004
1991	16.3	1999	2003
1988	14.5	1993	1996
1987	16.0	1992	1995
1986	17.0	1994	1998
1985	16.5	1993	1997
1984	17.3	1996	2001
1983	17.7	1995	2000

Region: Coonawarra Winemaker: David O'Leary
Viticulturist: Vic Patrick Chief Executive: Ray King

There's not much left of Mildara's historic white Coonawarra label other than its Cabernet Sauvignon which seemed to miss its cue in 1996. One hopes that Mildara, which appears to have invented a different Coonawarra brand for each month of the year, might yet preserve this last remaining link to its winemaking past.

CABERNET SAUVIGNON

Coonawarra $$$

1996	16.6	2004	2008
1995	16.3	2000	2003
1994	18.2	2002	2006
1993	18.7	2001	2005
1992	18.3	2000	2004
1991	17.0	1996	1999
1990	18.5	1995	1998
1989	16.0	1994	1997
1988	18.3	1996	2000

Region: Mudgee Winemaker: Ian MacRae
Viticulturist: Ian MacRae Chief Executive: Ian MacRae

Like several other smaller Mudgee makers, Miramar's robust and generously proportioned reds, citrusy chardonnay and tangy semillon offer genuine value for money at a time when most wine prices are simply spiralling upwards.

CABERNET SAUVIGNON

Mudgee $$

1997	16.6	2005	2009
1996	15.8	2001	2004
1995	15.0	2000	2003
1994	18.2		2006+
1991	16.8	1999	2003
1990	17.1	1995	1998

CHARDONNAY

Mudgee $$

1996	16.2	2001	2004
1995	16.7	2000	2003
1994	15.0	1996	1999
1993	17.7	1998	2001
1992	17.5	1997	2000
1991	17.9	1996	1999

Mildara Coonawarra

Riddoch Highway
Coonawarra SA 5263
Tel: (08) 8736 3380
Fax: (08) 8736 3307

Miramar

Henry Lawson Drive
Mudgee NSW 2850
Tel: (02) 6373 3874
Fax: (02) 6373 3854

SEMILLON
Mudgee $$

1997	17.5	2005	2009
1996	18.1	2004	2008
1995	17.9	2003	2007
1993	17.1	1998	2001
1992	16.5	1997	2000
1990	14.8	1995	1998

SHIRAZ
Mudgee $$

1997	15.7	2002	2005+
1996	15.3	2001	2004
1995	18.4	2003	2007
1994	17.6	2002	2006
1993	18.0		2005+
1991	17.4		2003+
1988	17.0	2000	2008
1986	17.0	1998	2006
1985	17.0	1997	2005

Mitchell

Hughes Park Rd
Sevenhill via
Clare SA 5453
Tel: (08) 8843 4258
Fax: (08) 8843 4340

Region: Clare Valley Winemaker: Andrew Mitchell
Viticulturist: Leon Schramm Chief Executive: Jane Mitchell

Andrew and Jane Mitchell's finely crafted wines include the two classic Clare Valley white styles of semillon and riesling, plus a group of tight-knit reds including the rather wild and exotic The Growers Grenache, the fine-grained Cabernet Sauvignon and my personal favourite, the ultra-spicy Peppertree Vineyard Shiraz.

CABERNET SAUVIGNON
Clare Valley $$$

1997	16.7	2002	2005+
1996	16.7	2004	2008
1995	15.0	2000	2003
1994	17.6	2002	2006
1992	17.4		2004+
1991	18.0		2003+
1990	18.5		2002+
1988	16.5	1996	2000

PEPPERTREE VINEYARD SHIRAZ

Clare Valley $$$

1997	16.0	1999	2002
1996	18.0	2001	2004
1995	15.0	2000	2003
1994	17.3	1999	2003
1993	18.0	2001	2005
1992	17.9	2000	2004
1991	17.5	1996	1999
1990	18.5	1998	2002
1989	18.0	1994	1997
1988	16.0	1993	1996

THE GROWERS GRENACHE

Clare Valley $$$

1998	16.5	2000	2003
1997	17.0	1999	2002
1996	15.7	1998	2001
1995	15.2	1997	2000

THE GROWERS SEMILLON/SAUVIGNON BLANC BLEND

Clare Valley $$

1998	16.6	2000	2003
1997	16.8	2002	2005
1996	17.2	2001	2004
1995	16.5	2000	2003
1994	18.2	2002	2006
1993	18.7	2001	2005
1992	16.5	1997	2000
1991	18.5	1996	1999
1990	18.0	1995	1998
1989	16.0	1995	1997

WATERVALE RIESLING

Clare Valley $$

1998	17.0	2003	2006+
1997	17.8	2005	2009
1996	16.0	2001	2004
1995	18.3	2003	2007
1994	16.5	1999	2003
1993	18.0	2001	2005
1992	17.4	1997	2000
1991	18.5	1996	1999
1990	18.5	1995	1998
1989	16.0	1997	2001
1988	16.0	1990	1993

Mitchelton

Mitchellstown via
Nagambie Vic 3608
Tel: (03) 5794 2710
Fax: (03) 5794 2615

Region: Goulburn Valley **Winemakers:** Don Lewis, Alan George
Viticulturist: John Beresford **Chief Executive:** Paul van der Lee

Don Lewis oversees the making of some of Victoria's most consistent and competent wines at Mitchelton, one of the state's more spectacular winery developments. Mitchelton's signature wines are its Blackwood Park Riesling, Marsanne and Print Label Shiraz. The Riesling has an enormous capacity to improve and endure in the bottle. Today Mitchelton is part of Petaluma Ltd.

BLACKWOOD PARK RIESLING

Goulburn Valley $$

1998	18.2	2006	2010
1997	17.0	2002	2005+
1996	18.0	2004	2008
1995	18.2	2000	2003
1994	18.0	1999	2002
1993	18.3	1998	2001
1992	17.7	1994	1997
1991	18.5	1999	2003
1990	17.5	1995	1998

CABERNET SAUVIGNON

Goulburn Valley $$$

1996	18.0	2004	2008+
1995	18.0		2007+
1994	18.2		2006+
1993	18.3		2005+
1992	18.1	2000	2004
1991	18.3	1999	2003
1990	17.6	1998	2002

CHARDONNAY

Goulburn Valley $$$

1997	18.3	2002	2005
1996	16.8	1998	2001
1994	18.2	1999	2002
1993	18.0	1998	2001
1992	18.5	1997	2000
1991	18.0	1996	1999
1990	17.5	1995	1998
1989	18.0	1994	1997
1988	17.9	1993	1996

MARSANNE
Goulburn Valley $$$

1996	17.0	2001	2004
1994	15.0	1995	1996
1993	18.6	1998	2001
1992	18.5	2000	2004
1991	16.6	1996	1999
1990	17.5	1998	2002
1989	15.8	1994	1997
1988	17.0	1996	2000
1987	15.0	1995	1999
1986	16.0	1994	1998

PRINT LABEL SHIRAZ
Goulburn Valley $$$$

1995	17.9	2003	2007
1994	16.6	2002	2006
1993	18.4		2005+
1992	17.8	2000	2004
1991	18.5		2003+
1990	17.2	1998	2002

Region: Barossa Valley Winemaker: Natasha Mooney
Chief Executive: Bruce Richardson

Formerly sold under the 'Barossa Valley Estate' label and made at Angle Vale, the Moculta wines are forward and fruity, destined for early enjoyment. The occasional wine like the vibrant, spicy Shiraz 1997, rises well above the average Moculta standard.

Moculta

Heaslip Road
Angle Vale SA 5117
Tel: (08) 8284 7000
Fax: (08) 8284 7219

CABERNET MERLOT
Barossa Valley $$

1997	16.6	1999	2002
1996	15.0	1998	2001
1995	16.0	1997	2000
1994	15.4	1996	1999
1993	15.0	1995	1998
1992	17.3	1994	1997
1990	16.3	1992	1995

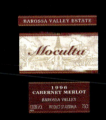

Montara

Chalambar Rd
Ararat Vic 3377
Tel: (03) 5352 3868
Fax: (03) 5352 4968

CHARDONNAY
Barossa Valley $$

1997	17.1	1998	1999
1996	15.6	1997	1998
1995	16.0	1996	1997
1994	17.0	1996	1999
1993	17.0	1995	1998

SHIRAZ
Barossa Valley $$

1997	17.8	1999	2002
1996	16.4	1998	2001
1995	16.0	2000	2003
1993	15.2	1998	2001
1992	17.5	1997	2000

Region: Grampians Winemaker: Mike McRae
Viticulturist: Mike McRae Chief Executive: Mike McRae

Montara is a long established vineyard just to the south of the Victorian western district town of Ararat which has specialised largely in red wines, with focus on shiraz and pinot noir. It's an unusual place to make pinot noir, but some vintages amply reward the McRaes' enthusiasm for their work. The Shiraz is usually the vineyard's best wine, full of small berries, spice, and pepper with a hint or two of regional eucalyptus and mint.

CABERNET SAUVIGNON
Grampians $$$

1996	14.8	1998	2001
1995	14.8	2000	2003
1994	16.9	2002	2006
1993	18.2		2005+
1992	16.5	2000	2004
1990	16.5	1995	1998

CHARDONNAY
Grampians

1996	14.8	1997	1998
1995	14.5	1996	1997
1994	15.0	1996	1999
1993	17.3	1998	2001

PINOT NOIR

Grampians $$$

1996	14.1	1998	2001
1995	16.7	2000	2003
1994	14.8	1996	1999
1993	15.8	2001	2005
1992	17.3	1997	2000

SHIRAZ

Grampians $$$

1996	16.0	2001	2004
1995	16.7	2000	2003
1994	17.4	2002	2006
1993	18.4		2005+
1992	17.2	2000	2004
1990	17.0	1992	1995
1989	16.5	1991	1994
1988	17.8		2000+

Region: Mudgee Winemaker: Brett McKinnon
Viticulturist: Stephen Guilbaud-Oulton Chief Executive: Andre Boucard

Montrose is another of Orlando Wyndham's substantial investments at Mudgee. It's a maker of sound, flavoursome and perfectly reliable table wines which occasionally rise well above the pack, like the 1996 Cabernet Sauvignon which gave me an enormous surprise. The Barbera is a delicious and simultaneously ripe and sour expression of this Italian grape variety.

Montrose

Henry Lawson Drive
Mudgee NSW 2850
Tel: (02) 6373 3853
Fax: (02) 6373 3795

BLACK SHIRAZ

Mudgee $$

1996	16.9	1998	2001
1995	16.5	1997	2000
1994	16.0	1996	1999

CABERNET SAUVIGNON

Mudgee $$

1996	18.5	2004	2008
1995	16.1	2000	2003
1994	17.6	2002	2006
1993	16.0	1998	2001
1992	17.3	2000	2004
1991	15.5	1993	1996
1990	16.2	1995	1998

THE ONWINE AUSTRALIAN WINE ANNUAL 2000

Moondah Brook Estate

Dale Rd
Middle Swan WA 6056
Tel: (08) 9274 5372
Fax: (08) 9274 5372

CHARDONNAY
Mudgee $$

1998	16.8	2000	2003
1997	17.5	2002	2005
1996	17.5	2001	2004
1995	17.5	2000	2003
1994	16.0	1996	1999
1993	17.6	1995	1998

POET'S CORNER RED
Mudgee $

1997	15.7	1999	2002
1996	16.4	2001	2004
1995	16.0	1997	2000
1994	14.0	1995	1996
1993	16.5	1998	2001
1992	15.0	1993	1994

POET'S CORNER WHITE
Mudgee $

1997	16.0	1998	1999
1996	16.0	1997	1998
1995	16.0	1996	1997

Region: Gingin Winemaker: Larry Cherubino
Viticulturist: Tony Kennar Chief Executive: Stephen Millar

From the rather warm region of Gingin, a short trip north of Perth, Moondah Brook's wines are clean, fresh and zesty. My favourite is the Verdelho which, typical of several Western Australian verdelhos, develops mouthfilling richness of flavour and texture after just a few short years in the bottle, a feat occasionally matched by the Chenin Blanc.

CABERNET SAUVIGNON
Gingin $$

1996	17.2	2004	2008
1995	16.0	2000	2003
1993	15.3	1995	1998
1992	17.7	1997	2000
1991	17.4	1999	2003
1990	15.6	1995	1998

CHARDONNAY

Gingin $$

1997	15.8	1998	1999
1996	15.0	1997	1998
1995	15.0	1996	1997
1993	16.9	1995	1998

CHENIN BLANC

Gingin $$

1996	16.0	2001	2004
1995	15.3	1997	2000
1994	16.5	1999	2002
1993	15.4	1994	1995
1992	16.2	1997	2000

VERDELHO

Gingin $$

1998	16.8	2000	2003+
1997	15.1	1999	2002
1996	15.6	1998	2001
1995	15.8	1997	2000
1994	17.5	1999	2002
1993	17.5	1998	2001
1992	17.4	1997	2000
1991	16.0	1993	1996

Region: Southern Tasmania Winemaker: Alain Rousso
Viticulturist: Alain Rousso Chief Executive: Tim Goddard

Despite a number of major recent changes at Moorilla Estate, which has vineyards near Hobart and in the Tamar Valley, it's hard to avoid the impression that life there is a constant battle against unripeness in the vineyard. Moorilla's winemaking is excellent, but the green thread beneath many of its red wines is often too hard simply to ignore. One wine which clearly shows what Moorilla is capable of in a warm year and worthy of great merit is the Winter Collection Merlot of 1997, which I rate at 18.6.

CABERNET SAUVIGNON

Southern Tasmania $$$

1997	15.8	2002	2005+
1995	14.8	2000	2003
1994	18.0	2002	2006
1993	15.0	2001	2005
1992	17.9	2000	2004
1991	16.5	1999	2003
1990	17.0	1998	2002

Moorilla Estate

655 Main Road
Berriedale Tas 7011
Tel: (03) 6249 2949
Fax: (03) 6249 4003

THE ONWINE AUSTRALIAN WINE ANNUAL 2000

CHARDONNAY
Southern Tasmania $$$$

1998	14.8	2000	2003+
1996	15.2	1998	2001
1995	18.4	2003	2007
1994	16.0	2002	2006
1993	17.0	1998	2001
1992	18.0	1997	2000
1991	17.0	1999	2003
1990	17.0	1998	2002
1989	18.0	1997	2001

GEWURZTRAMINER
Southern Tasmania $$$$

1998	16.8	2003	2006
1997	17.0	2002	2005
1996	15.0	1997	1998
1995	18.5	2003	2007
1994	17.5	2002	2006
1993	18.0	1998	2001
1992	16.8	1997	2000
1991	18.0	1993	1996

PINOT NOIR
Southern Tasmania $$$$

1998	15.3	2000	2003
1996	17.0	2001	2004
1995	16.5	2000	2003
1994	17.4	1999	2002
1993	13.5	1995	1998
1992	15.0	1994	1997
1991	17.0	1999	2003
1990	17.5	1995	1998

RESERVE PINOT NOIR
Southern Tasmania $$$$

1998	16.7	2000	2003
1997	15.2	1999	2002
1996	18.0	2001	2004

THE ONWINE AUSTRALIAN WINE ANNUAL

RIESLING
Southern Tasmania $$$

1997	16.0	1999	2002
1996	17.6	2001	2004
1995	16.6	1997	2000
1994	18.6		2006+
1993	18.2	1998	2001
1992	16.0	1997	2000
1991	17.5	1996	1999
1990	16.5	1995	1998
1989	17.0	1997	2001

Region: Mornington Peninsula **Winemaker:** Dr Richard McIntyre
Viticulturist: Ian Macrae **Chief Executive:** Dr Richard McIntyre

Rick McIntyre takes full advantage of his comparatively warm location on the Mornington Peninsula to develop succulent and fleshy table wines from Chardonnay and Pinot Noir which are right at the front of the region's quality leader-board. 1998 saw the release of two special wines, labelled as 'Wild Yeast' variants of Chardonnay and Pinot Noir. They look like a message in a bottle, if you were to ask me...

Moorooduc Estate

**501 Derril Road
Moorooduc Vic 3933
Tel: (03) 9696 4130
Fax: (03) 9696 2841**

CABERNET
Mornington Peninsula $$$$

1995	14.5	2000	2003
1994	14.5	1999	2002
1993	16.2	2001	2005
1992	16.7	2000	2004
1991	18.3	1999	2003
1990	18.0	1995	1998
1989	16.0	1991	1994
1988	17.0	1993	1997

CHARDONNAY
Mornington Peninsula $$$$

1998	16.8	2000	2003
1997	16.5	2002	2005
1996	18.2	2001	2004
1995	18.2	2000	2003
1994	18.7	1999	2002
1993	17.8	1998	2001
1992	17.7	1994	1997
1991	18.0	1996	1999
1990	18.3	1999	2002
1989	18.0	1994	1997

PINOT NOIR

Mornington Peninsula $$$$

1997	18.2	2002	2005
1996	16.0	2001	2004
1995	18.2	2000	2003
1994	17.8	1999	2002
1993	18.0	1998	2001
1992	18.7	2000	2004
1991	15.3	1996	1999

Morris

Mia Mia Road
Rutherglen Vic 3685
Tel: (02) 6026 7303
Fax: (02) 6026 7445

Region: NE Victoria Winemaker: David Morris
Viticulturist: Stephen Guilbaud-Oulton Chief Executive: Andre Boucard

There's a disarming honesty about the Morris table wines from Rutherglen in northeast Victoria. Don't for a moment go there looking for elegance and sophistication; you'd be taking the wrong bus. Instead, if the mood takes you, choose a Morris red wine for its richness and uncompromising ripeness and earthy, almost muddy regional character. But try leaving it for a few years first.

CABERNET SAUVIGNON

NE Victoria $$

1996	16.6	2004	2008+
1995	16.2	2003	2007
1994	16.8		2006+
1993	16.2		2005+
1992	16.6	2000	2004
1990	17.5		2002+
1989	17.5		2001+
1988	17.5	2000	2005
1987	16.5	1995	1999
1986	17.0	1994	1998

CHARDONNAY

NE Victoria $$

1997	15.1	1999	2002
1996	16.0	1998	2001
1995	15.7	1997	2000
1994	17.0	1999	2002
1991	15.0	1993	1996

DURIF
NE Victoria $$

1996	16.6	2004	2008+
1995	18.2		2007+
1994	18.1	2002	2006
1993	16.3	2001	2005
1992	17.0		2004+
1991	18.0		2003+
1990	18.2	2002	2010
1989	15.5	2001	2009
1988	16.5	2000	2005
1987	17.0	1999	2004
1986	16.5	1998	2003
1985	18.0	1997	2002
1984	17.0	1996	2001

SEMILLON
NE Victoria $$

1998	16.0	2000	2003
1996	17.1	2001	2004
1995	17.0	2000	2003
1994	16.5	1999	2002

SHIRAZ
NE Victoria $$

1996	16.8	2004	2008+
1995	16.0	2000	2003
1994	16.3	2002	2006
1993	15.0	1998	2001
1992	17.5		2004+
1991	17.0		2003+
1990	16.4	1998	2002
1989	15.8	1994	1997

Moss Wood

Metricup Road
Willyabrup via Cowaramup
WA 6284
Tel: (08) 9755 6266
Fax: (08) 9755 6303

Region: Margaret River Winemaker: Keith Mugford
Viticulturist: Ian Bell Chief Executive: Keith Mugford

Moss Wood has undertaken a change of direction with its long-awaited 1996 release, since this wine is the first so-called 'standard' Moss Wood Cabernet Sauvignon to have received the identical oak treatment previously only dished out to the domaine's now-extinct Reserve label. You'll notice more ripeness and sweetness and more assertive oak, but Keith Mugford has no doubt whatsoever it will age with all the grace and charm expected of a true Moss Wood. I tend to agree.

CABERNET SAUVIGNON
Margaret River $$$$$

1996	18.9	2008	2016
1995	19.0	2007	2015
1994	19.2		2014+
1993	18.0	2005	2013
1992	18.8	2004	2012
1991	19.5	2003	2011+
1990	19.0	2002	2010+
1989	18.3	2001	2009
1988	17.0		2000+
1987	18.3	1999	2007
1986	18.1	1998	2006
1985	17.3	1993	1997

CHARDONNAY
Margaret River $$$$

1998	17.0	2003	2006+
1997	18.7	2005	2009
1996	18.0	1998	2001
1995	18.2	2003	2007
1994	18.8	2002	2006
1993	17.8	1998	2001
1992	18.5	2000	2004
1991	17.5		2003+
1990	18.5		2002+
1989	17.0	1997	2001
1988	17.0	1996	2000

PINOT NOIR
Margaret River $$$$

1996	16.8	2001	2004
1995	18.0	2003	2007
1994	16.0	1999	2002
1993	15.2	1998	2001
1992	15.0	1997	2000
1991	15.5	1993	1998
1990	18.5	1998	2002

Mount Avoca

**Moates Lane
Avoca Vic 3467
Tel: (03) 5465 3282
Fax: (03) 5465 3544**

Region: Pyrenees Winemaker: Matthew Barry
Viticulturists: Matthew Barry & Graeme Miles Chief Executive: John Barry

Mount Avoca is a large-ish small vineyard and winery owned by the Barry family, which now has a greater collective role in wine production than ever before. Recent vintages of red wine appear very fast to develop and lack the customary freshness and vitality of the Sauvignon Blanc.

CABERNET
Pyrenees $$$

1996	15.0	1998	2001
1995	15.0	2000	2003
1994	15.0	1996	1999
1993	16.0	2001	2005
1992	18.5		2004+
1991	15.4	1999	2003
1990	17.8	1995	1998

CHARDONNAY
Pyrenees $$$

1998	16.0	2000	2003
1997	16.6	1999	2002+
1996	14.5	1998	2001

SAUVIGNON BLANC
Pyrenees $$$

1998	16.8	2000	2003
1997	17.8	1998	1999
1996	14.0	1996	1997
1995	17.5	1996	1997

SHIRAZ
Pyrenees $$

1997	15.0	2002	2005
1996	16.5	1998	2001
1995	15.0	1997	2000
1994	15.9	1996	1999
1993	16.0	1998	2001
1992	17.2	2000	2004
1991	17.0	1996	1999
1990	15.8	1995	1998
1989	15.5	1994	1997
1988	17.5	1993	1996

Mount Gisborne

**Waterson Road
Gisborne Vic 3437
Tel: 03 5428 2834
Fax: 03 5428 2834**

Mount Helen

**Northern Highway
Heathcote Vic 3523
Tel: (03) 5796 2236
Fax:**

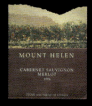

Region: Macedon Winemaker: Stuart Anderson
Viticulturist: David Ell Chief Executives: David and Mary Ell

David and Mary Ell own and manage an immaculate Macedon Ranges vineyard planted to pinot noir and chardonnay whose location is doubly fortunate in that it is both viticulturally suited to these grapes and within driving distance of home for winemaking sage Stuart Anderson. The Pinot Noir is heady, rich and bony, the Chardonnay retiring, complex and mineral.

CHARDONNAY
Macedon $$$$

1998	18.7	2003	2006+
1997	18.5	2002	2005
1995	18.0	2000	2003

PINOT NOIR
Macedon $$$$

1997	18.4	2002	2005+
1996	17.6	2004	2008
1995	18.1	2000	2003+

Region: Strathbogie Ranges Winemaker: Toni Stockhausen
Viticulturist: Damien de Castella Chief Executive: Ray King

Mount Helen is a Victorian brand owned by Mildara Blass, but the actual vineyard in the Strathbogie Ranges recently passed into the hands of Normans Wines Ltd. Although recent Chardonnay releases have been well below par, the 1997 Cabernet Merlot is one of the best red wines yet to come from Mount Helen fruit.

CABERNET MERLOT
Strathbogie Ranges $$$

1997	18.3	2005	2009
1996	17.3	2004	2008
1994	18.2		2006+
1991	17.6	1996	1999
1990	17.9	1995	1998

CHARDONNAY
Strathbogie Ranges $$$

1997	15.2	1998	1999
1996	15.0	1997	1998
1995	15.3	1997	2000
1994	18.3	1999	2002
1992	17.9	1997	2000
1991	16.7	1996	1999
1990	16.5	1995	1998

Region: Clare Valley Winemakers: Jeffrey Grosset, Stephanie Toole
Chief Executive: Stephanie Toole

Mount Horrocks' early-maturing table wines are the perfect answer for restaurant and bistro wine lists, although I rate the 1996 Cabernet Merlot as a more serious long-term prospect. Mount Horrocks' efforts are typically ready to drink at time of release.

CABERNET MERLOT

Clare Valley $$$

1996	18.4	2004	2008+
1995	17.0	2000	2003
1994	17.6	1999	2002
1993	16.0	1998	2001
1992	16.9	1997	2000

CORDON-CUT RIESLING

lare Valley $$$$

1998	17.2	1999	2000
1997	16.0	1999	2002
1996	18.2	2001	2004
1995	17.3	2000	2003
1994	18.8	1999	2002
1993	18.6	1998	2001
1992	17.1	1994	1997

RIESLING

Clare Valley $$

1998	18.1	2003	2006
1997	17.0	2002	2005
1996	17.3	1998	2001
1995	17.0	1997	2000
1994	18.0	1999	2002
1993	18.5	2001	2005
1992	17.5	2000	2004
1991	16.8	1996	1999

SEMILLON (SAUVIGNON BLANC)

Clare Valley $$$

1997	16.6	1999	2002
1996	16.4	1998	2001
1995	16.7	1997	2000
1994	18.5	2000	2006
1993	17.7	1998	2001
1992	18.4	2000	2004
1991	16.5	1996	1999
1990	16.5	1995	1998
1989	18.0	1994	1997

Mount Horrocks

**The Old Railway Station
Curling St
Auburn SA 5451
Tel: (08) 8849 2243
Fax: (08) 8849 2243**

Mount Ida

Northern Highway
Heathcote Vic 3523
Tel: (03) 5796 2236

Region: Bendigo Winemaker: Toni Stockhausen
Viticulturist: Damien de Castella Chief Executive: Ray King

Mildara Blass, not a company largely focused towards small production individual vineyard wines, must be absolutely delighted with the performance of the Mount Ida vineyard and its winemaker, Toni Stockhausen. Its wine is musky, spicy and brightly flavoured with red and dark berry/plum fruits, simply chock-full of pepper and spice, and married with well-handled oak.

SHIRAZ

Heathcote $$$

1997	17.6	2002	2005
1996	18.0	2001	2004
1995	18.9	2003	2007
1994	18.5	1999	2002
1992	18.6	1997	2000
1991	18.3	1999	2003
1990	18.1	1995	1998
1989	15.0	1991	1994

Mount Langi Ghiran

Vine Road
Buangor Vic 3375
Tel: (03) 5354 3207
Fax: (03) 5354 3277

Region: Grampians Winemakers: Trevor Mast, Andrew McLoughney
Viticulturist: Damias Sheehan Chief Executive: Trevor Mast

Mount Langi Ghiran is one of the premier vineyards in central and western Victoria. Best known for its remarkably spicy and peppery Langi Shiraz, it also makes an under-rated Cabernet Sauvignon Merlot Blend and a fragrant, limey Riesling. The company is expanding rapidly to take advantage of substantial export opportunities helped by flattering but deserved coverage in overseas media, especially within the United States.

CABERNET SAUVIGNON MERLOT

Grampians $$$$

1996	17.2	2004	2008+
1994	18.7		2006+
1993	18.5	2001	2005
1992	18.7	2000	2004
1991	18.2	1999	2003
1990	17.7	1995	1998
1989	17.5	1997	2001
1988	17.0	1993	1996

CHARDONNAY
Grampians $$$

1997	15.6	1999	2002+
1996	16.5	1998	2001
1995	16.2	1996	1997
1994	18.3	1999	2002
1993	18.5	1995	1998
1992	16.5	1994	1997

RIESLING
Grampians $$

1998	15.2	2000	2003
1997	15.0	1999	2002
1996	18.4	2004	2008
1995	18.3	2003	2007
1994	17.5	1999	2002
1993	18.5	1998	2001
1992	15.2	1994	1997

LANGI SHIRAZ
Grampians $$$$$

1997	18.6	2005	2009+
1996	18.5	2004	2008
1995	18.3	2003	2007
1994	19.3		2006+
1993	18.5	2001	2005
1992	18.0		2004+
1991	17.1	1999	2003
1990	18.0		2002+
1989	18.6		2001+
1988	17.5	1996	2000

Mount Mary

**Coldstream West Road
Lilydale Vic 3140
Tel: (03) 9739 1761
Fax: (03) 9739 0137**

Region: Yarra Valley Winemakers: John Middleton & Mario Marson
Viticulturists: John Middleton & Mario Marson Chief Executive: John Middleton

John Middleton's incredible attention to detail continues to inspire the making of some of Australia's greatest wines. While its reds are as well known and sought after as any made in Australia, Mount Mary's white wines are now approaching comparable stature. The Triolet blend of sauvignon blanc, semillon and muscadelle now rivals some of the most exceptional white Bordeaux wines. The Chardonnay, while stylistically about as far from the mainstream Australian example as it is possible to travel, has enjoyed a brilliant decade in the 1990s. It should be said that auction prices for the top years of Cabernet Quintet, possibly Australia's leading cabernet-based wine, are little short of hysterical.

CABERNET 'QUINTET'

Yarra Valley $$$$$

1996	18.7	2004	2008+
1995	17.8	2003	2007
1994	19.0		2006+
1993	16.8	2015	2013
1992	18.7	2000	2004
1991	18.8	1999	2003
1990	19.4		2002+
1989	15.5	1994	1997
1988	19.2	2000	2008
1987	17.3	1995	1999
1986	18.8		1998+
1985	17.5	1997	2002
1984	18.7		2004+
1983	16.0	1991	1995
1982	18.6	1994	1999
1981	16.5	1993	1998
1980	17.0	1992	1997

CHARDONNAY

Yarra Valley $$$$$

1997	18.6	2002	2005
1996	18.1	2004	2008
1995	18.7	2003	2007
1994	18.3	2002	2006
1993	17.2	1998	2001
1992	18.8	2000	2004
1991	17.9	1999	2003
1990	18.0	1998	2002
1989	16.0	1994	1997
1988	17.0	1993	1996

PINOT NOIR

Yarra Valley $$$$$

1996	16.7	1998	2001
1995	16.5	2000	2003
1994	18.4	2002	2006
1993	16.5	1998	2001
1992	18.2	2000	2004
1992	18.6	1997	2000
1991	18.2	1999	2003
1990	17.8	1995	1998
1989	18.7	1997	2001
1988	18.8	1996	2000

TRIOLET (FORMERLY SAUVIGNON)

Yarra Valley $$$$$

1997	17.9	2002	2005
1996	18.7	2001	2004
1995	18.6	2000	2003
1994	18.0	1999	2002
1993	18.6	1995	1998
1992	18.7	1997	2000+
1992	18.5	2000	2004
1991	18.3	1996	1999
1990	18.5	1998	2002
1989	18.0	1994	1997

Region: Lower Hunter Valley Winemaker: Phillip Ryan
Viticulturist: Graham Doran Chief Executive: Kevin McLintock

Mount Pleasant's benchmark Elizabeth (semillon) is consistently one of the best value buys in Australian wine. Its more illustrious stablemate, the Lovedale Semillon, is now being kept separate in more years than previously, spelling excellent news for enthusiasts of Hunter semillon. The Philip is also showing a return to form.

Mount Pleasant
Marrowbone Rd
Pokolbin NSW 2321
Tel: (02) 4998 7505
Fax: (02) 4998 7761

CHARDONNAY

Lower Hunter Valley $$

1997	16.6	1999	2002
1996	17.0	2001	2004
1995	16.2	2000	2003
1994	15.5	1996	1999
1993	17.6	1998	2001
1992	16.6	1997	2000
1991	17.8	1993	1996
1990	16.5	1995	1998

ELIZABETH

Lower Hunter Valley $$

1996	18.0	2004	2008+
1995	18.2	2003	2007+
1994	18.6		2006+
1993	18.6	2001	2005+
1992	17.9	2000	2004
1991	16.5	1993	1996
1990	15.4	1992	1995
1989	17.7	1994	1997
1988	16.6	1990	1993
1987	17.1	1995	1999
1986	18.6	1994	1998+
1985	14.0	1990	1993
1984	18.0	1996	2001

LOVEDALE SEMILLON

Lower Hunter Valley $$$$

1996	18.7		2008+
1995	18.7	2003	2007+
1986	18.8	1998	2006+
1984	19.0	1997	2005+

MAURICE O'SHEA SHIRAZ

Lower Hunter Valley $$$

1996	16.6	2001	2004+
1994	18.0	2002	2006
1993	17.6	1998	2001

OLD PADDOCK & OLD HILL SHIRAZ

Lower Hunter Valley $$$

1997	16.6	2002	2005
1996	17.8	2004	2008+
1995	17.2	2003	2007

PHILIP

Lower Hunter Valley $$

1996	15.4	1998	2001
1995	16.5	2000	2003
1994	15.2	1999	2002
1993	14.0	1995	1998

ROSEHILL SHIRAZ
Lower Hunter Valley $$$

1997	18.0	2002	2005
1996	18.2	2004	2008
1995	15.3	1997	2000
1991	17.6	1996	1999
1990	14.6	1992	1995
1988	15.8	1990	1993
1987	17.6	1992	1995

Region: Eden Valley Winemakers: Adam Wynn, Andrew Ewart
Viticulturist: Adam Wynn Chief Executive: Adam Wynn

Mountadam sits comfortably amongst Australia's leading makers of chardonnay. Adam Wynn's wine leaves little to the imagination, for he pioneered the full orchestral barrel fermented style in Australia, creating a wine of enormous richness, power and alcohol, which from time to time can become intrusive. Many other makers have since followed suit. I retain a soft spot for the self-confident, rather strident and pink-amber coloured Pinot Noir Chardonnay sparkling wine which is only released after considerable age.

Mountadam

**High Eden Road
Eden Valley SA 5235
Tel: (08) 8564 1101
Fax: (08) 8361 3400**

CHARDONNAY
Eden Valley $$$$

1997	18.7	2002	2005
1996	17.2	1998	2001
1995	16.0	2000	2003
1994	18.3	2002	2006
1993	18.6	2001	2005
1992	18.2	2000	2004
1991	18.8		2003+
1990	18.2	1998	2002
1989	17.3	1994	1997

PINOT NOIR
Eden Valley $$$$

1997	16.3	2002	2005
1996	16.0	2004	2008
1995	16.3	2000	2003
1994	16.7	1999	2002
1993	17.0	2001	2005
1992	16.9	1997	2000
1991	18.0	1999	2002
1990	18.0	1995	1998

Murrindindee

**RMB 6070 Cummins Lane
Murrindindee Vic 3717
Tel: (03) 5797 8217
Fax: (03) 5797 8422**

PINOT NOIR CHARDONNAY
Eden Valley $$$$

1992	18.4	1997	2000
1991	18.2	1996	1999
1990	18.4	1995	1998
1989	17.6	1994	1997
1987	17.5	1992	1995

THE RED
Eden Valley $$$$

1995	17.0	2000	2003
1994	18.4		2006+
1992	16.7	2000	2004
1990	18.0	1995	1998
1989	16.0	1994	1997
1988	17.0	1996	2000
1987	16.0	1992	1995
1986	18.0	1994	1998

Region: Central Victoria Winemaker: Hugh Cuthbertson
Viticulturist: Alan Cuthbertson Chief Executive: Janet Cuthbertson

Murrindindee is a small specialist maker of Chardonnay and a red Bordeaux blend sited in the foothills of the Great Dividing Range in Victoria. Its Chardonnay is given the full leesy Burgundian treatment, while the red is an elegant, supple and finely-tuned wine of some style and longevity.

CABERNETS
Central Victoria $$$$

1995	18.1	2003	2007
1994	17.1	2002	2006
1992	15.1	1994	1997
1985	15.3	1993	1997

CHARDONNAY
Central Victoria $$$$

1997	18.3	2002	2005+
1996	17.1	2001	2004
1994	17.3	1999	2002

Region: McLaren Vale Winemakers: Roger Harbord & Peter Fraser
Viticulturist: Roger Polkinghorn Chief Executive: Rob Byrne

Normans is a medium-sized winery which has based its success on providing sound, flavoursome wine at a fair price. The Merlot is an honest, true-to-type expression of this popular variety, but I'm a little concerned at what I perceive as a broad drop in quality at a time when the company is seeking rather rapid and dramatic expansion.

Normans

**Grants Gully Road
Clarendon SA 5157
Tel: (08) 8383 6138
Fax: (08) 8383 6089**

CABERNET SAUVIGNON

South Australia $$

1998	14.9	2000	2003
1997	14.7	1999	2002+
1996	16.0	2001	2004
1995	15.4	1997	2000
1994	15.0	1996	1999

CHAIS CLARENDON CABERNET SAUVIGNON

McLaren Vale $$$$

1996	16.6	2004	2008
1995	15.7	1997	2000
1994	18.0	2000	2006
1992	17.3	2000	2004
1991	18.4		2003+
1990	18.2		2002+
1989	18.0	1997	2001
1988	18.0	1996	2000
1987	15.0	1992	1995
1986	16.0	1994	1998
1984	18.0	1992	1996

CHAIS CLARENDON CHARDONNAY

Padthaway $$$

1997	17.2	1999	2002
1996	17.2	2001	2004
1995	17.7	2000	2003
1994	17.5	1999	2002
1991	17.5	1996	1999
1990	18.5	1998	2002
1989	16.0	1994	1997

Oakridge Estate

864 Maroondah Highway
Coldstream Vic 3770
Tel: (03) 9739 1920
Fax: (03) 9739 1923

CHAIS CLARENDON SHIRAZ

McLaren Vale $$$$

1996	17.1	2001	2004
1995	18.2	2003	2007
1994	16.7	1999	2002
1992	17.3	1997	2000
1991	18.0	1999	2003
1990	18.2		2002+
1989	18.0	1997	2001
1988	18.5		2000+

MERLOT

South Australia $$

1998	16.7	2000	2003
1997	16.5	1999	2002
1996	16.0	1998	2001

Region: Yarra Valley Winemaker: Michael Zitzlaff
Viticulturist: Michael Zitzlaff Chief Executive: Michael Zitzlaff

Oakridge has successfully moved its base onto the Yarra Valley floor and adjacent to the Maroondah Highway. Its new Reserve wines would appear to be full of potential, although the price asked for the 1995 Reserve Merlot was stretching the envelope beyond any inherent quality of the wine.

CABERNET SAUVIGNON MERLOT

Yarra Valley $$$

1997	15.4	2002	2005
1995	16.0	1997	2000
1994	15.0	1996	1999
1993	16.3	1998	2001
1992	18.2	2000	2004
1991	17.8	1999	2003
1990	16.5	1992	1995

CHARDONNAY

Yarra Valley $$$$

1998	16.8	2003	2006
1997	18.2	2002	2005
1996	18.3	2001	2004
1995	15.6	1997	2000
1994	16.0	1996	1999

RESERVE CABERNET SAUVIGNON

Yarra Valley $$$$

1995	16.8	2000	2003+
1994	18.0	2002	2006
1991	18.9	2003	2011
1990	18.5	2002	2010
1987	15.0	1992	1995
1986	18.5	1994	1998

Region: Barossa Valley Winemaker: Philip Laffer
Viticulturist: Joy Dick Chief Executive: Andre Boucard

Orlando is one of the three largest wine companies in Australia, a position it maintains with a relatively small number of large-selling mid-priced brands. The 'Saint series' offers exceptional value, especially with white wine, while the RF and Jacobs Creek range maintain their standards despite enormous increases in scale of production. Jacobs Creek is presently the largest-selling brand of bottled wine in the entire UK wine market. I'm very impressed with the new premier Centenary Hill Barossa Shiraz.

CENTENARY HILL SHIRAZ

Barossa Valley $$$$$

1996	18.2	2004	2008
1995	17.6	2000	2003+
1994	18.9	2002	2006+

JACARANDA RIDGE CABERNET SAUVIGNON

Coonawarra $$$$$

1994	18.8		2006+
1992	16.8	2000	2004
1991	18.3		2003+
1990	18.5		2002+
1989	18.1	1997	2001
1988	17.4	1993	1996
1987	17.5	1995	1999
1986	16.0	1991	1994
1982	17.8	1987	1990

JACOB'S CREEK CHARDONNAY

Southern Australia $

1998	15.0	1999	2000
1997	15.6	1997	1998
1996	15.4	1997	1998

Orlando

Barossa Valley Way
Rowland Flat SA 5352
Tel: (08) 8521 3111
Fax: (08) 8521 3100

JACOB'S CREEK RIESLING

Southern Australia $

1998	15.6	1999	2000
1997	16.7	2002	2005
1996	16.7	1998	2001
1995	15.0	1997	2000
1994	15.8	1996	1999

JACOB'S CREEK SHIRAZ CABERNET

Southern Australia $

1997	15.6	2002	2005
1996	15.0	1998	2001
1995	16.0	2000	2003
1994	15.5	1999	2002

LAWSON'S SHIRAZ

Padthaway $$$$$

1994	17.3	2002	2008+
1993	18.0	2001	2005
1992	17.7	2000	2004
1991	18.8	1999	2003
1990	18.2		2002+
1989	17.5	1997	2001
1988	18.1	1996	2000
1987	17.7	1999	2007
1986	17.5	1994	1998

RUSSET RIDGE

Coonawarra $$

1996	17.8	2001	2004+
1995	15.6	2000	2003
1994	17.8	1999	2002
1993	17.2	2001	2005
1992	16.8	2000	2004
1991	17.6	1996	1999

RUSSET RIDGE CHARDONNAY

Coonawarra $$$

1998	16.5	2000	2003
1997	16.1	1998	1999
1996	15.6	1997	1998

ST HELGA RIESLING
Eden Valley $$

1998	17.3	2003	2006+
1997	18.0	2002	2005
1996	16.5	2001	2004
1995	16.0	2000	2003
1994	17.0	1999	2002
1993	17.8	1998	2001
1992	18.0	1997	2000
1991	17.7	1999	2003+
1990	18.0	1995	1998
1989	17.0	1991	1994

ST HILARY CHARDONNAY
Padthaway $$

1998	17.3	2003	2006
1997	17.0	1999	2002
1996	17.2	2001	2004
1995	15.6	1996	1997
1994	16.7	1996	1999

ST HUGO CABERNET SAUVIGNON
Coonawarra $$$

1996	18.7	2004	2008+
1994	18.4	2002	2006+
1993	17.6	2001	2005
1992	16.5	1997	2000
1991	18.5		2003+
1990	18.5		2002+
1989	18.3	1997	2001
1988	17.5	1996	2000
1987	16.8	1995	1999
1986	17.0	1994	1998
1985	17.8	1990	1993
1984	18.0	1989	1992
1983	15.5	1985	1988
1982	18.4	1990	1994

THE ONWINE AUSTRALIAN WINE ANNUAL 2000

STEINGARTEN RIESLING

Eden Valley $$$

1998	18.2	2006	2010
1997	18.7		2009+
1996	18.4		2008+
1995	18.5	2003	2007
1994	18.6	2002	2006
1992	17.2	1997	2000
1991	18.2	1996	1999
1990	18.3	1995	1998
1989	16.5	1991	1994
1988	17.0	1993	1996
1987	17.0	1999	2004

Oxford Landing

**PMB 31
Waikerie SA 5330
Tel: (08) 8561 3200
Fax: (08) 8561 3393**

Region: Riverlands Winemaker: Hugh Reimers
Viticulturist: Bill Wilksch Chief Executive: Robert Hill Smith

Oxford Landing is owned by S. Smith & Son, whose leading brand is Yalumba. It offers some of the best value around in the 'fighting varietal' section of the market, especially with a red blend of cabernet sauvignon and shiraz that does justice to some time in the cellar.

CABERNET SHIRAZ

Riverlands $

1998	14.8	1999	2000
1997	16.7	1998	1999
1996	16.1	1998	2001
1995	14.5	1996	1997
1994	15.0	1996	1999
1993	16.0	1998	2001
1992	16.0	1997	2000
1991	16.0	1999	2003

CHARDONNAY

Riverlands $

1998	16.0	1999	2000+
1997	16.0	1998	1999
1996	15.9	1998	2001
1995	14.5	1996	1997
1994	16.3	1996	1999
1993	15.8	1994	1995

Region: Mornington Peninsula Winemaker: Lindsay McCall
Viticulturist: Lindsay McCall Chief Executives: Lindsay and Margaret McCall

Paringa Estate has enjoyed the two best Mornington Peninsula vintages for pinot noir and chardonnay with some fine wines from its two most recent vintages. With its brilliant Pinot Noir and intensely flavoured Chardonnay to partner its piercingly sour and spicy Shiraz, Paringa produced an exceptional series of 1997 Peninsula wines. Its red wines remain its principal focus, based as they are around penetrative ripe fruit and smoky mocha oak.

Paringa Estate

44 Paringa Rd
Red Hill South Vic 3937
Tel: (03) 5989 2669
Fax: (03) 5989 2669

CHARDONNAY
Mornington Peninsula $$$$

1998	17.5	2003	2006
1997	18.2	2002	2005
1996	15.4	1997	1998
1995	17.8	2000	2003
1994	18.2	1996	1999
1993	17.9	1998	2001
1992	16.9	1997	2000

PINOT NOIR
Mornington Peninsula $$$$$

1998	18.6	2003	2006+
1997	19.0	2005	2009
1996	16.0	1998	2001
1995	18.0	2000	2003
1994	16.0	1996	1999
1993	18.2	1998	2001
1992	17.7	1997	2000
1991	14.7	1996	1999

SHIRAZ
Mornington Peninsula $$$$$

1998	16.6	2003	2006
1997	18.7	2005	2009
1996	16.5	2001	2004
1995	16.4	2000	2003
1994	18.4	1999	2002
1993	19.0	2001	2005
1992	15.8	2000	2004
1991	17.4	1999	2003
1990	17.5	1995	1998

THE ONWINE AUSTRALIAN WINE ANNUAL

Parker Coonawarra Estate

**Riddoch Highway
Coonawarra SA 5263
Tel: (02) 9357 3376
Fax: (02) 9358 1517**

Region: Coonawarra Winemaker: Chris Cameron
Viticulturist: Doug Balnaves Chief Executive: John Parker

Parker's Terra Rossa First Growth only appears in years of sufficient quality to justify this self-imposed form of appellation. The Cabernet Sauvignon is the fall-back position, although it rarely achieves the standard one might expect of a second label to a very significant vineyard.

CABERNET SAUVIGNON

Coonawarra $$$

1997	15.8	1999	2002+
1996	15.3	1998	2001
1995	16.1	2000	2003
1994	15.4	1999	2002
1992	15.0	1997	2000
1991	16.5	1999	2003
1989	16.0	1991	1994

TERRA ROSSA FIRST GROWTH

Coonawarra $$$$$

1996	18.8	2008	2016
1994	15.1	1999	2002
1993	18.5	2001	2005
1991	19.0		2003+
1990	18.8		2002+
1989	17.0	1994	1997
1988	18.5		2000+

Passing Clouds

**RMB 440 Kurting Road
Kingower Vic 3517
Tel: (03) 5438 8257
Fax: (03) 5438 8246**

Region: Bendigo Winemakers: Graeme Leith, Greg Bennett
Viticulturists: Graeme Leith, Greg Bennett
Chief Executives: Graeme Leith, Sue Mackinnon

Passing Clouds is a mature central Victorian vineyard that crops low yields of intensely flavoured fruit which consistently imparts significant regional eucalypt and mint flavours to its robust, firm and long-living wines. Give them all the time you can.

ANGEL BLEND

Bendigo $$$$

1997	18.1	2005	2009+
1996	17.0		2008+
1995	18.4		2007+
1994	17.4		2006+
1992	18.2	2000	2004
1991	17.3	1999	2003
1990	16.8		2002+
1987	16.0	1995	1999
1985	18.0	1993	1997

GRAEME'S BLEND

Bendigo $$$

1997	17.2	2005	2009
1996	16.9	2004	2008+
1995	18.3	2003	2007
1994	16.4		2006+
1992	18.3		2004+
1991	17.5	1996	1999
1990	18.0	1995	1998
1989	15.5	1994	1997

SHIRAZ

Bendigo $$$$

1997	16.0	2005	2009
1996	16.8	2004	2008
1994	18.0	2002	2006+

Region: Clare Valley **Winemaker:** Neil Paulett
Viticulturist: Neil Paulett **Chief Executive:** Neil Paulett

Neil Paulett is one a group of skilled Clare Valley winemakers who fashion sophisticated reds with delightful clarity of fruit, minty regional influences and fine-grained tannins plus, of course, the regional speciality of riesling. This is typically a zesty, citrusy wine which usually appreciates at least five years in the bottle.

Pauletts

Polish Hill Road
Polish Hill River SA 5453
Tel: (08) 8843 4328
Fax: (08) 8843 4202

CABERNET MERLOT

Clare Valley $$

1997	16.5	2002	2005
1996	18.2	2004	2000
1995	16.7	2000	2003
1994	17.0	1996	1999
1993	15.3	1995	1998
1992	18.2	2000	2004
1991	18.1	1999	2003
1990	18.5	1995	1998
1989	18.0	1994	1997
1988	17.0	1993	1996
1987	16.0	1992	1995

Peel Estate

**Fletcher Road
Baldivis WA 6210
Tel: (09) 9524 1221
Fax: (08) 9524 1625**

RIESLING

Clare Valley $

1998	16.8	2000	2003+
1997	15.0	2002	2005
1996	16.6	2001	2004
1995	18.0	2003	2007
1994	18.2	2002	2006
1993	17.0	1995	1998
1992	18.2	2000	2004
1991	17.3	1999	2003
1990	18.0	1998	2002
1989	15.0	1994	1997
1988	16.5	1996	2000
1987	17.0	1999	2004

SHIRAZ

Clare Valley $$

1997	15.9	2002	2005
1996	16.4	2001	2004
1995	16.8	2000	2003
1994	17.4	1999	2002
1993	18.5	2001	2005
1992	17.6	2000	2004
1991	17.5	1996	1999
1990	17.5	1995	1998
1989	17.0	1994	1997

**Region: South West Coastal Winemaker: Will Nairn
Viticulturist: Matt Banovich Chief Executive: Will Nairn**

Peel Estate's reds are given substantially extended oak maturation which helps define Will Nairn's house style. The Wood-Matured Chenin Blanc is somewhat controversial. Richly textured, very ripe and concentrated, it's by no means a technically perfect wine, but just happens to go superbly with Asian food! Try to leave it for five to eight years for it to develop rare complexity and character.

CABERNET SAUVIGNON

South West Coastal $$$$

1996	15.0	2001	2004
1995	14.0	2000	2003
1994	16.7	2002	2006
1993	18.0		2005+
1992	16.4	1997	2000
1991	18.4	1999	2003
1990	17.8	1998	2002
1989	17.8		2001+

CHARDONNAY

South West Coastal $$$

1997	14.5	1998	1999
1996	15.3	1998	2001
1995	17.7	2000	2003
1994	18.4	1999	2002
1993	17.0	1998	2001
1992	17.3	1997	2000
1991	18.2	1996	1999
1990	18.5	1998	2002

SHIRAZ

South West Coastal $$$

1995	16.7	2003	2007
1994	15.7	1999	2002
1993	18.2		2005+
1992	17.0	2000	2004
1991	15.0	1993	1996
1990	18.0	1998	2002
1989	18.0		2001+

VERDELHO

South West Coastal $$$

1998	15.7	2000	2003
1997	15.0	1998	1999
1996	18.0	1998	2001
1995	16.2	1997	2000
1994	16.8	1999	2002
1993	17.0	1998	2001
1992	14.7	1994	1997

WOOD-MATURED CHENIN BLANC

South West Coastal $$$

1997	16.0	2002	2005
1996	18.4	2004	2008
1995	16.8	2000	2003
1994	18.3	2002	2006
1993	17.3	1998	2001
1992	16.5	1997	2000
1991	17.7	1999	2003
1990	16.3	1995	1998
1989	15.0	1994	1997

Pendarves

110 Old North Rd
Belford NSW 2335
Tel: (02) 9913 1088
Fax: (02) 9970 6152

Region: Lower Hunter Valley Winemaker: Greg Silkman
Viticulturist: Ray Dibley Chief Executive: Dr Philip Norrie

Dr Philip Norrie, GP, wine historian and author, and one of the medical front men in the ongoing tussle with Australia's neo-prohibitionist movement, is also a tireless worker in his vineyard, Pendarves Estate. My pick of his wines remains the Chardonnay and Verdelho, although some of the reds made with the Bordeaux blend of cabernet sauvignon, merlot and malbec pack an arresting intensity of sweet berry fruits.

CHARDONNAY
Lower Hunter Valley $$

1998	16.8	2000	2003
1997	15.3	1999	2002
1996	16.3	1998	2001
1995	17.8	2000	2003
1994	17.8	1999	2002
1993	16.9	1998	2001

Penfolds

Tanunda Road
Nuriootpa SA 5355
Tel: (08) 8560 9389
Fax: (08) 8560 9494

Region: Barossa Valley Winemaker: John Duval
Viticulturist: Andrew Pike Chief Executive: Bruce Kemp

Although it's worth noting the very fine quality of the classic 1994 Grange, the biggest thing about Penfolds, Australia's most identifiable maker of red wine, is the sheer outright excellence of its 1996 reds. I believe these wines will ultimately surpass the 1994s and in most cases have pointed them accordingly. The wines which have given me the greatest excitement are the 1996 Bin 389 and Bin 407, both of which have tended to fall into the shadow of the more expensive Penfolds labels. They're affordable, they're out there and they're great. Although I have to admit that the 1996 Bin 707 is better. And just for the record, the 1996 Yattarna is a step up from the 1995 wine which, adequate though it was, simply fell short of the massive expectations placed before it. And also for the record, keep an eye out for the forthcoming once-off Block 42 Kalimna Cabernet Sauvignon from 1996, sourced from the same vineyard responsible for the once-off Grange Cabernet of 1953 and the first vintage of Bin 707. There's nothing more than a Barossa cabernet could possibly do!

ADELAIDE HILLS CHARDONNAY (FORMERLY TRIAL BIN)
Adelaide Hills $$$

1997	16.4	2002	2005
1996	18.2	2001	2004
1995	16.7	1997	2000

ADELAIDE HILLS SEMILLON (FORMERLY TRIAL BIN)

Adelaide Hills $$$

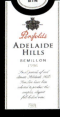

1997	16.4	1999	2002
1996	17.5	1998	2001
1995	16.8	1997	2000
1994	16.5	1996	1999
1993	18.5	2001	2005

BIN 128 COONAWARRA SHIRAZ

Coonawarra $$$

1996	18.4		2008+
1995	15.9	2000	2003
1994	18.2	2002	2006
1993	16.4	2001	2005
1992	18.0	2000	2004
1991	16.8	1999	2003
1990	17.9	1998	2002
1989	15.8	1994	1997
1988	17.0	2000	2005
1987	15.0	1992	1995
1986	18.0	1994	1998
1985	16.5	1993	1997

BIN 389 CABERNET SHIRAZ

South Australia $$$

1996	19.2		2008+
1995	17.7	2004	2008
1994	18.2		2006+
1993	18.1		2005+
1992	17.8		2004+
1991	18.4		2003+
1990	18.7		2002+
1989	16.0	1994	1997
1988	18.0	1996	2000
1987	17.5	1995	1999
1986	18.6	1998	2006
1985	15.7	1993	1997
1984	15.0	1989	1992
1983	18.2	1995	2003

BIN 407 CABERNET SAUVIGNON

Barossa Valley $$$

1996	18.6	2004	2008
1995	17.0	2000	2003
1994	18.3	2002	2006
1993	18.1	2001	2005
1992	16.5	1997	2000
1991	18.3		2003+
1990	18.0		2002+

BIN 707 CABERNET SAUVIGNON

Barossa Valley & Coonawarra $$$$$

1996	19.5		2016+
1994	18.8		2004+
1993	18.8		2005+
1992	18.4		2004+
1991	19.2	2003	2011+
1990	18.9		2002+
1989	17.5	1997	2001
1988	18.7	2000	2008
1987	18.0	1999	2007
1986	18.8		2006+
1985	17.5	1997	2005
1984	18.0	1996	2004
1983	17.5	1995	2003
1982	16.8	1994	2002
1980	18.2	1992	2000
1978	17.5	1990	1998
1977	17.5	1989	1997
1964	19.0	1994	1999

CLARE ESTATE

Clare Valley $$$

1996	18.2	2004	2008+
1995	18.2	2003	2007
1994	18.1	2002	2006
1993	18.2		2005+
1992	17.5	2000	2004
1991	18.2	1999	2003
1990	16.8	1998	2002
1989	16.0	1994	1997
1988	17.5	1993	1996
1987	16.5	1992	1995
1986	18.1	1994	1998

CLARE ESTATE CHARDONNAY

Clare Valley $$

1996	16.4	1998	2001
1995	16.3	1997	2000
1994	17.6	1999	2002
1993	17.5	1998	2001
1992	16.4	1994	1997

GRANGE

Barossa Valley (predominantly) $$$$$

1994	19.3	2006	2014+
1993	18.6		2013+
1992	18.8	2004	2012
1991	18.6		2011+
1990	19.1		2010+
1989	18.3	2001	2006
1988	18.2	2000	2005
1987	17.8	1999	2007
1986	19.0		2006+
1985	18.0	1997	2005
1984	18.2	1996	2004
1983	19.0		2003+
1982	17.8	1994	2002
1981	16.4	1993	2001
1980	18.1	2000	2005
1979	17.7	1987	1991
1978	18.5	1998	2003
1977	16.0	1989	1994
1976	18.4	1996	2006
1975	17.7	1995	2000
1974	15.0	1982	1986
1973	15.3	1985	1990
1972	17.2	1984	1989
1971	19.0	2001	2006
1970	17.0	1982	1990
1969	17.5	1989	1994
1968	18.0	1988	1998
1967	18.7	1987	1997
1966	19.0	1996	2001
1965	17.8	1985	1995
1964	17.5	1984	1989
1963	18.6	1993	2003
1962	19.0	1992	1997
1961	17.2	1981	1986
1960	18.0	1990	1995
1959	16.2	1979	1984
1958	15.6	1978	1983
1957	18.2	1977	1982
1956	16.4	1976	1981
1955	19.0	1985	1990
1954	18.6	1974	1979
1953	19.6	1983	1988
1952	18.8	1972	1982
1951	16.0	1963	1971

KALIMNA BIN 28 SHIRAZ

Barossa Valley $$$

1996	18.5		2008+
1995	17.0	2003	2007
1994	17.8	2002	2006
1993	15.3	1998	2001
1992	17.9	2000	2004
1991	18.0	1999	2003
1990	18.1	1998	2002
1989	16.0	1994	1997
1988	16.7	1996	2000
1987	16.5	1995	1999
1986	18.2	1998	2003
1985	16.0	1993	1997
1984	15.5	1989	1992
1983	15.0	1995	2000
1982	16.5	1990	1994

KOONUNGA HILL SHIRAZ CABERNET SAUVIGNON

South Australia $$

1997	15.9	2002	2005
1996	17.2	2004	2008
1995	16.0	2000	2003
1994	16.2	1999	2002
1993	16.5	2001	2005
1992	16.6	2000	2004
1991	17.7	1999	2003
1990	17.1	1998	2002
1989	16.4	1997	2001
1988	17.0	1996	2000
1987	15.0	1995	1999
1986	18.2	1998	2006
1985	15.3	1993	1997
1984	17.0		1996+
1983	16.7		1995+
1982	17.3	1994	2002
1981	16.5		1993+
1980	16.7	1992	2000+
1979	16.0	1987	1991
1978	18.2	1990	1998
1977	17.5	1989	1997
1976	16.5	1988	1996

MAGILL ESTATE SHIRAZ

Adelaide Metropolitan $$$$$

1996	18.6		2008+
1995	18.2	2003	2007
1994	18.4	2002	2006+
1993	18.2		2005+
1992	17.2	2000	2004
1991	18.8		2003+
1990	18.5		2002+
1989	18.0	1997	2001
1988	17.6	2000	2005
1987	18.2	1995	1999
1986	18.5	1998	2003
1985	18.2	1993	1997
1984	17.2	1989	1992
1983	17.9	1995	2000

OLD VINE RED RHONE BLEND

Barossa Valley $$$

1996	17.9	2004	2008
1995	15.8	1997	2000
1994	17.7	2002	2006
1993	16.8	2001	2005

RAWSON'S RETREAT RED

South Australia $

1998	15.8	2000	2003
1997	15.0	1998	1999
1996	15.0	1998	2001
1995	16.2	1997	2000
1994	15.3	1996	1999

ST HENRI SHIRAZ (SHIRAZ CABERNET IN 1995)

Barossa Valley, Clare Valley, Coonawarra $$$$

1995	17.6	2003	2007+
1994	18.3		2006+
1993	17.9	2003	2007
1992	17.0	2000	2004
1991	18.3		2003+
1990	18.9		2002+
1989	18.3		2001+
1988	18.0	2000	2005
1987	18.0	1999	2004
1986	17.5	1998	2003
1985	17.6	1997	2002
1984	14.5	1992	1996
1983	17.0	1995	2003
1982	17.0	1990	1994
1981	15.0	1993	1998
1980	17.0	1992	1997
1979	14.0	1987	1991
1978	14.5	1990	1995
1977	15.0	1989	1994
1976	18.0	1996	2001

THE VALLEYS CHARDONNAY

Clare and Eden Valleys $$

1997	17.9	1999	2002
1996	16.5	1998	2001
1995	16.4	1997	2000
1994	17.8	1999	2002
1993	17.5	1998	2001
1992	17.0	1997	2000
1991	16.9	1993	1996

Region: Coonawarra Winemaker: Kym Tolley
Viticulturist: Michael Wetherall Chief Executive: Kym Tolley

Penley Estate has emerged in recent years as one of the leading red wine estates of Coonawarra. Given his background and breeding, it's hardly surprising that Kym Tolley, related to the Penfold family, fashions his best wines in a Penfolds-like style, based around fruit richness and ripeness almost bordering on the over-ripe, with an excellent integration of assertive chocolate oak. The Chardonnay is a full-blown, citrusy and creamy style which doesn't require cellar patience at all.

Penley Estate

McLeans Rd
Coonawarra SA 5263
Tel: (08) 8231 2400
Fax: (08) 8231 0589

CABERNET SAUVIGNON

Coonawarra $$$$$

1996	17.5	2004	2008
1995	16.2	2000	2003
1994	17.0	1998	2002
1993	18.0		2005+
1992	18.1	2000	2004
1991	18.8		2003+
1990	18.3	1998	2002
1989	17.5	1994	1997

CHARDONNAY

Coonawarra $$$

1997	17.0	1999	2002+
1996	16.3	1998	2001
1995	17.0	1997	2002
1994	16.5	1996	1999
1993	15.8	1995	1998
1991	15.0	1996	1999
1990	16.5	1995	1998
1989	15.3	1994	1997

HYLAND SHIRAZ

Coonawarra $$$

1997	16.7	1999	2002+
1996	16.9	2001	2004
1994	14.9	1996	1999
1993	15.0	1995	1998

Pepper Tree

**Halls Road
Pokolbin NSW 2320
Tel: (02) 4998 7539
Fax: (02) 4998 7746**

PHOENIX CABERNET SAUVIGNON

Coonawarra $$$

1997	16.7	1999	2002+
1996	17.1	1998	2001+
1995	15.6	1997	2000

SHIRAZ CABERNET

Coonawarra $$

1996	16.3	1998	2001
1995	16.9	1997	2000
1994	17.8	2002	2006
1993	16.8	1995	1998
1992	17.0	1997	2000
1991	18.2	1999	2003
1990	17.5	1995	1998

Region: Lower Hunter Valley Winemakers: Chris Cameron, Chris Archer
Viticulturist: Carl Davies Chief Executive: Chris Cameron

Pepper Tree is an ambitious Hunter Valley-based winery which not only sources fruit from a number of regions in several states, but is actually able to manage its Coonawarra vineyard by computer from Pokolbin! Its flagship wine is the Coonawarra Reserve Merlot, possibly Australia's finest example of this variety.

CHARDONNAY

Various $$$

1998	17.4	2000	2003
1997	15.7	1998	1999
1996	15.3	1997	1998

COONAWARRA RESERVE MERLOT

Coonawarra $$$$$

1998	18.9	2006	2010
1996	18.7	2001	2004+
1995	16.5	1997	2000

RESERVE SEMILLON

Lower Hunter Valley $$$

1998	16.6	2006	2010
1997	18.2	2005	2009
1996	17.3	2004	2008
1995	18.6	2003	2007
1994	17.2	1999	2002
1993	16.5	1998	2001

Petaluma

Spring Gully Road
Piccadilly SA 5151
Tel: (08) 8339 4122
Fax: (08) 8339 5253

Region: Adelaide Hills Winemakers: Brian Croser, Con Moshos
Viticulturist: Mike Harms Chief Executive: Brian Croser

Petaluma is now enjoying doing what it does best without having to look too far over its shoulder. Although the refinement of style is a never-ending process, especially for a mind as restless as Brian Croser's, each of Petaluma's wines is now established in the market and has reached a clear quality standard around which it will deviate from season to season. To release the 1996 premier Tiers Chardonnay without upsetting the bulk of the Petaluma Chardonnay of that year was an outstanding effort and it will be fascinating to watch how Croser treats this and other of the 'distinguished' chardonnay sites to which he has access. Meantime, it's steady as she goes with the cutting-edge Riesling and the polished Coonawarra blend.

CHARDONNAY

Adelaide Hills $$$$$

1997	18.9	2005	2009
1996	18.7	2004	2008
1995	18.8	2003	2007
1994	18.5	2002	2006
1993	18.2	1995	1998
1992	18.8	2000	2004
1991	16.0	1996	1999
1990	18.2	1998	2002
1989	17.0	1991	1994
1988	18.0	1993	1996

COONAWARRA

Coonawarra $$$$$

1996	18.6	2008	2010
1995	18.4	2003	2007+
1994	19.0	2006	2014+
1993	18.2	2005	2013
1992	18.2	2004	2012
1991	18.3	2003	2011
1990	19.1	2002	2010+
1988	19.0	2000	2008
1987	17.6	1999	2007
1986	18.0	1998	2006
1985	15.0	1993	1997
1984	14.0	1989	1992
1982	15.0	1990	1994
1981	16.7	1986	1989
1980	14.5	1985	1988
1979	19.0	1991	1999+

CROSER
Adelaide Hills $$$$

1996	18.2	1998	2001
1995	18.0	1997	2000
1994	18.3	1996	1999
1993	18.2	1995	1998
1992	18.4	1997	2000
1991	17.0	1993	1996
1990	18.3	1995	1998
1988	18.5	1990	1993
1987	17.5	1995	1999

MERLOT
Coonawarra $$$$$

1996	18.1	2004	2008
1994	16.0	1999	2002
1993	18.3	2001	2005
1992	18.6	2000	2004
1991	16.8	1996	1999
1990	18.9	1998	2002

RIESLING
Clare Valley $$$

1998	18.4	2006	2010
1997	18.8	2005	2009+
1996	18.1	2004	2008
1995	18.6	2003	2007+
1994	18.6	2002	2006
1993	18.4	2001	2005
1992	18.1	1997	2000
1991	18.0	1996	1999
1990	18.8	1998	2002
1989	16.5	1991	1994
1988	17.0	1993	1996
1987	17.7	1999	2004
1986	19.0	1991	1994
1985	18.2	1993	1997

Region: Barossa Valley Winemakers: Andrew Wigan, Peter Lehmann,
Peter Scholz, Ian Hongell & Leonie Lange
Viticulturist: Peter Nash Chief Executive: Douglas Lehmann

Peter Lehmann has become synonymous with the sumptuous flavours of Barossa red wine, especially from shiraz. The Stonewell Shiraz is one of the very finest in Australia, while the two Barossa red releases from 1997 and the Clancy's each offer simply extraordinary value for money. Peter Lehmann's next self-imposed challenge is to do to Barossa semillon what he and others have accomplished with its shiraz.

Peter Lehmann

**Off Para Road
Tanunda SA 5352
Tel: (08) 8563 2500
Fax: (08) 8563 3402**

CABERNET SAUVIGNON

Barossa Valley $$

1997	18.1	2002	2005+
1996	17.2	2001	2004
1995	16.6	2000	2003
1994	18.1	1999	2002
1993	18.0	2001	2005
1992	18.3	2000	2004
1991	16.9	1999	2003
1990	18.2		2002+
1989	17.5	1997	2001
1988	18.0		2000+
1987	17.0	1995	1999
1986	18.0	1998	2003

CHARDONNAY

Barossa Valley $$

1997	16.5	1998	1999
1996	15.2	1997	1998
1995	15.0	1996	1997
1994	16.0	1996	1999
1993	16.0	1995	1990
1992	16.5	1994	1997
1991	16.3	1993	1996
1990	17.5	1998	2002

CLANCY'S

Barossa Valley $$

1997	17.9	2002	2005
1996	16.8	1998	2001
1995	16.8	1997	2000
1994	17.0	1996	1999
1993	15.3	1995	1998
1992	16.4	1994	1997
1991	17.3	1993	1996

EDEN VALLEY RIESLING

Eden Valley $

1998	17.0	2003	2006
1997	16.0	1999	2002
1996	17.2	2001	2004
1995	15.0	1997	2000
1994	16.5	1999	2002
1993	18.0	1998	2001
1992	17.9	1997	2000
1991	17.5	1996	1999
1990	17.0	1995	1998

MENTOR (FORMERLY CELLAR COLLECTION CABERNET BLEND)

Barossa Valley $$$$

1995	16.8		2007+
1994	18.0		2006+
1993	16.0	2001	2005+
1992	16.5	2000	2004
1991	18.2	1999	2003
1990	18.4		2002+
1989	18.4	2001	2006
1986	18.6	1998	2003

NOBLE SEMILLON

Barossa Valley $$$$

1998	15.4	2003	2006
1997	15.8	1999	2002
1996	14.8	1997	1998
1995	16.0	2000	2003
1994	17.4	1999	2002
1992	15.4	1997	2000
1990	16.0	1995	1998
1989	16.0	1994	1997

RESERVE RIESLING

Eden Valley $$

1994	18.0	2002	2006
1993	18.5	2001	2005+
1992	16.4	1994	1997
1991	18.0	1996	1999
1990	17.8	1992	1997
1989	17.5	1991	1996
1987	17.5	1992	1995

THE ONWINE AUSTRALIAN WINE ANNUAL

SEMILLON

Barossa Valley $

1998	16.8	2000	2003
1997	17.1	1999	2002
1996	16.8	1998	2001
1995	16.5	2000	2003
1994	18.0	1999	2002
1993	16.5	2001	2005
1992	17.0	2000	2004
1990	16.0	1995	1998

SHIRAZ

Barossa Valley $$

1997	18.0	2002	2005+
1996	17.5	1998	2001
1995	16.2	1997	2000
1994	17.5	1999	2002
1993	17.3	2001	2005
1992	18.2	2000	2004
1991	17.4	1996	1999
1990	17.0	1995	1998
1989	16.0	1994	1999
1988	18.5	1996	2000

STONEWELL SHIRAZ

Barossa Valley $$$$$

1994	19.0	2002	2006+
1993	18.6	2005	2013
1992	18.2	2000	2004
1991	18.7	1999	2003
1990	17.0		2002+
1989	18.8	2001	2006+
1988	18.6		2000+
1987	18.5	1999	2004

Pewsey Vale

Brownes Rd
Pewsey Vale SA 5353
Tel: (08) 8561 3200
Fax: (08) 8561 3393

Region: Eden Valley Winemaker: Louisa Rose
Viticulturist: Robin Nettelbeck Chief Executive: Robert Hill Smith

The Eden Valley has long been rated as one of the most suitable regions in Australia for riesling and several wine brands have a stellar history of fine, steely long-term examples. Pewsey Vale, one of the S Smith & Son brands made at the Yalumba winery at Angaston, is one of these. Its wine is long, limey and crisply finished. The beneficiary of recent developments in Pewsey Vale's vineyard, the Cabernet is a tight, fine-grained wine given smoky coffee oak influences to complement its sweet berry flavours.

CABERNET

Eden Valley $$

1997	18.2	2005	2009+
1996	17.3	2004	2008
1995	16.0	2003	2007
1994	18.2	2002	2006
1993	17.8		2005+
1992	16.6	2000	2004
1991	17.8	1999	2003
1990	17.5	1998	2002
1989	15.3	1990	1991
1988	16.0	1996	2000
1986	17.0	1991	1994

RIESLING

Eden Valley $

1998	16.6	2003	2006
1997	18.3	2005	2009
1996	18.3		2008+
1995	17.8	2003	2007
1994	18.1		2006+
1993	18.3	1998	2001
1992	18.0	1997	2000
1991	18.1	1999	2003
1990	18.5	1998	2002
1989	16.7	1997	2001
1988	17.0	1993	1996
1987	17.0	1992	1995
1986	18.0	1991	1994
1985	16.8	1993	1997
1984	18.7	1996	2004
1983	16.8	1991	1995
1981	16.6	1989	1993
1979	18.3	1991	1999
1978	18.5	1990	1998
1973	17.8	1985	1993
1969	18.6	1981	1989

Pierro

**Caves Road
Willyabrup via
Cowaramup WA 6284
Tel: (08) 9755 6220
Fax: (08) 9755 6308**

Region: Margaret River Winemaker: Mike Peterkin
Viticulturist: Mike Peterkin Chief Executive: Mike Peterkin

Pierro's Chardonnay is the Margaret River's small-maker rival to Leeuwin Estate. It's made in more of a full orchestra style, although the richness of fruit achieved by Mike Peterkin and its powerful depth of flavour handles in its stride the full-on oak and lees treatment it receives in the winery. Pierro's Cabernets is a firm, astringent wine, its Semillon Sauvignon Blanc one of Australia's best oak-matured and fermented expressions of this blend, while the Pinot Noir settles with time into a flavoursome, leathery wine of rustic, earthy charm.

CABERNETS

Margaret River $$$$$

1997	15.8	2002	2005
1996	18.2	2004	2008+
1995	16.0	2000	2003

CHARDONNAY

Margaret River $$$$$

1997	18.6	2002	2005+
1996	19.2	2004	2008
1995	18.2	2000	2003
1994	19.1	2002	2006
1993	18.8	2001	2005
1992	19.0	2000	2004
1991	18.5	1996	1999
1990	18.5	1998	2002
1989	17.6	1994	1997
1988	16.5	1990	1995
1987	18.3	1995	1999
1986	18.7	1994	1998

PINOT NOIR

Margaret River $$$$

1997	16.8	2002	2005
1996	16.5	2001	2004
1995	15.3	2000	2003
1994	16.0	1999	2002
1993	17.2	2001	2005
1992	17.0	2000	2004
1990	18.5	1995	1998
1988	15.0	1989	1990
1987	18.0	1992	1995

Pikes

Polish Hill River Road
Sevenhill SA 5453
Tel: (08) 8843 4370
Fax: (08) 8843 4353

SEMILLON SAUVIGNON BLANC

Margaret River $$$

1998	17.5	2000	2003
1997	18.0	2002	2005
1996	18.2	2001	2004
1995	18.2	1997	2000
1994	18.0	1999	2002
1993	18.2	1998	2001
1992	17.5	1997	2000
1991	17.5	1996	1999
1990	17.0	1998	2002
1989	16.5	1994	1997

Region: Clare Valley Winemaker: Neil Pike
Viticulturist: Andrew Pike Chief Executive: Neil Pike

Now a worthy entrant in the Australian sangiovese stakes, Pikes is a successful small Clare Valley winery which specialises in all the right things for this region: riesling, shiraz and cabernet. The 1998 Riesling is a very fine wine with all the limey citrus flavours Clare Riesling is noted for. Reserve editions of Riesling and Shiraz may be a little hard to trace, but are worth every effort to do so.

CABERNET

Clare Valley $$$

1997	16.8	2005	2009
1996	17.6	2004	2008+
1995	16.0	1997	2000
1994	18.3	2002	2006
1993	18.0	1998	2001
1992	18.4	2000	2004
1991	18.2	1999	2003
1990	18.0	1998	2002

RIESLING

Clare Valley $$

1998	18.1	2003	2006+
1997	16.7	2002	2005
1996	17.2	2001	2004
1995	14.7	1997	2000
1992	16.1	1997	2000
1990	18.0	1998	2002
1988	18.0	1993	1996

SHIRAZ
Clare Valley $$$

1997	17.0	2005	2009
1996	16.0	2001	2004
1995	18.2	2000	2003
1994	17.6	1999	2002
1993	17.2	2001	2005
1992	18.3	2000	2004
1991	18.5		2003+
1990	18.3		2002+

Pipers Brook

Pipers Brook Road
Pipers Brook Tas 7254
Tel: (03) 6332 4444
Fax: (03) 6334 9112

Region: Pipers River Winemaker: Andrew Pirie
Viticulturist: Andrew Pirie Chief Executive: Andrew Pirie

Pipers Brook is Tasmania's most important winery. While it produces wines from a broad array of grapes whose precise vineyard sourcing has been paired by Andrew Pirie to meet the ripening requirements of each variety, its most successful wines of present times are made from Riesling and Gewürztraminer. Pipers Brooks' latest major release is the Pirie sparkling wine, a 1995 vintage blend of pinot noir with chardonnay that has justifiably earned substantial praise. I am less convinced by recent Chardonnay vintages and releases of The Summit (Chardonnay), wines I find simply too evolved to justify Pirie's hopes for them.

CHARDONNAY
Pipers River $$$$

1998	17.0	2003	2006
1997	17.8	1999	2002
1996	15.8	1998	2001
1995	18.4	2003	2007
1994	15.0	1996	1999
1993	18.2	1998	2001
1992	18.0	1997	2000
1991	18.5	1999	2003

GEWURZTRAMINER
Pipers River $$$

1998	18.5	2003	2006+
1997	17.2	1999	2002
1996	18.3	2001	2004
1995	18.3	2000	2003
1993	17.0	1995	1998
1992	18.2	2000	2004
1991	17.0	1999	2003
1990	16.8	1995	1998
1989	16.0	1994	1997

OPIMIAN (FORMERLY CABERNET SAUVIGNON)

Northern Tasmania $$$$

1997	15.3	2002	2005
1995	18.4	2003	2007
1992	16.3	1994	1997
1991	17.0	1999	2003
1989	16.0	1994	1997
1988	17.0	1996	2000
1987	15.0	1992	1995
1986	15.5	1994	1998

PELLION (FORMERLY PINOT NOIR)

Northern Tasmania $$$$

1998	16.3	2000	2003+
1997	16.8	2002	2005
1996	15.0	2001	2004
1995	16.8	1997	2000
1994	17.3	1999	2002
1993	16.8	1995	1998
1992	17.5	1997	2000
1991	18.0	1999	2003
1990	16.5	1992	1995
1988	17.0	1993	1996

RIESLING

Pipers River $$$

1998	18.6	2006	2010
1997	17.2	2002	2005
1996	18.1	2004	2008
1995	18.2	2003	2007
1994	17.5	2002	2006
1993	18.3	1998	2001
1992	18.8		2004+
1991	16.5	1996	1999
1990	17.0	1995	1998
1989	18.0	1994	1997
1988	16.5	1993	1996

Region: Great Southern Winemakers: Gavin Berry, Gordon Parker
Viticulturists: Roger Pattenden, Peter Glen Chief Executive: Tony Smith

Recent vintages are moving towards the very ripe flavour spectrum and finding strong favour amongst the US wine media, but Plantagenet's ground-breaking Shiraz (1994 vintage, especially) is still a wine of rare intensity and complexity. But its best performing wine, year in, year out is its superlative Riesling, of which the 1998 edition presents a superb length of piercingly clear fruit and floral, spicy jasmine-like complexity.

Plantagenet
Albany Highway
Mount Barker WA 6324
Tel: (08) 9851 2150
Fax: (08) 9851 1839

CABERNET SAUVIGNON
Great Southern $$$$

1996	15.8	2001	2004
1995	16.5	2003	2007
1994	18.2	2002	2006
1993	17.3	2001	2005
1992	18.5		2004+
1991	17.9		2003+
1990	18.3		2002+
1989	18.0		2001+
1988	17.5		2000+
1987	16.5		2007+
1986	18.0	1998	2003
1985	18.0	1997	2002

CHARDONNAY
Great Southern $$$

1998	16.8	2003	2006
1997	17.5	2002	2005
1996	16.0	2001	2004
1995	18.1	2000	2003
1994	17.0	1996	1999
1993	18.2	1998	2001
1992	16.7	1994	1997
1991	18.0	1996	1999
1990	18.0	1995	1998

PINOT NOIR
Great Southern $$$$

1997	17.0	1999	2002+
1996	17.5	2001	2004
1995	17.4	2000	2003
1994	16.7	1996	1999
1993	17.0	1998	2001
1991	16.6	1999	2003
1990	16.5	1995	1998

Poole's Rock

229 Woolombi Rd
Broke NSW 2330
Tel: (02) 9667 1622
Fax: (02) 9667 1442

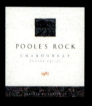

RIESLING
Great Southern $$

1998	18.7	2006	2010
1997	18.5	2005	2009
1996	18.5	2004	2008
1995	18.3	2003	2007
1994	18.5		2006+
1993	18.4	1998	2001
1992	18.1	1997	2000
1991	17.8	1996	1999
1990	16.5	1992	1995
1989	18.5	1991	1994

SHIRAZ
Great Southern $$$$

1997	16.5		2009+
1996	16.0	2002	2008
1995	18.2	2003	2007
1994	19.0	2002	2006
1993	18.5		2005+
1991	17.4	1999	2003
1990	18.0	1998	2002
1989	17.0		2001+
1988	17.0		2000+
1987	17.0	1999	2007
1986	16.5	1998	2007

Region: Lower Hunter Valley Winemaker: Phil Ryan
Viticulturist: Evan Powell Chief Executive: David Clarke

Poole's Rock is a highly rated Hunter Valley vineyard owned by Sydney merchant banker David Clarke. The Chardonnay is a typically generous, mouthfilling Hunter style based around ripe peachy, melon and tobaccoey fruit.

CHARDONNAY
Lower Hunter Valley $$$$

1998	17.2	2003	2006
1997	17.0	2002	2005
1996	17.8	1998	2001
1995	16.0	1997	2000

Preece

Mitchellstown via
Nagambie Vic 3608
Tel: (03) 5794 2710
Fax: (03) 5794 2615

Region: Goulburn Valley Winemakers: Don Lewis, Alan George
Viticulturist: John Beresford Chief Executive: Paul van der Lee

Preece is a mid-priced Mitchelton label which stands for several attractive early-drinking bistro styles of wine. Look out for the occasional surprise under the Cabernet Sauvignon label and some supple and intense varietal Merlot releases of great appeal.

CABERNET SAUVIGNON

Goulburn Valley $$

1997	15.2	2002	2005
1996	15.7	1998	2001
1995	16.2	2000	2003
1994	16.7	1999	2002
1993	16.2	1998	2001
1992	17.5	1997	2000
1991	17.2	1996	1999

CHARDONNAY

Goulburn Valley $$

1998	15.8	1999	2000
1997	16.4	1998	1998
1996	15.0	1997	1998
1995	15.7	1997	2000
1994	16.5	1996	1999
1993	15.9	1995	1998

MERLOT (FORMERLY SOLD AS CHINAMAN'S BRIDGE)

Goulburn Valley $$

1997	16.8	2002	2005
1995	17.2	2000	2003
1994	16.5	1999	2002
1993	16.0	1998	2001
1992	17.7	1997	2000

SAUVIGNON BLANC (FORMERLY SOLD AS CHINAMAN'S BRIDGE)

Goulburn Valley $$

1997	15.0	1998	1999
1996	15.0	1997	1998
1995	15.4	1995	1996
1994	16.5	1996	1999

Primo Estate

Old Port Wakefield Rd
Virginia SA 5120
Tel: (08) 8380 9442
Fax: (08) 8380 9696

Region: Adelaide Winemakers: Joe Grilli, Grant Harrison
Viticulturist: Peter Cox Chief Executive: Joe Grilli

Joe Grilli is one of Australia's most innovative winemakers. He pioneered the use of the northern Italian 'amarone' technique of leaving harvested bunches of red grapes to develop and shrivel further before making into wine, the now celebrated 'Joseph' Moda Amarone Cabernet Merlot. It remains one of the most distinctive but interesting of all Australian cellaring red styles. The Joseph label has been extended to include one of Australia's most bizarre and simply delicious sparkling red wines, plus the long-established Botrytis Riesling, now know as 'La Magia'.

JOSEPH CABERNET SAUVIGNON MERLOT

Adelaide Plains $$$$$

1997	18.5		2009+
1996	18.2		2008+
1995	16.5	2000	2003
1994	19.2		2006+
1993	18.7		2005+
1992	17.8		2004+
1991	19.2		2003+
1990	18.5		2002+
1989	18.5		2001+
1988	17.0	1996	2000
1987	16.6	1995	1999

JOSEPH 'LA MAGIA' BOTRYTIS RIESLING

Adelaide Plains $$$

1998	15.7	2003	2006
1996	17.2	2001	2004
1995	18.6	2000	2003
1994	18.3	1999	2002
1993	18.8	2001	2005
1991	18.4	1999	2003
1989	16.5	1994	1998

Region: Geelong Winemaker: Bruce Hyett
Viticulturist: Bruce Hyett Chief Executive: Bruce Hyett

Prince Albert is a small vineyard in Victoria's Geelong region planted exclusively to pinot noir, from which Bruce Hyett makes a delicate, willowy wine with genuine varietal qualities. The two most recent vintages attest volumes to the quality of fruit of which Prince Albert is clearly capable.

Prince Albert

100 Lemins Rd
Waurn Ponds Vic 3216
Tel: (03) 5241 8091
Fax: (03) 5241 8091

PINOT NOIR

Geelong $$$$

1998	17.5	2003	2006
1997	18.0	2002	2005
1996	15.0	1998	2001
1995	18.0	2000	2003
1994	17.0	1999	2002
1993	15.8	1995	1998
1992	18.3	1997	2000
1991	15.5	1996	1999
1990	15.5	1992	1995

Region: Pyrenees Winemaker: Neill Robb
Viticulturist: Neill Robb Chief Executive: Neill Robb

Sally's Paddock is the small dry land in front of Neill and Sally Robb's winery at Redbank, planted to a largely Bordeaux-based mix of red varieties. While the 1997 vintage looks a little disjointed at present, Neill Robb's eclectic Sally's Paddock blend has displayed very convincing form in recent years. Without sacrificing a minute of the wine's legendary longevity, Robb has given it more flesh and body, allied with more assertive oak treatment.

Redbank

Sunraysia Highway
Redbank Vic 3478
Tel: (03) 5467 7255
Fax: (03) 5467 7248

SALLY'S PADDOCK

Pyrenees $$$$

1997	16.5	2005	2009
1996	18.0	2008	2016
1995	18.8		2007+
1994	18.5		2006+
1993	18.5		2005+
1992	17.9	2000	2004
1991	17.2	2003	2011
1990	18.6	1998	2002
1989	16.0		2001+
1988	16.6	2000	2008
1987	15.0	1999	2004
1986	18.2		2006+
1985	16.6	1997	2005
1984	15.5	1989	1992
1983	16.0		2003+

Redgate

**Boodjidup Road
Margaret River WA 6285
Tel: (08) 9757 6488
Fax: (08) 9757 6308**

Region: Margaret River Winemaker: Andrew Forsell
Viticulturist: Jeffrey Cottle Chief Executive: Bill Ullinger

Redgate is another of Margaret River's group of emerging top-class wineries which tends to specialise in the Bordeaux varieties, red and white. As the quality of the Cabernet Sauvignon and Cabernet Franc from the 1995 vintage attests, Redgate deserves attention.

CABERNET FRANC
Margaret River $$$$

1996	16.2	1998	2001
1995	18.2	2000	2003+
1994	14.8	1996	1999

CABERNET SAUVIGNON
Margaret River $$$$

1996	15.8	2001	2004
1995	18.5	2003	2007
1994	17.8	2002	2006
1993	15.3	1995	1998

SAUVIGNON BLANC RESERVE
Margaret River $$$

1998	17.2	1999	2000
1997	16.1	1998	1999
1996	16.5	1998	2001

Redman

**Riddoch Highway
Coonawarra SA 5263
Tel: (08) 8736 3331
Fax: (08) 8736 3013**

Region: Coonawarra Winemakers: Bruce & Malcolm Redman
Viticulturists: Bruce & Malcolm Redman
Chief Executives: Bruce & Malcolm Redman

Redman's wines have faded in and out rather more than they might have over recent vintages, with the Redman brothers focusing on restrained, more reserved expressions of Coonawarra red wine.

CABERNET SAUVIGNON
Coonawarra $$$

1997	16.5	2002	2005
1996	16.7	2004	2008
1994	18.0	2002	2006
1993	18.2	2001	2005
1992	17.8		2004+
1991	15.3		2003+
1990	18.0		2002+
1989	15.0	1997	2001
1988	16.5		2000+
1987	16.5	1999	2004

CABERNET SAUVIGNON MERLOT

Coonawarra $$$

1996	17.3	2004	2008+
1995	15.9	2000	2003
1994	18.1		2006+
1993	18.2	2001	2005
1992	18.4	2000	2004
1991	17.6	1999	2003
1990	16.0	1995	1998

SHIRAZ (FORMERLY CLARET)

Coonawarra $$

1997	14.8	1998	1999
1996	15.3	2001	2004+
1995	15.8	1997	2000
1994	15.4	1996	1999
1993	17.0	2001	2005
1992	17.5	2000	2004
1991	16.5	1993	1996
1990	17.5	1995	1998
1989	15.0	1991	1994
1988	17.0	1993	1996

Region: Margaret River Winemakers: Mike & Jan Davies
Viticulturist: John James Chief Executive: John James

Ribbon Vale is home to a range of earthy, rustic red wines of powerful extract and several racy, spotlessly clean unwooded white wines from semillon and sauvignon blanc which are so philosophically removed from the reds it's a wonder they're from the same winery. Of particular zest and flavour are the Semillon and delightfully intense Semillon Sauvignon Blanc from 1998.

CABERNET SAUVIGNON

Margaret River $$$

1996	14.7	2001	2004
1995	17.0	2003	2007
1994	17.2	2002	2006
1993	17.2	2001	2005
1992	15.8	2000	2004
1991	16.8	1999	2003
1990	18.0	1998	2002

Ribbon Vale

Lot 5 Caves Rd
Willyabrup via Cowramup
WA 6284
Tel: (08) 9755 6272
Fax: (08) 9755 6337

CABERNET SAUVIGNON MERLOT

Margaret River $$$

1996	17.0	2004	2008+
1995	16.0	2003	2007+
1994	16.3	2002	2006
1993	15.3	1995	1998
1992	16.8	1997	2000
1991	16.5		2003+
1990	18.0	1995	1998
1989	17.0	1994	1997

MERLOT

Margaret River $$$

1997	14.7	1999	2002
1996	17.0	2004	2008
1995	17.3	2000	2003
1994	14.5	1999	2002
1993	16.8	2001	2005
1992	17.7	2000	2004
1991	18.1	1999	2003
1990	16.5	1995	1998

SAUVIGNON BLANC

Margaret River $$$

1998	15.3	1999	2000
1997	17.5	1998	1999
1996	17.8	1997	1998
1995	18.4	1996	1997

SEMILLON

Margaret River $$$

1998	18.0	1999	2000
1997	16.7	1999	2002
1996	18.3	1998	2001
1995	17.3	1997	2000
1994	17.4	1999	2002
1993	18.0	1995	1998
1992	18.3	1997	2000
1991	18.0	1996	1999

SEMILLON SAUVIGNON BLANC

Margaret River $$$

1998	18.4	2000	2003
1997	15.2		1998
1996	17.9	1998	2001

Richmond Grove

Para Rd
Tanunda SA 5352
Tel: (08) 8563 7300
Fax: (08) 8563 2804

Region: Various Winemaker: John Vickery
Viticulturist: Joy Dick Chief Executive: Andre Boucard

Richmond Grove is a major national brand owned by Orlando Wyndham. It retains a few labels from the days of its Hunter origins, but the real excitement lies elsewhere. Take for example the pair of rieslings made by John Vickery, one of the foremost riesling specialists in Australia, the Coonawarra Cabernet Sauvignon, the Barossa Shiraz and the refreshingly flavoured white wines sourced from the company's massive developments at Cowra. The Watervale Riesling is clearly the brand's leading wine.

BAROSSA RIESLING

Barossa Valley $$

1998	16.3	2000	2003+
1997	16.5	2002	2005
1996	18.0	2004	2008
1995	17.4	2000	2003
1993	16.9	1995	1998

BAROSSA SHIRAZ

Barossa Valley $$

1996	17.0	1998	2001
1995	16.0	1997	2000
1994	17.6	1999	2002

CABERNET MERLOT

Hunter Valley $$

1996	15.3	2001	2004
1995	14.7	1997	2000
1994	15.0	1996	1999
1993	15.6	1999	2002
1992	15.8	1994	1997
1990	15.6	1992	1995

COONAWARRA CABERNET SAUVIGNON

Coonawarra $$

1996	16.4	1998	2001
1995	16.0	2000	2003
1994	18.3	2002	2006
1993	16.5	1998	2001
1992	16.8	1997	2000

COWRA CHARDONNAY

Cowra $$

1998	15.8	1999	2000
1997	16.6	1999	2002
1996	16.0	1998	2001
1995	15.0	1996	1997

COWRA VERDELHO

Cowra $$

1998	16.0	1999	2000
1997	15.0	1998	1999
1996	16.8	1998	2001
1995	16.0	2000	2003
1994	17.5	1996	1999
1993	17.1	1995	1998

WATERVALE RIESLING

Clare Valley $$

1998	18.4	2006	2010
1997	18.5	2005	2009
1996	16.8	2001	2004
1995	18.1	2003	2007
1994	16.4	1999	2002

Region: Coonawarra Winemaker: Wayne Stehbens
Viticulturist: Leon Oborne Chief Executive: David Yunghanns

Owned and made by the Wingara Wine Group at their Katnook Estate winery, Riddoch offers two fine early-drinking red wines in its Cabernet Shiraz and Shiraz, both spicy, silky-smooth and intensely flavoured. The whites are clean and refreshing, but not as exciting.

Riddoch

**Riddoch Highway
Coonawarra SA 5263
Tel: (08) 8737 2394
Fax: (08) 8737 2397**

CABERNET SHIRAZ
Coonawarra $$

1997	14.8	1998	1999
1996	16.6	1998	2001
1995	15.3	1997	2000
1994	17.0	1996	1999
1993	16.4	1998	2001
1992	17.4	1997	2000
1991	18.3	1996	1999
1990	17.7	1995	1998

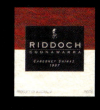

CHARDONNAY
Coonawarra $$

1997	15.6	1999	2002
1996	15.0	1997	1998
1995	14.5	1996	1997

SAUVIGNON BLANC
Coonawarra $$

1998	15.0	1999	2000
1997	15.5		1998
1996	16.2	1997	1998
1995	16.7	1996	1997
1994	16.6	1996	1999

SHIRAZ
Coonawarra $$

1997	15.2	1999	2002
1996	17.0	1998	2001
1995	15.5	1996	1997
1994	17.0	1999	2002
1993	15.0	1995	1998
1992	16.6	1997	2000
1991	18.0	1999	2003
1990	17.5	1995	1998

Robertson's Well

Riddoch Highway
Coonawarra SA 5263
Tel: (08) 8736 3380
Fax: (08) 8736 3307

Region: Coonawarra Winemaker: David O'Leary
Viticulturist: Vic Patrick Chief Executive: Ray King

Robertson's Well is a premium Mildara Blass label given to a finely crafted and long-living Coonawarra cabernet sauvignon. Recent vintages haven't quite lived up to the promise of the 1994 wine.

CABERNET SAUVIGNON
Coonawarra $$$

1996	16.2	2001	2004
1995	16.0	1997	2000
1994	18.3	2002	2006
1993	17.5	2001	2005
1992	17.8	2000	2004

Rosemount Estate

Rosemount Road
Denman NSW 2328
Tel: (02) 6549 6400
Fax: (02) 6547 2742

Region: Upper Hunter Valley Winemaker: Philip Shaw
Viticulturist: Richard Hilder Chief Executives: Sandy Oatley, Keith Lambert

Rosemount Estate has just completed its 25th year, frankly a short time given what the Oatley family has achieved with this major national brand. Rosemount Estate draws fruit from a large number of wine regions to put together its extensive wine portfolio which ranges from the excellent and more affordable blends of shiraz with grenache and cabernet, the popular 'Diamond Series', all the way to the Show Reserve wines and the individual 'specials', such as the Balmoral Syrah (McLaren Vale), Roxburgh Chardonnay (Upper Hunter) and the latest arrival, the simply wonderful Mountain Blue (Mudgee). Toss in wines like the superbly complex and evolved Yarra Valley Chardonnay, the Chardonnay and Cabernet Sauvignon from Orange and you could be forgiven for thinking that Rosemount has its bases well and truly loaded.

BALMORAL SYRAH
McLaren Vale $$$$$

1996	18.4	2004	2008
1995	19.2		2007+
1994	18.7	2002	2006+
1993	16.5	1998	2001
1992	19.0	2000	2004+
1991	18.8		2003+
1990	18.5	2002	2010
1989	18.4	1997	2003+

CABERNET SAUVIGNON

South Australia $$

1998	16.2	2000	2003
1996	15.3	1998	2001
1995	15.0	1997	2000
1994	16.5	1999	2002
1993	16.6	1998	2001
1992	17.0	1997	2000
1991	16.5	1999	2003

CHARDONNAY

Upper Hunter Valley $$

1998	17.3	2000	2003
1997	16.2	1999	2002
1996	16.5	1998	2001
1995	15.5	1996	1997
1994	17.0	1996	1999
1993	17.5	1998	2001
1992	15.1	1994	1997

GIANT'S CREEK CHARDONNAY

Upper Hunter Valley $$$$

1997	18.3	2005	2009+
1996	17.2	2001	2004
1995	16.7	1997	2000
1994	17.3	1999	2002
1993	18.5	1998	2001
1992	15.3	1994	1997
1989	17.0	1997	2001
1988	16.8	1996	2000
1987	17.8	1995	1999

GSM

McLaren Vale $$$

1996	17.0	2001	2004
1995	15.9	2003	2007
1994	16.4	1999	2002

MCLAREN VALE SHIRAZ

McLaren Vale $$$$

1994	17.9	2002	2006
1993	15.5	1998	2001
1992	17.0	2000	2004

MOUNTAIN BLUE

Mudgee $$$$$

1997	18.6	2009	2017
1996	18.8		2008+
1995	18.6		2007+
1994	18.2		2006+

ORANGE VINEYARD CABERNET SAUVIGNON

Orange $$$

1998	18.0	2006	2010
1997	16.7	2005	2009
1996	17.5	2004	2008
1995	16.0	2003	2007

ORANGE VINEYARD CHARDONNAY

Upper Hunter Valley $$$

1997	18.5	2005	2009
1996	18.0	2001	2004
1995	18.0	2003	2007
1994	18.4	1999	2002
1993	18.2	1995	1998
1992	18.2	1997	2000

ROXBURGH CHARDONNAY

Upper Hunter Valley $$$$$

1997	18.2	2002	2006
1996	18.5	2002	2006
1995	18.5	2000	2003
1994	17.6	1999	2001
1993	16.6	1998	2001
1992	16.5	1997	2000
1991	18.3		2003+
1990	17.9	1998	2002
1989	18.3	1997	2001

THE ONWINE AUSTRALIAN WINE ANNUAL

SHIRAZ
McLaren Vale $$

1998	16.8	2000	2003+
1997	16.3	1999	2002
1995	16.8	1997	2000
1994	15.7	1996	1999
1993	17.0	1998	2001
1992	16.5	1997	2000
1991	16.3	1996	1999
1990	17.9	1998	2003

SHOW RESERVE CABERNET SAUVIGNON
Coonawarra $$$$

1996	18.7	2004	2008+
1995	16.5	2000	2003
1994	18.8	2006	2014
1993	18.0	2001	2005
1992	18.3		2004+
1991	16.0	2003	2011
1990	18.1	2002	2010
1989	16.3	1994	1997
1988	17.5	1996	2000+
1987	18.0	1999	2004
1986	18.2	1998	2006
1985	18.1	1993	1997+

SHOW RESERVE CHARDONNAY
Upper Hunter Valley $$$$

1997	18.0	2002	2005+
1996	18.8	2004	2008+
1995	18.1	2003	2007
1994	17.1	2002	2006
1993	17.6	1998	2001
1992	17.2	1997	2000
1991	16.1	1999	2003+
1990	18.4	1998	2002

SHOW RESERVE SEMILLON
Upper Hunter Valley $$$$

1996	18.0	2004	2008
1995	18.2	2003	2007
1991	16.8	1996	1999
1990	18.1	1998	2002
1989	18.3	1997	2001+

Rothbury Estate

**Broke Rd
Pokolbin NSW 2320
Tel: (02) 4998 7555
Fax: (02) 4998 7553**

Region: Lower Hunter Valley Winemaker: Adam Eggins
Viticulturist: Roger Dixon Chief Executive: Ray King

Rothbury Estate is Mildara Blass' winemaking base in the Hunter Valley. Originally the brainchild of Len Evans, it experienced a turbulent financial history which penultimately led to its listing on the Stock Exchange and ultimately to its purchase by Fosters Brewing, owners of Mildara Blass. Its relentless pursuit of its own identity has seen a significant number of changes in both wine labels and also in fruit sourcing. Rothbury's present range includes several non-Hunter wines (a concept initiated during the Evans period of tenure), plus the top regional Hunter wines which are now labelled under the 'Brokenback Range' label.

BROKENBACK SHIRAZ (FORMERLY RESERVE SHIRAZ)

Lower Hunter Valley $$$

1996	15.6	1998	2001
1995	14.5	1997	2000
1994	18.0		2006+
1993	18.6	2001	2005+
1993	18.9		2008+
1991	18.3		2003+
1989	18.4		2001+

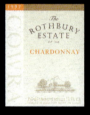

COWRA CHARDONNAY

Cowra $$

1998	15.0		1999
1997	17.0	1999	2002
1996	16.6	1998	2001
1995	17.0	2000	2003
1994	15.0	1995	1996
1993	17.0	1998	2001

HUNTER VALLEY CHARDONNAY (FORMERLY BARREL FERMENT CHARDONNAY)

Lower Hunter Valley $$

1997	16.6	1998	1999
1996	17.5	2001	2004
1994	18.4	1996	1999
1993	16.3	1995	1998
1992	17.2	1997	2000
1991	17.0	1996	1999
1990	17.0	1992	1995

HUNTER VALLEY SEMILLON

Lower Hunter Valley $$

1997	17.5	2004	2009
1996	18.2	2004	2008
1995	17.7	2000	2003
1994	16.9	1999	2002
1993	18.0		2005+
1992	15.0	1994	1997
1991	18.1	1999	2003
1990	16.0		2002+
1989	18.1		2001+
1988	15.0	1990	1995
1987	16.0	1995	1999
1986	18.6	1994	1998

MUDGEE CABERNET MERLOT

Mudgee $$

1997	14.5	1998	1999
1996	15.0	1998	2001
1995	15.3	2000	2003

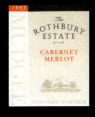

Region: Tamar Valley Winemaker: Greg O'Keefe
Viticulturist: John Vincent Chief Executives: John & Denise Vincent

Now in the hands of John and Denise Vincent, who have wisely employed Greg O'Keefe as winemaker, Rotherhythe has every opportunity to cement the fine start to its history created by Steve Hyde. From time to time this vineyard has made exceptional wines from chardonnay, pinot noir and cabernet sauvignon.

CABERNET SAUVIGNON

Tamar Valley $$$$

1994	16.8	2002	2006
1993	15.0	1998	2001
1992	15.6	2000	2004
1991	18.1	1999	2003
1990	18.3	1995	1998
1989	14.7	1994	1997
1988	17.0	1996	2000

Rotherhythe

**Henderson Lane
Gravelly Beach
Exeter Tasmania Tas 7251
Tel: (03) 6394 4869
Fax: (03) 6331 1977**

Rouge Homme

**Riddoch Highway
Coonawarra SA 5263
Tel: (08) 8736 3205
Fax: (08) 8736 3250**

CHARDONNAY

Tamar Valley $$$$

1995	17.3	2000	2003
1994	18.5	1999	2002
1993	16.8	1998	2001
1992	15.4	1994	1997
1991	17.3	1996	1999

PINOT NOIR

Tamar Valley $$$$

1994	18.7	2002	2006
1993	14.7	1995	1998
1992	17.5	1997	2000
1991	16.5	1996	1999

**Region: Coonawarra Winemaker: Paul Gordon
Viticulturist: Max Arney Chief Executive: Bruce Kemp**

A delightful 1996 Cabernet Sauvignon gives renewed credibility and stature to what was once a leading Coonawarra label. Rouge Homme's wines have been deliberately made in earlier-drinking styles, offering uncomplicated, easy-drinking marriages of fruit and oak, if deployed. It's sometimes hard not to wonder if more could not be made from the vineyard resources the brand has access to.

CABERNET SAUVIGNON

Coonawarra $$$

1997	16.8	1999	2002+
1996	18.2		2008+
1995	17.0	2000	2003
1994	16.1	1999	2002
1993	14.5	2001	2005
1992	17.7	2000	2004
1991	16.8	1999	2003
1990	16.8	1995	1998
1989	16.0	1994	1997
1988	17.0	1996	2000

PINOT NOIR

Coonawarra $$

1997	16.0	1999	2002
1996	14.0	1997	1998
1995	15.7	1997	2000
1994	16.0	1996	1999

CABERNET MERLOT (FORMERLY RICHARDSON'S RED BLOCK)

Coonawarra $$$

1996	16.6	2001	2004
1995	16.0	2000	2003
1994	15.3	1996	1999
1993	16.5	1995	1998
1992	15.0	1994	1997

CHARDONNAY (FORMERLY RICHARDSON'S WHITE BLOCK CHARDONNAY)

Coonawarra $$

1998	16.0	1999	2000
1995	15.8	1997	2000
1994	14.5	1995	1996

SHIRAZ CABERNET

Coonawarra $$

1997	16.9	2002	2005
1996	17.0	1998	2001
1995	14.8	1997	2000

Region: Coonawarra Winemaker: John Innes
Viticulturist: Grant Oschar Chief Executive: Peter Rymill

Rymill is a relative newcomer to the Coonawarra scene which since the early 1990s has set and maintained a healthy standard of quality and consistency. A recently tasted Sauvignon Blanc 1992 was a delightful surprise, while the Merlot Cabernets is a personal tip for every-day enjoyment.

CABERNET SAUVIGNON

Coonawarra $$$$

1997	16.8	2005	2009
1996	16.0	2001	2004
1995	16.2	2000	2003
1994	16.4	2002	2006

MERLOT CABERNETS

Coonawarra $$$

1997	17.4	1999	2002
1996	16.8	1998	2001
1995	16.6	1997	2000
1994	16.0	1996	1999

Rymill

The Riddoch Run Vineyard
Coonawarra SA 5263
Tel: (08) 8736 5001
Fax: (08) 8736 5040

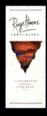

Saltram

**Angaston Road
Angaston SA 5353
Tel: (08) 8564 3355
Fax: (08) 8564 2209**

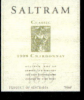

SAUVIGNON BLANC
Coonawarra $$

1998	15.7		1999
1997	16.8	1998	1999
1996	15.4	1997	1998
1992	17.5	1994	1997+

SHIRAZ
Coonawarra $$$

1997	17.4	2002	2005
1995	16.5	2000	2003
1994	15.0	1999	2002+

Region: Barossa Valley Winemaker: Nigel Dolan
Viticulturist: Murray Heidenreich Chief Executive: Ray King

It's really only for the No. 1 reds of Cabernet Sauvignon and Shiraz that Saltram remains of interest to the drinker of serious wine. The Classic label of cheaper varietal wines has lost its early gloss and now hosts a set of uninteresting, if sound and drinkable beverage wines, but Nigel Dolan deserves every encouragement to keep up his excellent work with the very ripe, concentrated and assertively oaked No. 1 reds.

CLASSIC CHARDONNAY
South Australia $

1998	15.3	1999	2000
1997	15.0		1998
1996	15.7	1997	1998
1995	16.5	1997	2000
1994	16.5	1996	1999
1993	16.3	1995	1998
1992	17.0	1994	1997

NO. 1 SHIRAZ
Barossa Valley $$$$

1996	18.4	2002	2006
1995	17.2	2000	2003
1994	18.2	2002	2006

246 2000 THE ONWINE AUSTRALIAN WINE ANNUAL

Region: Various, WA Winemaker: Bill Crappsley
Viticulturist: Ian Davies Chief Executive: Peter Prendiville

It's something of a mystery to me why recent Sandalford releases appear to have rather gone off the boil, just when the brand was making strong headway with its Cabernet Sauvignon, Chardonnay, Shiraz and Verdelho. Sandalford does have access to fruit from several premium Western Australian wine regions, so one would have thought that it had more scope than most WA makers to better absorb variations from vintage to vintage.

CABERNET SAUVIGNON
Mount Barker, Margaret River $$$$

1997	16.6	2005	2009
1996	18.2	2004	2008
1995	17.8	2000	2003
1994	17.7	2002	2006
1993	14.8	1998	2001
1992	16.0	1994	1997
1991	16.2	1999	2003
1990	17.0		2002+
1989	15.5		2001+

CHARDONNAY
Margaret River, Mount Barker, Pemberton blend $$$

1997	16.6	1999	2002+
1996	16.9	1998	2001
1995	18.3	2000	2003
1994	17.2	1999	2002
1993	18.5	1998	2001
1992	15.4	1993	1994

SHIRAZ
Margaret River, Mount Barker $$$$

1997	15.0	1999	2002+
1996	16.3	2001	2004
1995	16.7	2003	2007
1994	17.3	2002	2006
1993	16.8	1998	2001
1992	14.5	1994	1997
1991	14.7	1996	1999

Sandalford

3210 West Swan Road
Caversham WA 6055
Tel: (08) 9274 5922
Fax: (08) 9274 2154

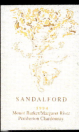
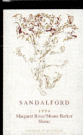

Sandstone

PO Box 558
Busselton WA 6280
Tel: (08) 9755 6271
Fax: (08) 9755 6292

VERDELHO
Margaret River $$$

1998	16.4	2003	2006
1997	15.2	1998	1999
1996	17.4	1998	2001
1995	15.7	1997	2000
1994	16.2	1999	2002
1993	18.0	2001	2005
1992	16.0	1997	2000
1991	16.5	1996	1999
1990	17.7	1998	2002

Region: Margaret River Winemakers: Mike & Jan Davies
Chief Executive: Mike Davies

Sandstone's Semillon is one of the finest of the wood-matured Margaret River styles, with distinctive richness derived from fruit quality, oak and yeast lees contact after fermentation. Ripe and alcoholic, they develop in the bottle for at least five years. The pungent and slightly rusticated Cabernet Sauvignon reflects a very natural approach to winemaking.

CABERNET SAUVIGNON
Margaret River $$$$

1996	16.9	2004	2008
1995	16.0	2003	2007
1993	16.4	2001	2005
1992	17.9		2004+
1991	17.0		2003+
1990	16.8	1998	2002
1989	17.5	1997	2001
1988	16.3	1993	1996

SEMILLON
Margaret River $$$$

1998	18.3	2003	2006
1997	18.5	2002	2005
1995	18.5	2003	2007
1994	18.0	1999	2002
1993	18.2	2001	2005
1992	18.2	1994	1997

Region: McLaren Vale   Winemakers: Michael & Filippo Scarpantoni
Viticulturist: Filippo Scarpantoni   Chief Executive: Domenico Scarpantoni

Scarpantoni's red wines are rich, rustic and generous. Like many other McLaren Vale makers this vineyard struggled to achieve consistently ripe fruit in 1997, but has released two honest wines in the Block 3 Shiraz and Cabernet Sauvignon.

Scarpantoni

**Scarpantoni Drive
McLaren Flat SA 5171
Tel: (08) 8383 0186
Fax: (08) 8383 0490**

BLOCK 3 SHIRAZ
McLaren Vale $$$

1997	16.2	2002	2005
1996	17.0	2001	2004
1995	16.3	1997	2000
1994	16.5	1999	2002
1993	16.3	1998	2001
1992	16.5	1997	2000

CABERNET SAUVIGNON
McLaren Vale $$$

1997	16.6	2002	2005
1996	15.4	1998	2001
1995	15.3	1997	2000
1994	18.3	2002	2006
1993	16.5	1998	2001
1992	16.9	2000	2004
1991	17.2		2003+

Region: Geelong   Winemakers: Robin Brockett, Matthew Browne
Viticulturist: Robin Brockett   Chief Executive: Matthew Browne

Scotchmans Hill is a booming small winery on Victoria's Bellarine Peninsula whose wines have a devoted market and are found on dozens of cafe wine lists, where their early-maturing qualities are best appreciated. The 1997 Pinot Noir and Chardonnay have both developed very well over the last twelve months into the most convincing examples of these varieties yet from this winery.

Scotchmans Hill

**Scotchmans Road
Drysdale Vic 3222
Tel: (03) 5251 3176
Fax: (03) 5253 1743**

CABERNET SAUVIGNON MERLOT
Geelong $$$$

1996	14.7	1998	2001
1995	15.8	2000	2003
1994	14.4	1996	1999
1993	18.1	2001	2005
1992	15.2	1994	1997

CHARDONNAY
Geelong $$$$

1998	16.4	1999	2000
1997	17.6	1998	2002
1996	15.6	1997	1998
1995	16.5	1996	1997
1994	16.0	1996	1999
1993	18.3	1998	2001
1992	15.9	1994	1997
1991	17.0	1993	1996
1990	16.0	1995	1998

PINOT NOIR
Geelong $$$$

1998	15.8	1999	2000
1997	17.6	1999	2002
1996	15.0	1998	2001
1995	17.5	1996	1997
1994	16.0	1995	1996

SAUVIGNON BLANC
Geelong $$$

1998	15.2		1998
1997	16.6	1998	1999
1996	16.8	1997	1998
1995	15.5	1996	1997

Seaview

Chaffeys Road
McLaren Vale SA 5171
Tel: (08) 8323 8250
Fax: (08) 8323 9308

Region: McLaren Vale Winemaker: Steve Chapman
Viticulturist: Brian Hill Chief Executive: Bruce Kemp

Seaview's split personality offers several fine choices at different pricing levels from the ripe and generous basic range of McLaren Vale to the Edwards & Chaffey premium collection of ripe, chunky regional red wines of great strength and endurance, plus a Chardonnay which appears to have been taken as a willing and grateful participant to every winemaking artefact in the textbook.

CHARDONNAY
McLaren Vale $

1998	16.6	2000	2003
1997	15.4	1998	1999
1996	16.3	1998	2001
1995	15.0	1996	1997
1994	16.0	1996	1999
1993	16.5	1995	1998

EDWARDS & CHAFFEY CABERNET SAUVIGNON

McLaren Vale $$$$

1996	18.6	2004	2008+
1994	17.8	2002	2006+
1992	18.0	2000	2004

EDWARDS & CHAFFEY CHARDONNAY

McLaren Vale $$$$

1997	17.3	1999	2002+
1996	17.0	1998	2001
1995	18.0	1997	2000
1994	17.2	1996	1999

EDWARDS & CHAFFEY PINOT NOIR CHARDONNAY (FORMERLY EDMOND MAZURE)

South Australia $$$$

1995	18.4	1997	2000+
1993	16.7	1995	1998
1992	18.7	1997	2000
1991	17.5	1993	1996
1990	18.3	1995	1998
1989	18.5	1991	1994

EDWARDS & CHAFFEY SHIRAZ

McLaren Vale $$$$

1997	16.2	2002	2005
1996	18.0	2001	2004+
1995	16.8	1997	2000
1994	18.0	2002	2006

PINOT NOIR CHARDONNAY

South Australia $$$

1994	18.1	1999	2002
1993	17.6	1995	1998
1992	18.2	1997	2000
1991	17.0	1993	1996
1990	18.6	1995	1998
1989	18.0	1991	1994

Seppelt

Great Western Vic 3377
Tel: (03) 5361 2222
Fax: (03) 5361 2200

SHIRAZ
McLaren Vale $$

1997	16.7	2002	2005+
1996	16.2	2001	2004
1995	16.0	2000	2003
1994	16.7	2002	2006
1993	16.2	1998	2001
1992	16.7	1997	2000

Regions: Great Western, Barooga, Barossa
Winemakers: Ian McKenzie, James Godfrey, Andrew Fleming
Viticulturist: Fiona Wigg Chief Executive: Bruce Kemp

Seppelt's wild and rambling range of wines, including a number made at the famous headquarters at Great Western, is tending to polarise between a collection of accessibly priced and highly decorative Victorian labels and a legendary series of Barossa fortifieds. I keep a soft spot for the Sunday Creek Pinot Noir, which even if made in an up-front show style still offers true pinot noir flavour at a very cheap rate. Next come several premium individual vineyard wines like the cabernets from Dorrien and Drumborg, plus the excellent Great Western Shiraz, while there's also the first-rate family of sparkling wines headed by the resurgent Salinger. It's pleasing to be able to report that the two most recent vintages of Salinger have re-established it amongst the very finest of Australian sparkling wines.

CHALAMBAR SHIRAZ
Great Western $$

1997	16.8	2002	2005+
1996	15.2	1998	2001
1995	17.5	2003	2007
1994	16.5	1999	2002
1993	15.4	1995	1998
1992	17.2	1997	2000
1991	17.0	1999	2003
1990	17.8	1998	2002
1989	17.0	1998	2001

CORELLA RIDGE CHARDONNAY
Victoria $$

1998	16.3	2000	2003
1997	16.6	1999	2002
1996	16.4	1998	2001
1995	16.0	1996	1997

252   2000   THE ONWINE AUSTRALIAN WINE ANNUAL

DORRIEN CABERNET SAUVIGNON

Barossa Valley $$$$

1994	18.7	2006	2014
1993	17.0	2001	2005
1992	17.8	2000	2004
1991	18.6		2003+
1990	18.0		2002+
1989	17.9	1997	2001
1988	15.3	1993	1996
1987	17.4	1995	1999
1986	17.5	1998	2003
1984	18.3	1996	2001
1982	18.0	1990	1994

DRUMBORG CABERNET SAUVIGNON

Western Districts $$$$

1993	17.1	2001	2005
1991	17.2	1999	2003
1989	18.2		2001+
1985	18.5	1997	2002
1982	18.0	1990	1994

FLEUR-DE-LYS VINTAGE BRUT

Southern Australia $$

1993	16.8	1995	1998
1992	16.5	1994	1997
1991	17.8	1993	1996
1990	17.2	1992	1995

GREAT WESTERN SHIRAZ

Great Western $$$$

1995	18.0		2007+
1993	17.6	1998	2001
1992	18.0	2000	2004
1991	18.4		2003+
1988	16.5	1993	1996
1987	14.5	1992	1995
1986	17.0	1998	2003
1985	16.5	1997	2002

HANS IRVINE BRUT

Great Western $$$

1990	16.8	1995	1998
1988	18.1	1996	2000
1987	16.8	1995	1999
1986	16.6	1991	1994

HARPERS RANGE CABERNET BLEND

Victoria $$$

1997	17.4	2002	2005+
1996	16.3	2001	2004
1995	16.9	2003	2007
1994	16.4	1999	2002
1993	15.0	1995	1998
1992	17.0	1997	2000
1991	18.2	1996	1999
1990	16.5	1995	1998

ORIGINAL SPARKLING SHIRAZ (FORMERLY HARPERS RANGE SPARKLING BURGUNDY

Victoria $$$

1994	18.0	2002	2006+
1993	17.8	2001	2005
1992	16.0	1997	2000
1991	18.0		2003+
1990	17.6	1998	2002
1989	15.5	1997	2001
1988	16.5	1996	2000
1987	16.5	1995	1999
1986	16.8	1994	1998
1985	17.0	1993	1997

SALINGER

Southern Australia $$$$

1993	18.7	1998	2001
1992	18.7	1997	2000
1991	18.3	1996	1999
1990	18.6	1995	1998
1989	17.0	1991	1994

THE ONWINE AUSTRALIAN WINE ANNUAL

SHOW SPARKLING SHIRAZ

Great Western $$$$$

1987	17.0	1995	1999+
1986	18.7	1998	2006
1985	17.0	1993	1997
1984	18.3	1999	2001
1983	17.6	1995	2000
1982	18.3	1990	1994
1972	18.2	1992	1997

SUNDAY CREEK PINOT NOIR

Victoria $$$

1998	16.8	2000	2003
1997	17.5	1999	2002
1996	17.7	1998	2001

TERRAIN CABERNET SAUVIGNON

Southern Australia $

1997	15.8	2002	2005
1996	15.2	1998	2001
1995	15.4	1997	2000
1994	15.0	1996	1999
1993	17.7	1998	2001

Region: Clare Valley Winemakers: Brother John May & John Monten
Viticulturist: Brother John May Chief Executive: Brother John May

Although Sevenhill has made riesling from its Clare Valley vineyards for several decades, recent years have shown new refinements to the wine, which tends to develop honeyed and toasty complexity after a few years in the bottle. Sevenhill's red wines have also developed nicely in recent years and didn't suffer too much of a dip with the 1997 vintage.

Sevenhill

College Rd
Sevenhill via
Clare SA 5453
Tel: (08) 8843 4222
Fax: (08) 8843 4382

CABERNET SAUVIGNON

Clare Valley $$$

1997	15.8	2002	2005+
1996	16.6	2004	2008
1995	15.3	1997	2000
1994	17.0		2006+
1993	17.3		2005+
1992	17.2	2000	2004
1991	16.3	1999	2003
1990	16.0	1998	2002

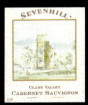

DRY RED (FORMERLY SHIRAZ TOURIGA GRENACHE)

Clare Valley $$

1997	15.7	2002	2005
1996	16.6	2001	2004
1995	16.5	2002	2006
1994	16.8	2002	2006
1993	17.2		2005+
1992	17.2	2000	2004
1991	19.0	1996	1999
1990	16.0	1995	1998

RIESLING

Clare Valley $$

1998	17.5	2003	2006
1997	18.1	2002	2005
1996	18.2	2004	2008
1995	18.3	2000	2003
1994	18.2	2002	2006
1993	16.8	1998	2001
1992	18.5	1997	2000
1991	17.0	1993	1996
1990	15.0	1995	1998

SEMILLON

Clare Valley $$

1998	16.8	2003	2006
1996	16.0	1998	2001
1995	15.0	1997	2000
1994	16.0	1999	2002
1993	17.2	1998	2001

SHIRAZ

Clare Valley $$$

1997	16.7	2002	2005+
1996	17.6	2001	2004
1995	17.4	2003	2007
1994	17.5	2002	2006
1993	18.2		2005+
1992	17.3	2000	2004
1991	18.0		2003+
1990	15.8	1995	1998

ST. ALOYSIUS
Clare Valley $$

1998	15.2	1999	2000
1997	16.0	1998	1999
1996	15.2	1997	1998
1995	16.6	1997	2000
1994	16.7	1996	1999
1993	16.8	1995	1998
1992	16.2	1997	2000
1991	18.0	1996	1999
1990	15.5	1992	1995

ST. IGNATIUS
Clare Valley $$

1997	15.6	2002	2005
1996	15.8	1998	2001
1995	16.2	1997	2000
1994	17.3	1999	2002
1993	17.8		2005+

Region: Yarra Valley   Winemaker: Iain Riggs
Viticulturist: Alaister Butt   Chief Executive: Iain Riggs

An excellent series of recent Shiraz vintages from Seville Estate has fully justified Iain Rigg's expectations, with deliciously dark, savoury, spicy medium-weight wines which do justify their increased prices. Seville has released a GP range of wines sourced from various regions, firstly as a means of generating additional revenue, secondly as a mark of respect to the vineyard's founder, Dr Peter McMahon.

CABERNET SAUVIGNON
Yarra Valley $$$$

1995	15.8	2000	2003+
1994	16.7	2002	2006
1992	18.3	2004	2012
1991	18.0	1999	2003
1990	17.5	1994	1998
1989	16.0	1993	1997
1988	18.0	1992	1996
1987	15.0	1991	1995
1986	17.0	1990	1994

Seville Estate

Linwood Road
Seville Vic 3139
Tel: (03) 5964 4556
Fax: (03) 5964 3585

CHARDONNAY
Yarra Valley $$$

1997	18.3	2002	2005+
1996	17.5	2001	2004
1995	17.8	2000	2003
1994	18.3	2002	2006
1993	17.7	1998	2001
1992	17.6	2000	2004
1991	18.2	1996	1999
1990	17.5	1995	1998
1989	16.0	1991	1994

PINOT NOIR
Yarra Valley $$$$

1995	16.3	2000	2003
1993	18.1	1998	2001
1992	16.5	2000	2004
1991	18.2	1996	1999

SHIRAZ
Yarra Valley $$$$

1996	18.0	2004	2008
1995	18.2	2003	2007
1994	16.7	1996	1999
1993	18.6	2001	2005
1992	18.4	1997	2000
1991	18.3	1996	1999
1990	18.0	1995	1998
1989	15.0	1991	1994
1988	17.5	1996	2000
1986	17.6	1994	1998

Region: Yarra Valley Winemakers: Shan & Turid Shanmugam
Viticulturists: Shan & Turid Shanmugam Chief Executive: Turid Shanmugam

It's typically one of the Yarra Valley's finer Chardonnays, but Shantell's is made without a malolactic fermentation, giving it a distinctive mineral feel and freshness. As much of an individual, the Cabernet Sauvignon harks back to an older style, with eucalypt/mint flavours and a long, linear tannic backbone. Shantell's Pinot Noir frequently tastes highly spiced, with fruit flavours of cherries and cooked plums.

Shantell

1974 Melba Highway
Dixons Creek Vic 3775
Tel: (03) 5965 2264
Fax: (03) 5965 2331

CABERNET SAUVIGNON
Yarra Valley $$$$

1996	15.4	2001	2004
1995	15.3	2000	2003
1994	17.4	2002	2006
1993	16.4	1998	2001
1992	18.6		2004+
1991	18.0	1999	2003
1990	18.0	1998	2002
1989	16.5	1991	1994
1988	18.1	1993	1996
1987	16.0	1992	1995

CHARDONNAY
Yarra Valley $$$

1997	16.3	2002	2005
1996	16.7	1998	2001
1995	18.2	2000	2003
1994	18.4	1999	2002
1993	18.4	1998	2001
1992	18.2	1997	2000
1991	17.8	1996	1999
1990	18.7	1995	1990

PINOT NOIR
Yarra Valley $$$$

1997	16.2	2002	2005
1996	16.4	2001	2004
1995	16.0	2000	2003
1994	15.0	1996	1999
1993	17.6	1998	2001
1992	16.0	1994	1997
1991	17.3	1996	1999
1990	17.4	1995	1998

Sharefarmers

c/- Spring Gully Road
Piccadilly SA 5151
Tel: (08) 8339 4122
Fax: (08) 8339 5253

Region: Coonawarra Winemakers: Brian Croser, Con Moshos
Viticulturist: Mike Harms Chief Executive: Brian Croser

At time of writing objections still remain, but Brian Croser's biggest PR win in years has been to have the Sharefarmers Vineyard accepted into the Geographical Indication (the official term for wine region) of Coonawarra. The Sharefarmers wines are light-bodied, clean and early-drinking entrants in the bistro stakes.

MERLOT MALBEC CABERNET SAUVIGNON

Coonawarra $$

1996	15.2	1998	2001
1995	15.7	1997	2000
1994	16.9	1999	2002+

SEMILLON SAUVIGNON BLANC (FORMERLY CHARDONNAY SAUVIGNON BLANC)

Coonawarra $$

1998	16.4	1999	2000
1997	15.8	1998	1999
1996	15.5	1997	1998

Shaw and Smith

PO Box 172
Stirling SA 5152
Tel: (08) 8370 9911
Fax: (08) 8370 9339

Region: Adelaide Hills Winemaker: Martin Shaw
Viticulturist: Martin Shaw Chief Executives: Martin Shaw, Michael Hill Smith

A white wine specialist, Shaw and Smith combines the winemaking and marketing talents of two cousins, Martin Shaw and Michael Hill Smith. Its leading wine is the Reserve Chardonnay, a superbly complex and elegant wine of genuine finesse. The Sauvignon Blanc is a benchmark in the less overtly grassy style while the Unoaked Chardonnay, as much as the idea fills me with inertia, is still probably the best going around today.

RESERVE CHARDONNAY

Adelaide Hills $$$$

1997	18.4	2002	2005+
1996	17.5	2001	2004
1995	18.6	2000	2003
1994	17.0	1999	2002
1993	19.0	2001	2005
1992	18.9	2000	2004
1991	17.0	1993	1996

SAUVIGNON BLANC

Adelaide Hills $$$

1998	17.5	1998	1999
1997	17.2	1998	1999
1996	18.1	1998	2001
1995	18.2	1997	2000
1994	18.5	1995	1996

UNOAKED CHARDONNAY

Adelaide Hills $$$

1998	17.0	1999	2000
1997	17.5	1998	1999
1996	17.3	1997	1998
1995	16.5	1996	1997

Region: McLaren Vale Winemaker: Nick Holmes
Viticulturist: Nick Holmes Chief Executive: Nick Holmes

Maker of some of the McLaren Vale's most elegant and refined red wines, Nick Holmes has shown a deft touch with recent vintages of Sauvignon Blanc and Merlot. Shottesbrooke's reds tend to be a little tight and unexpressive when they are released at just one year of age, but usually develop more character and body with time in the bottle.

CABERNET SAUVIGNON MERLOT MALBEC

McLaren Vale $$$

1997	16.3	2002	2005
1996	15.8	2001	2004
1995	18.1	2003	2007
1994	17.8	2002	2006
1993	16.0	1998	2001
1992	18.1	2000	2004
1991	18.5	1999	2003
1990	17.4	1998	2002
1989	17.2	1997	2001
1988	18.0	1993	1996
1987	14.5	1989	1992
1986	18.0	1994	1998

Shottesbrooke

**Bagshaws Road
McLaren Flat SA 5171
Tel: (08) 8383 0002
Fax: (08) 8383 0222**

CHARDONNAY
McLaren Vale $$

1998	16.8	2000	2003+
1997	16.0	1999	2002
1996	17.0	2001	2004
1995	15.0	1997	2000
1994	18.2	1999	2002
1993	18.5	2001	2005
1992	16.0	1997	2000

MERLOT
McLaren Vale $$$

1997	17.9	2002	2005
1996	17.0	2001	2004
1995	17.2	2000	2003
1994	17.2	1999	2002
1993	18.0	2001	2005
1992	18.0	1997	2000
1991	17.0	1993	1996

SAUVIGNON BLANC
Fleurieu $$

1998	17.8	1999	2000
1997	17.3	1998	1999
1996	16.7	1998	2001
1995	16.7	1997	2000
1994	18.5	1996	1999
1993	18.3	1994	1995

Skillogalee

Trevarrick Road
Sevenhill via
Clare SA 5453
Tel: (08) 8843 4311
Fax: (08) 8843 4343

Region: Clare Valley Winemaker: David Palmer
Viticulturist: David Chandler Chief Executive: David Palmer

A most reliable small specialist maker of Clare Valley riesling and dry red, Skillogalee's wines are usually elegant, crystal-clear in their fruit expression and ideally suited to medium-term cellaring. Its reds often reveal regional minty and eucalyptus flavours.

RIESLING
Clare Valley $$

1998	17.0	2003	2006
1997	17.8	2005	2009
1996	17.5	2001	2004
1995	18.0	2003	2007
1994	18.5		2006+
1993	17.3	2001	2005
1992	18.0	1997	2000
1991	17.0	1996	1999
1990	18.5	1998	2002
1989	16.5	1991	1994

SHIRAZ

Clare Valley $$$

1997	17.9	2002	2005+
1996	16.4	1998	2001
1995	17.0	2000	2003
1994	17.6	1999	2002
1993	17.4	2001	2005
1992	17.5	2000	2004
1991	17.3	1996	1999
1990	18.0	1995	1998

THE CABERNETS

Clare Valley $$$

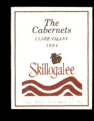

1997	17.5	2002	2005+
1996	17.8	2004	2008
1995	16.0	2000	2003
1994	17.5	2002	2006
1993	16.4	2001	2005
1992	16.8	2000	2004
1991	17.0	1996	1999
1990	17.0	1998	2002

Region: East Coast   Winemaker: Andrew Hood
Viticulturist: Rodney Lyne   Chief Executive: Rodney Lyne

Spring Vale has its settings all worked out. Its tiny vineyard is situated near Freycinet on Tasmania's warm east coast, where fruit usually ripens more regularly than in much of Tasmania. Its wine is being made by consultant Andrew Hood, whose pinot noirs for Winstead and Wellington are already raising the levels of expectation in Tasmania. Furthermore, it has a great label.

CHARDONNAY

East Coast $$$

1998	16.6	2000	2003
1997	18.0	2002	2005
1994	16.4	1996	1999
1993	16.4	1995	1996

Spring Vale

130 Spring Vale Road
Cranbrook Tas 7190
Tel: (03) 6257 8208
Fax: (03) 6257 8598

St Hallett

**St Hallett's Road
Tanunda SA 5352
Tel: (08) 8563 2319
Fax: (08) 8563 2901**

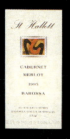

PINOT NOIR
East Coast $$$$

1998	17.5	2003	2006
1997	17.8	2002	2005
1996	14.5	1998	2001
1995	15.0	1997	2000
1994	16.5	1996	1999
1993	16.8	1998	2001
1992	16.8	1997	2000
1991	16.5	1996	1999
1990	16.0	1992	1995

Region: Barossa Valley Winemakers: Stuart Blackwell, Cathy Spratt
Viticulturist: Carl Lindner Chief Executive: Bob McLean

While its Old Block Shiraz is becoming increasingly difficult to find, I enjoy the ripeness, depth and softness of St Hallett's Blackwell Shiraz, a wine you can enjoy immediately upon release. The Faith Shiraz is a lighter wine again, with about the weight of a Cru Beaujolias. The Chardonnay and Semillon are made in the soft, broad and generous style you'd expect from the Barossa floor.

BLACKWELL SHIRAZ
Barossa Valley $$$$

1996	17.5	2004	2008
1995	16.0	2000	2003
1994	17.9	1999	2002+

CABERNET MERLOT
Barossa Valley $$$

1996	16.1	2001	2004
1995	16.0	1997	2000
1994	16.8	1996	1999
1993	17.0	1998	2001
1992	17.5	2000	2004
1991	16.4	1999	2003
1990	17.3	1995	1998

CHARDONNAY
Barossa Valley $$$

1997	15.6	1999	2002
1996	15.3	1997	1998
1995	16.1	1997	2000
1994	17.1	1996	1999
1993	16.5	1995	1998
1992	15.5	1994	1997
1991	18.0	1996	1999

EDEN VALLEY RIESLING
Eden Valley $$$

1998	17.2	2003	2006+
1997	18.2	2002	2005+
1996	16.6	2001	2004

FAITH SHIRAZ
Barossa Valley $$$

1997	16.5	1998	1999
1996	15.8	1998	2001
1995	16.6	2000	2003
1994	16.9	1996	1999+

OLD BLOCK SHIRAZ
Barossa Valley $$$$

1995	16.8	2000	2003+
1994	18.5	2002	2006
1993	17.0	1998	2001
1992	17.8	1997	2000
1991	18.6	2003	2011
1990	10.2	1998	2002
1989	17.6	1997	2001
1988	18.6	2000	2008
1987	17.0	1995	1999
1986	18.5	1998	2003
1985	17.5	1993	1997

SEMILLON SELECT
Barossa Valley $$$

1997	17.1	1999	2002
1996	16.5	1998	2001
1995	15.1	1996	1997

St Huberts

St Huberts Rd
Coldstream Vic 3770
Tel: (03) 9739 1118
Fax: (03) 9739 1096

Region: Yarra Valley Winemaker: Fi Purnell
Viticulturist: Damien de Castella Chief Executive: Ray King

Since the early 1970s, when the Cester family adopted the name of one of Victoria's largest vineyards of last century for their Yarra Valley venture (the present vineyard is not believed to be planted on the previous St Huberts vineyard site), the property has had one of the most chequered careers imaginable, despite making the occasional head-turning wine in the process. Mildara Blass is talking up its determination to restore St Huberts to the Yarra's elite, making its wines in a longer-living style than its near neighbour and stablemate of Yarra Ridge.

CABERNET SAUVIGNON
Yarra Valley $$$

1997	17.9	2005	2009+
1996	16.0	1998	2001
1995	17.9	2000	2003
1994	18.3	2002	2006
1993	17.0	1998	2003
1992	18.2	2000	2004
1991	18.2	1999	2003
1990	16.8	1998	2002

CHARDONNAY
Yarra Valley $$$

1997	15.3	1999	2002
1996	16.0	1998	2001
1995	17.5	2000	2003
1994	17.8	1999	2002
1993	17.4	1998	2001
1992	18.6	1997	2000+
1991	17.5	1996	1999

PINOT NOIR
Yarra Valley $$$

1998	16.0	2000	2003
1997	16.0	2002	2005
1996	16.3	1998	2001
1995	16.8	2000	2003
1994	14.5	1995	1996
1993	18.1	1998	2001
1992	16.3	1994	1997
1991	18.1	1993	1996
1990	17.0	1992	1995

St Leonards

Wahgunyah Vic 3687
Tel: (02) 6033 1004
Fax: (02) 6033 3636

Region: NE Victoria Winemaker: Peter Brown
Viticulturist: Peter Brown Chief Executive: Peter Brown

Peter Brown, one of Milawa's Brown Brothers, has purchased St Leonards from the family business together with the historic and adjacent All Saints property. It's too early to see precisely where he intends to take the brand, which is still fondly regarded as a fine maker of regional northeast Victorian table wines.

WAHGUNYAH SHIRAZ

NE Victoria $$$

1997	17.5	2005	2009
1996	16.7	1998	2001
1995	15.7	2000	2003
1994	17.4	2004	2008

Stanton & Killeen

Murray Valley Highway
Rutherglen Vic 3685
Tel: (02) 6032 9457
Fax: (02) 6032 8018

Region: NE Victoria Winemaker: Chris Killeen
Viticulturist: Lynton Enever Chief Executive: Norm Killeen

Stanton & Killeen's red wines exemplify the richness, softness and generosity of the best from northeast Victoria, while its Vintage Port is the only serious Australian rival to that of Chateau Reynella.

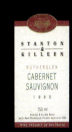

CABERNET SAUVIGNON

NE Victoria $$$

1996	16.0	2000	2003
1995	16.5	2000	2003
1992	17.8		2004+
1991	17.5	1999	2003
1990	16.4		2002+
1988	15.0	1996	2000
1987	17.0	1995	1999
1986	17.1	1994	1998
1985	16.1	1993	1997

DURIF

NE Victoria $$$

1997	16.7		2009+
1996	17.0		2007+
1995	17.1		2007+
1994	16.4		2006+
1992	17.8		2004+
1991	15.8	1999	2003
1990	18.0		2002+
1988	18.0		2000+
1987	16.5	1999	2004
1986	17.0	1998	2003

SHIRAZ
NE Victoria $$$

1996	17.2	2004	2008
1995	16.8		2005+
1993	17.5		2005+
1992	18.3		2004+
1991	16.6	1999	2003
1990	17.8		2002+
1988	15.5	1996	2000
1987	17.5	1995	1999
1985	16.5	1993	1997

SHIRAZ CABERNET BLEND
NE Victoria $$$

1997	17.0	2005	2009+
1996	17.0	2004	2008+
1995	16.6		2007+
1994	16.5		2006+
1992	17.6		2004+

VINTAGE PORT
NE Victoria $$$

1993	18.4		2005+
1992	18.6		2004+
1991	18.5		2003+
1990	18.2	1998	2002
1989	17.2	1997	2001
1988	18.5	2000	2005
1987	16.5	1999	2004
1986	18.6		2006+
1985	17.0	1997	2002
1984	16.0	1996	2001

Region: Mornington Peninsula Winemaker: Tod Dexter
Viticulturist: Stuart Marshall Chief Executive: Tod Dexter

The Stonier wines are amongst the finest and most consistent of those from Victoria's Mornington Peninsula region and are graded into early-drinking regional wines plus the sought-after Reserve label, whose Pinot Noir and Chardonnay are right up there with the finest Australian cool climate examples of these varieties. Stonier still makes far too much Cabernet from my point of view, but are hardly likely to scale down this somewhat errant use of their resources while Melburnians take the stuff away in truckloads from the cellar door!

Stonier

362 Frankston-Flinders Rd
Merricks Vic 3916
Tel: (03) 5989 8300
Fax: (03) 5989 8709

CABERNET

Mornington Peninsula $$$

1997	15.0	1999	2002+
1995	14.5	1997	2000
1994	15.0	1998	2001
1993	16.7	1998	2001
1992	16.5	2000	2004
1991	17.0	1999	2003
1990	16.5	1992	1995

CHARDONNAY

Mornington Peninsula $$$

1998	16.5	1999	2000
1997	16.5	1998	2001
1996	17.0	1998	2001
1995	17.0	1997	2000
1994	16.5	1996	1999
1993	17.0	1995	1998
1992	16.6	1997	2000
1991	10.5	1996	1999

PINOT NOIR

Mornington Peninsula $$$

1998	16.6	1999	2000
1997	16.5	1999	2002
1996	17.6	2001	2004
1995	16.0	1997	2000
1994	16.8	1996	1999
1993	17.4	1995	1998
1992	16.5	1994	1997
1991	17.0	1993	1996
1990	16.0	1992	1995

RESERVE CABERNET
Mornington Peninsula $$$$

1995	14.8	2000	2003
1993	17.6	2001	2005
1992	17.5	2000	2004
1991	16.6	1999	2003
1990	17.0	1998	2002
1989	16.0	1994	1997
1988	18.2	1996	2000
1987	15.7	1992	1995

RESERVE CHARDONNAY
Mornington Peninsula $$$$

1997	18.6	2002	2005
1996	17.8	1998	2001
1995	17.8	2003	2007
1994	18.2	1996	1999
1993	17.5	1998	2001
1992	18.2	1994	1997
1991	17.0	1996	1999
1990	18.0	1995	1998
1989	16.0	1991	1994

RESERVE PINOT NOIR
Mornington Peninsula $$$$

1997	18.7	2002	2005
1995	14.0	1997	2000
1994	17.2	1996	1999
1993	18.6	1998	2001
1992	18.2	1997	2000
1991	16.6	1993	1996
1990	17.5	1992	1995

Region: Lower Hunter Valley Winemaker: Neil Sutherland
Viticulturist: Nicholas Sutherland Chief Executive: Neil Sutherland

Sutherland's traditional Hunter portfolio of Shiraz, Chardonnay and unwooded Semillon evolve in the classic Hunter style, creating generous, complex wines after around five years in the bottle.

Sutherland

**Deasey's Road
Pokolbin NSW 2320
Tel: (02) 4998 7650
Fax: (02) 4998 7603**

CHARDONNAY
Lower Hunter Valley $$$

1996	14.9	1997	1998
1994	16.5	1999	2002
1993	14.5	1994	1995
1992	15.8	1997	1997

SEMILLON
Lower Hunter Valley $$

1995	16.5	2003	2007
1994	17.7	1999	2002
1993	17.0	2001	2005
1991	17.3	1996	1999
1990	14.8	1992	1995
1989	18.0	1994	1997

SHIRAZ
Lower Hunter Valley $$

1994	18.1	2002	2006
1993	15.0	1995	1998
1992	15.8	1997	2000
1991	17.1	1999	2003
1990	15.5	1992	1995
1989	18.5	1994	1997

Region: Pyrenees Winemaker: Shane Clohesy
Viticulturist: Philippe Bru Chief Executive: Chris Markell

The man instrumental to its name and the very personal identity of its wines, Dominique Portet, has left the company, leaving a fresh challenge to the team headed by Chris Markell. There's been a gradual move in Taltarni's reds to a softer and more approachable style which, while still able to appreciate cellaring, does not demand it in the nature of vintages past.

Taltarni
Taltarni Road
Moonambel Vic 3478
Tel: (03) 5467 2218
Fax: (03) 5467 2306

CABERNET SAUVIGNON
Pyrenees $$$$

1996	16.8	2004	2008
1995	18.0	2007	2015
1994	18.2	2006	2014+
1993	17.6	2005	2013
1992	18.0	2004	2012+
1991	18.3	2003	2011+
1990	18.0	2002	2010+
1989	16.1	1997	2001
1988	18.5	2000	2008
1987	16.7	1999	2007
1986	16.8	1998	2006
1985	17.3	1987	2005
1984	18.2	1996	2004
1983	16.8		2003+
1982	17.5		2002+
1981	15.8	1989	1993
1980	16.0	1988	1992
1979	19.2		1999+

MERLOT (MERLOT CABERNET FRANC 1988 TO 1990)

Pyrenees $$$$

1996	17.3	2001	2004
1995	17.9	2003	2007
1994	18.0	2002	2006
1993	17.9	2001	2005
1992	16.8	2000	2004
1991	16.8	1999	2003+
1990	18.2	1988	2002
1989	17.0	1994	1997
1988	18.3	2000	2008

RESERVE CABERNET SAUVIGNON

Pyrenees $$$$$

1994	18.1		2004+
1992	18.6		2012+
1988	18.3		2008+
1984	18.4		2004+
1979	19.2	1999	2009

SAUVIGNON BLANC (FORMERLY FUME BLANC)

Pyrenees $$$

1998	16.3	1999	2000
1997	15.8	1997	1998
1996	16.5	1998	2001
1995	15.0	1997	2000
1994	17.9	1996	1999
1993	16.5	1998	2001
1992	17.0	1994	1997

SHIRAZ (FORMERLY FRENCH SYRAH)

Pyrenees $$$$

1997	18.7	2005	2009+
1996	18.6	2004	2008
1995	16.0	2000	2003
1994	17.8	1999	2002
1993	18.4	2001	2005
1992	18.5		2004+
1991	18.2		2003+
1990	16.7	1998	2002+
1989	16.5	1997	2001
1988	18.5	2000	2008
1987	16.5	1995	1999
1986	18.5	1994	1998
1985	18.7	1997	2005+
1984	17.0	1992	1996
1983	16.5		2003+
1982	17.5	1990	1994
1981	18.0	1989	1993

Region: Yarra Valley Winemaker: Clare Halloran
Viticulturist: Lindsay Corby Chief Executive: Daniel Besen

Despite some regular baton changes in the winemaking position Tarrawarra has consistently made excellent Chardonnay and Pinot Noir from its mature Yarra Valley vineyard. While the Chardonnay's style has barely altered from the richly structured, creamy and secondary wines on which Tarrawarra first made its name, the Pinot Noir has steadily acquired more suppleness and fleshiness. Recent tastings of the 1992 stamp it as one of the true Yarra classics.

CHARDONNAY

Yarra Valley $$$$

1997	18.6	2005	2009
1996	17.5	2001	2004
1995	17.5	2000	2003+
1994	16.5	1996	1999
1993	18.3	1998	2001+
1992	18.8	2000	2004
1991	18.5	1996	1999
1990	17.6	1995	1998
1989	17.7	1997	2001
1988	18.5	1993	1996
1987	17.0	1995	1999
1986	17.3	1991	1994

Tarrawarra

Healesville Road
Yarra Glen Vic 3775
Tel: (03) 5962 3311
Fax: (03) 5962 3887

PINOT NOIR

Yarra Valley $$$$

1997	17.3	1992	1995
1996	18.6	2001	2004+
1995	18.2	2000	2003
1994	18.2	1999	2002
1993	16.7	1998	2001
1992	18.8	2000	2004
1991	16.5	1999	2003
1990	15.0	1998	2002
1989	15.3	1994	1997
1988	15.0	1993	1996

Tatachilla

151 Main Road
McLaren Vale SA 5171
Tel: (08) 8323 8656
Fax: (08) 8323 9096

Region: McLaren Vale Winemaker: Justin McNamee
Viticulturist: Vic Zerella Chief Executive: Keith Smith

Tatachilla is a successful wine producer in McLaren Vale which from time to time augments its fruit with that from other South Australian regions, especially in its cheaper labels. The Foundation Shiraz is a typical contemporary expression of the variety: very thick, concentrated and chock-full of American oak.

FOUNDATION SHIRAZ

McLaren Vale $$$$

1997	16.8	1999	2002+
1996	16.7	2001	2004
1995	16.0	1997	2000

Taylors

Mintaro Road
Auburn SA 5451
Tel: (08) 8849 2008
Fax: (08) 8849 2240

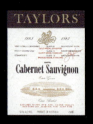

Region: Clare Valley Winemakers: Susan Mickan, Kelvin Budarick
Viticulturists: Ken Noack, Kate Strachan Chief Executive: Neil Jericho

Taylors is a large Clare Valley vineyard which successfully goes about its business of making early-drinking regional wines and selling them to those content to stay with a label they have learned to trust. I can't help thinking it should do more.

CABERNET SAUVIGNON

Clare Valley $$

1997	14.8	1999	2002
1996	15.0	1998	2001
1995	15.7	1997	2000
1994	16.3	1999	2002
1993	14.8	2001	2005
1992	15.2	2000	2004
1991	16.7	1999	2003
1990	16.0	1995	1998
1989	15.1	1997	2001

CHARDONNAY

Clare Valley $$

1996	16.4	2001	2004
1995	16.2	2000	2003
1994	15.0	1996	1999
1993	16.5	1995	1998
1992	17.3	1997	2000
1991	16.0	1993	1996

CLARE RIESLING (FORMERLY RHINE RIESLING)

Clare Valley $

1998	15.6	2000	2003
1997	15.6	1999	2002
1996	17.8	2004	2008
1994	18.2	2002	2006
1993	16.8	1995	1998

SHIRAZ (FORMERLY HERMITAGE)

Clare Valley $$

1997	16.5	2002	2005
1996	16.0	2001	2004
1995	16.5	2000	2003
1994	16.0	1996	1999
1993	16.3	1998	2001
1992	16.7	1997	2000
1991	17.5	1999	2003
1990	14.0	1995	1998
1989	16.5	1994	1997
1988	15.0	1993	1996

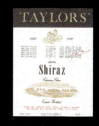

Region: Mudgee Winemaker: David Robertson
Viticulturist: David Robertson Chief Executive: David Robertson

I really enjoy the way David Robertson puts together his muscular, earthy and robust Cabernet Sauvignon and figgy, chalky Chardonnay, with its typically regional zesty citrus marmalade fruit.

CABERNET SAUVIGNON

Mudgee $$$

1995	17.5	2003	2007
1994	16.8	2002	2006+
1993	15.8	2001	2005
1992	16.8		2004+
1991	17.8		2003+
1990	18.2	1998	2002

Thistle Hill

McDonalds Road
Mudgee NSW 2850
Tel: (02) 6373 3546
Fax: (02) 6373 3540

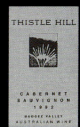

Thomas Mitchell

**Mitchellstown via
Nagambie Vic 3608
Tel: (03) 5794 2710
Fax: (03) 5794 2615**

CHARDONNAY
Mudgee $$$

1997	15.2	2002	2005
1996	17.3	2004	2008
1994	14.5	1999	2002
1993	16.9	2001	2005
1992	17.3	2000	2004
1991	16.4	1993	1996
1990	18.3	1995	1998

Region: Goulburn Valley Winemakers: Don Lewis, Alan George
Viticulturist: John Beresford Chief Executive: Paul van der Lee

The Thomas Mitchell blend of cabernet sauvignon, cabernet franc and shiraz frequently displays attractive ripe cassis-like fruit and regional mint/menthol overtones. The more affordable of Mitchelton's tier of labels, this range usually offers attractive value for the drinking dollar.

CABERNET SHIRAZ CABERNET FRANC
Goulburn Valley $$

1997	14.8	1998	1999
1995	16.2	1997	2000
1994	16.2	1999	2002
1993	15.1	1995	1998
1992	16.6	1997	2000
1991	17.8	1996	1999
1990	16.5	1995	1998

CHARDONNAY
Goulburn Valley $$

1998	16.7	1999	2002
1997	17.0	1999	2002
1996	15.3	1998	2001

Region: Clare Valley Winemaker: Tim Adams
Viticulturist: Tim Adams Chief Executives: Tim Adams, Pam Goldsack

Tim Adams commitment towards the traditional wines of the Clare Valley is expressed not only in the choice of wines he makes, but in the finely crafted manner he goes about it. His wines show considerably more restraint and tightness than the fleshy and highly oaked wines so popular in the mass market, even with the cult-like The Fergus, made from old grenache vines. Together with the new release of the premier Aberfeldy red (shiraz), each of Tim Adams' latest wines from semillon, dry and sweet, is of particular quality, even if there's not much evidence of botrytis in the 1998 Botrytis Affected Semillon.

ABERFELDY
Clare Valley $$$$$

1997	19.0	2005	2009+
1996	18.3	2004	2008
1995	18.7		2007+
1994	19.2		2006+
1993	18.9		2005+
1992	18.5		2004+
1991	17.0	1999	2003
1990	18.0		2002+

BOTRYTIS AFFECTED SEMILLON
Clare Valley $$$

1998	18.3	2003	2006
1997	17.0	2002	2005
1994	17.0	2002	2006
1992	17.6	1997	2000
1991	17.5	1999	2003
1990	16.7	1995	1998

CABERNET
Clare Valley $$

1997	16.8	2002	2005
1996	16.9	2004	2008
1995	16.8	2003	2007
1994	16.5	2002	2006
1993	17.1	2001	2005
1992	17.7	2000	2004
1991	17.2		2003+
1990	17.2	1998	2002

Tim Adams
**Warenda Rd
Clare SA 5453
Tel: (08) 8842 2429
Fax: (08) 8842 3550**

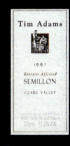

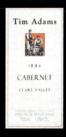

THE ONWINE AUSTRALIAN WINE ANNUAL **2000** 27

RIESLING
Clare Valley $$

1998	17.7	2006	2010
1997	18.5	2005	2009
1996	17.5	2004	2008
1995	15.3	1997	2000
1994	18.2	2002	2006
1993	18.2	2001	2005
1992	18.5	2000	2004
1991	17.0	1999	2003
1990	18.0		2002+

SEMILLON
Clare Valley $$

1997	18.5	2002	2005+
1996	17.9	2004	2008
1995	15.4	1997	2000
1994	18.3		2006+
1993	17.6	2001	2005
1992	17.7	2000	2004
1991	18.0	1999	2003
1990	17.5		2002+

SHIRAZ
Clare Valley $$

1997	17.8	2002	2005
1996	15.9	2001	2004
1995	17.4	2003	2007
1994	17.8	1999	2002
1993	17.2	1995	1998
1992	17.9	2000	2004
1991	17.5	1999	2003
1990	18.1	1998	2002
1989	17.2	1997	2001
1988	18.0	1996	2000
1987	17.7	1995	1999
1986	17.0	1994	1998

THE FERGUS GRENACHE
Clare Valley $$

1998	18.2	2003	2006+
1997	17.8	2002	2005
1996	17.4	2001	2004
1995	18.0	2000	2003
1994	17.9	2002	2006
1993	18.1	1998	2001

Region: Barossa Valley Winemaker: Neville Falkenberg
Viticulturist: Allen Jenkins   Chief Executive: Bruce Kemp

Tollana is a lesser-feted portion of the Southcorp Empire, but that doesn't mean it's not worth taking seriously. The TR222 Cabernet Sauvignon is a comparatively lean, reserved but polished act that is designed for the cellar, while the TR16 Shiraz is a spicy, savoury faster-maturing wine finished in creamy vanilla oak. Tollana's crisp dry whites are usually ready to enjoy at release, while the intensity and quality of its Botrytis Riesling often belies its affordable price.

Tollana

**Tanunda Road
Nuriootpa SA 5355
Tel: (08) 8560 9389
Fax: (08) 8560 9494**

BOTRYTIS RIESLING
Coonawarra and Eden Valley $$$

1997	15.3	1999	2002
1996	16.0	1998	2001
1995	18.5	2000	2003
1994	17.0	1997	2000
1993	15.6	1995	1998
1992	18.3	1997	2000
1991	16.7	1996	1999
1990	17.5	1995	1998

CABERNET SAUVIGNON BIN TR222
Adelaide Hills $$$

1997	18.5	2005	2009+
1996	17.4	2004	2008
1994	18.3		2006+
1993	18.1		2005+
1992	17.8	2000	2004
1991	17.0	2003	2011
1990	14.5	1992	1995
1988	17.8	1096	2000
1987	17.7	1992	1995
1986	18.0	1994	1998

CHARDONNAY
Eden Valley $$

1998	15.6	2000	2003
1997	18.2	2002	2005
1996	16.3	1998	2001
1995	15.3	1996	1997
1994	16.8	1996	1999
1993	17.0	1995	1998

Trentham Estate

**Sturt Highway
Trentham Cliffs NSW 2738
Tel: (03) 5024 8888
Fax: (03) 5024 8800**

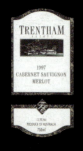

EDEN VALLEY RIESLING

Eden Valley $

1998	16.7	2000	2003
1995	16.5	1997	2000
1994	17.0	2002	2006
1993	16.6	1995	1998
1992	15.6	1993	1994

SHIRAZ BIN TR16

Eden Valley $$$

1996	16.2	2001	2004
1995	15.8	1997	2000
1994	15.8	1999	2002
1993	16.5	1998	2001
1992	18.4	2000	2004
1991	16.5	1999	2003
1990	16.0	1995	1998
1988	18.5	1993	1996

Region: Murray River Valley Winemaker: Anthony Murphy
Viticulturist: Pat Murphy Chief Executive: Anthony Murphy

While 1997 vintage conditions didn't make life easy for Tony Murphy, Trentham Estate well deserves its reputation for its soft, approachable red wines, most of which develop quite readily with bottle-aged complexity after just a couple of years. The 1996 Shiraz shows just how good they can be.

CABERNET SAUVIGNON MERLOT

Murray River $$

1997	15.0	1999	2002
1996	16.5	2001	2004
1995	15.0	1997	2000
1994	14.0	1995	1996
1993	16.6	1998	2001
1992	15.5	1994	1997
1991	16.1	1993	1996
1990	18.0	1992	1995

CHARDONNAY
Murray River $$

1998	15.0	1999	2000
1997	15.3	1998	1999
1996	17.0	1998	2001
1995	15.8	1997	2000
1994	16.5	1996	1999
1993	17.8	1995	1998
1992	16.2	1994	1997

MERLOT
Murray River $$

1997	15.6	1999	2002
1996	15.7	1998	2001
1995	16.0	1997	2000
1994	16.9	1996	1999
1993	16.2	1995	1998
1992	16.5	1993	1994
1991	17.0	1996	1999

SHIRAZ
Murray River $$

1997	16.3	1999	2002
1996	18.1	2001	2004
1995	16.7	2000	2003
1994	16.0	1996	1999
1993	16.5	1995	1998
1992	16.8	1997	2000

Region: Mornington Peninsula Winemaker: Daniel Greene
Viticulturist: Shane Strange Chief Executive: Peter Hollick

It's taken time and effort at Tuck's Ridge for it to make wines that perform to the expectations of owner Peter Hollick. Hopefully the rich, concentrated and complex 1997 Pinot Noir will prove to be something of a turning point.

PINOT NOIR
Mornington Peninsula $$$$

1998	16.9	2000	2003
1997	17.5	1999	2002
1996	16.2	1998	2001

Tuck's Ridge

37 Red Hill/Shoreham Rd
Red Hill South Vic 3937
Tel: (03) 5989 8660
Fax: (03) 5989 8579

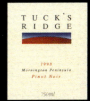

Tulloch

"Glen Elgin"
De Beyers Road
Pokolbin NSW 2321
Tel: (02) 4998 7503
Fax: (02) 4998 7682

Region: Lower Hunter Valley Winemaker: Pat Auld
Viticulturist: Jerome Scarborough Chief Executive: Bruce Kemp

Other than the excellent Hector of Glen Elgin, an old-fashioned Hunter red with several modern attachments, it's difficult to get too excited about the Tulloch range of wines, which seems to depend excessively on an outdated sparkling wine from semillon, a lean and ungenerous Verdelho and a simple and unsatisfying Unwooded Chardonnay. Surely it deserves better than this.

HECTOR OF GLEN ELGIN
Lower Hunter Valley $$$$ 4

1995	16.6	2003	2007
1994	18.2	2002	2006
1991	17.9		2003+
1989	16.5	1997	2001
1987	18.6	1999	2004
1986	16.7	1994	1998

HUNTER CUVÉE
Lower Hunter Valley $$ 5

1994	16.0	1996	1999
1992	16.5	1997	2000
1991	16.0	1993	1996
1990	17.7	1992	1995

VERDELHO
Lower Hunter Valley $$

1998	16.5	2000	2003
1997	14.5	1998	1999
1996	15.3	1996	1997
1995	16.6	1996	1997
1994	16.8	1996	1999
1993	16.3	1995	1998

Tunnel Hill

**Healesville Road
Yarra Glen Vic 3775
Tel: (03) 5962 3311
Fax: (03) 5962 3887**

Region: Yarra Valley Winemaker: Clare Halloran
Viticulturist: Lindsay Corby Chief Executive: Daniel Besen

By its own standards Tunnel Hill, Tarrawarra's once-feted second label, has not performed to par over the last two releases. The Chardonnay is especially disappointing, even to the extent that its requires some serious remedy.

PINOT NOIR
Yarra Valley $$$

1998	16.1	1999	2000
1997	16.7	1999	2002
1996	17.0	1998	2001
1995	15.4	1996	1997
1994	18.4	1996	1999
1993	17.0	1995	1998
1992	15.7	1994	1997
1991	15.5	1996	1999
1990	17.0	1992	1995

Tyrrell's

**Broke Road
Pokolbin NSW 2320
Tel: (02) 4993 7000
Fax: (02) 4998 7723**

Region: Lower Hunter Valley Winemakers: Andrew Spinaze, Andrew Thomas
Viticulturist: Cliff Currie Chief Executive: Bruce Tyrrell

Tyrrell's is one of the Hunter Valley's most illustrious winemakers and has enjoyed an exceptional decade in the 1990s with both red and white Hunter wines, principally from shiraz, semillon and chardonnay. The company is presently shifting its focus towards other wine regions, especially McLaren Vale and Heathcote. Its 1997 Rufus Stone Shiraz from Heathcote should greatly encourage Tyrrell's, which has invested heavily in a large vineyard there.

BROKENBACK SHIRAZ
Lower Hunter Valley $$$

1997	16.0	1999	2002
1996	15.1	1998	2001
1995	16.8	2000	2003
1994	17.2	2002	2006

LOST BLOCK SEMILLON
Lower Hunter Valley $$$

1998	18.3	2003	2006+
1997	17.1	2002	2005+
1996	17.8	2004	2008
1995	16.7	2000	2003+

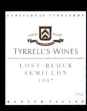

MOON MOUNTAIN CHARDONNAY

Lower Hunter Valley $$$

1998	17.0	2000	2003+
1997	17.4	1999	2002
1996	17.0	1998	2001

OLD WINERY CABERNET MERLOT

Various $$

1997	15.3	1999	2002
1996	15.0	1998	2001
1995	15.8	1997	2000
1994	16.2	1996	1999
1993	15.8	1998	2001
1991	17.1	1996	1999

OLD WINERY CHARDONNAY

Lower Hunter Valley $$

1998	14.0	1998	1999
1997	15.7	1998	1999
1996	15.6	1997	1998
1995	16.5	1997	1998

OLD WINERY PINOT NOIR

Lower Hunter Valley $$

1998	15.0	1999	2000
1997	15.6	1999	2002
1996	15.2	2001	2004
1995	15.0	2000	2003

OLD WINERY SHIRAZ

Lower Hunter Valley $$

1997	15.2	1999	2002
1996	17.3	2001	2004
1995	16.8	1997	2000
1993	14.5	1995	1998
1992	17.0	2000	2004
1991	15.3	1996	1999

284 2000 THE ONWINE AUSTRALIAN WINE ANNUAL

RUFUS STONE CABERNET SAUVIGNON

Coonawarra $$$$

1996	15.2	2001	2004
1995	15.1	2000	2003
1994	16.6	2002	2006
1993	16.0	1998	2001
1992	14.8	1994	1997

SHEE-OAK CHARDONNAY

Lower Hunter Valley $$$

1998	15.4	1999	2000
1997	17.0	1998	1999
1996	16.8	1997	1998

VAT 1 SEMILLON

Lower Hunter Valley $$$

1998	17.9	2006	2010+
1997	18.7		2009+
1996	18.5		2008+
1995	18.6		2007+
1994	18.0	2002	2006
1993	16.8	1998	2001
1992	18.6	2004	2012
1991	17.4	1999	2003
1990	16.6	1998	2002
1989	15.8	1991	1994
1988	16.5	1993	1996
1987	17.8	1999	2007
1986	18.8	1998	2008
1985	16.5	1993	1997
1984	18.2	1996	2004
1983	16.7	1995	2003
1982	18.0	1994	2002
1981	17.0	1989	1993
1980	18.0	1992	2000

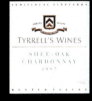

VAT 5 NVC SHIRAZ
Lower Hunter Valley $$$

1998	16.5	2003	2006
1996	16.7	1998	2001
1995	17.7	2000	2003
1994	16.6	1996	1999
1993	16.2	1998	2001
1992	16.5	1997	2000
1990	16.5	1998	2002
1989	17.0	1997	2001
1988	14.5	1993	1996
1987	17.5	1995	1999
1986	14.0	1991	1994

VAT 6 PINOT NOIR
Lower Hunter Valley $$$$

1997	17.9	2002	2005
1996	15.3	2001	2004
1994	17.2	1999	2002
1993	14.5	1995	1998
1992	15.6	1997	2000
1991	14.5	1993	1996
1990	16.9	1995	1998
1989	17.6	1994	1997

VAT 8 SHIRAZ CABERNET
Lower Hunter Valley, Coonawarra $$$

1997	17.8	2005	2009+
1996	17.5	2001	2004
1995	18.1	2003	2007
1994	17.8	2002	2006
1993	18.0	2001	2005
1992	18.0	1997	2000
1991	17.5	1999	2003

VAT 9 SHIRAZ
Lower Hunter Valley $$$$

1997	18.4	2005	2009
1996	16.4	2004	2008
1995	18.1	2003	2007
1994	17.6	1999	2002
1993	16.3	1998	2001
1992	18.0	1997	2000
1991	18.8		2003+
1990	17.2	2002	2007

VAT 11 BAULKHAM SHIRAZ

Lower Hunter Valley $$$$

1998	18.5	2006	2010+
1996	17.6	2004	2008
1995	18.6	2003	2007
1994	18.1	2002	2006
1993	17.3	1998	2001
1992	18.2	2000	2004

VAT 47 PINOT CHARDONNAY

Lower Hunter Valley $$$$

1997	18.1	2005	2009
1996	18.4	2004	2008
1995	18.3	2000	2003
1994	18.0	1999	2002
1993	18.5	2001	2005
1992	18.5	1997	2000
1991	17.5	1999	2003
1990	18.0		2002+
1989	18.1	1997	2001
1988	14.0	1990	1993
1987	16.5	1995	1999
1986	18.6	1994	1998

Region: Margaret River Winemaker: Clive Otto
Viticulturist: Bruce Pearce Chief Executive: Bob Baker

Owned by Janet Holmes a Court, Vasse Felix is a rapidly expanding Margaret River vineyard with a brand new winery overlooking the lake on its original property. Its leading current releases include the spicy 1997 Shiraz and the very promising Heylesbury dry red blend of the same year, a classy, polished and balanced wine displaying pristine small red and black berry fruit.

Vasse Felix

**Cnr Caves Road and
Harmans Road South
Cowaramup WA 6284
Tel: (08) 9755 5242
Fax: (08) 9755 5425**

CABERNET MERLOT (FORMERLY CLASSIC DRY RED)

Margaret River $$$

1997	16.4	2002	2005
1996	16.5	2001	2004
1995	16.2	2000	2003
1994	16.6	1996	1999
1993	16.0	1995	1998
1992	17.5	2000	2004
1991	16.8	1999	2003
1990	16.0	1995	1998

THE ONWINE AUSTRALIAN WINE ANNUAL **2000**

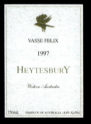

CABERNET SAUVIGNON

Margaret River $$$$

1997	16.7	2002	2005+
1996	17.5	2001	2004+
1995	17.8	2003	2007
1994	18.2		2006+
1993	16.5	1995	1998
1991	18.0		2003+
1990	17.9	1998	2002
1989	17.5	1997	2001
1988	18.5	1996	2000

CHARDONNAY

Margaret River $$$

1997	16.0	1999	2002
1996	16.6	1998	2001
1995	17.4	2000	2003
1994	18.1	1999	2002
1993	18.5	1998	2001
1992	16.0	1997	2000
1991	16.5	1993	1996
1990	16.5	1995	1998

CLASSIC DRY WHITE

Margaret River $$$

1998	16.0	1999	2000
1997	15.0	1998	1999
1996	15.7	1998	2001
1995	14.8	1996	1997
1994	16.2	1996	1999
1993	17.5	1995	1998

HEYTESBURY

Margaret River $$$$$

1997	18.2	2005	2009
1996	16.7	2002	2008
1995	18.4	2003	2007+

SHIRAZ
Margaret River $$$$

1997	18.0	2005	2009
1996	17.1	2001	2004
1995	18.3	2000	2003
1994	18.2	2002	2006
1993	16.1	1998	2001
1992	16.7	2000	2004
1991	16.5	1999	2003

Region: Macedon Winemaker: Mark Sheppard
Viticulturist: Mark Sheppard Chief Executive: John Quirk

Its linear, lightly greenish and finely astringent 1997 'V' wine is the best Virgin Hills release for several seasons. Now under new ownership but back in the winemaking hands of Mark Sheppard, there's every reason to expect big things from this former icon amongst small Victorian wine brands.

VIRGIN HILLS
Macedon $$$$

1997	17.2	2005	2009
1995	14.8	1997	2000
1994	16.5	2002	2006
1993	16.3	2001	2005
1992	18.6	2000	2004
1991	18.4		2003+
1990	16.5	1998	2002
1988	18.2	1996	2000
1987	16.8	1999	2004
1985	18.3	1993	1997

Region: Margaret River Winemaker: Stuart Pym
Viticulturist: Michael Melsom Chief Executive: Michael Wright

Michael Wright has poured millions into Voyager Estate and the results are now coming through and into the bottle. The Chardonnay is becoming a consistent performer in the ripe, generous Margaret River style, but it's even more significant that 1994 and 1995 have produced two very classy, very polished Cabernet Merlot blends.

CHARDONNAY
Margaret River $$$$

1997	17.0	1999	2002
1996	17.6	1998	2001
1995	16.0	1997	2000
1994	17.0	1996	1999

THE ONWINE AUSTRALIAN WINE ANNUAL 2000

Virgin Hills

Piper Street
Kyneton Vic 3444
Tel: (03) 5422 7444
Fax: (03) 5422 7400

Voyager Estate

Lot 1 Gnarawary Rd
Margaret River WA 6285
Tel: (08) 9385 3133
Fax: (08) 9383 4029

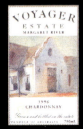

Wantirna Estate

10 Bushy Park Lane
Wantirna South Vic 3152
Tel: (03) 9801 2367
Fax: (03) 9887 0225

Region: Yarra Valley Winemakers: Reg Egan, Maryann Egan
Viticulturist: Reg Egan Chief Executive: Reg Egan

A welcome inclusion in this edition, Wantirna Estate is certainly one of the jewels in the Yarra Valley's crown. In particular, the 1997 wines reveal a rare combination of pure varietal intensity with finely honed balance. The 1997 Lily Pinot Noir and Amelia Cabernet Sauvignon Merlot provided one of the highlights in researching this edition.

AMELIA CABERNET SAUVIGNON MERLOT

Yarra Valley $$$$

1997	19.0	2005	2009
1996	15.2	1998	2001
1995	18.0	1998	2001

ISABELLA CHARDONNAY

Yarra Valley $$$$

1998	18.9	2003	2006+
1997	18.2	2002	2005+
1996	18.7	2001	2004+

LILY PINOT NOIR

Yarra Valley $$$$

1998	17.8	2003	2006
1997	18.7	2002	2005+
1996	17.9	2001	2004

Warramate

27 Maddens Lane
Gruyere Vic 3770
Tel: (03) 5964 9219
Fax: (03) 5964 9219

Region: Yarra Valley Winemakers: Jack Church, David Church
Viticulturist: Jack Church Chief Executive: Jack Church

Warramate is a small family-owned vineyard sited above the same slope as the Yarra Yering and Underhill vineyards and below that of the Coldstream Hills 'amphitheatre' block. Its red wines are generally light and herby.

CABERNET SAUVIGNON

Yarra Valley $$$

1996	14.5	1998	2001
1995	15.2	1997	2000+
1994	15.0	1999	2002
1992	15.0	1994	1997
1991	16.6	1996	1999
1990	17.5	1998	2002
1989	16.5	1997	2001
1988	16.5	1993	1996

RIESLING
Yarra Valley $$

1998	16.6	2003	2006+
1997	15.1	2002	2005
1996	15.3	1998	2001
1995	16.7	2000	2003
1994	18.2	2002	2006
1993	17.7	2001	2005
1991	17.4	1999	2003

Region: Pyrenees Winemaker: Luigi Bazzani
Viticulturist: Luigi Bazzani Chief Executive: Luigi Bazzani

Warrenmang is a brilliant little wine village complete with small conference centre, guest cottages and one of the best restaurants not only in provincial Australia but anywhere in Terra Australis. Its peppery, minty Shiraz is its most consistent wine, although the Grand Pyrenees has developed a loyal following for its robust, earthy style.

Warrenmang
Mountain Creek Road
Moonambel Vic 3478
Tel: (03) 5467 2233
Fax: (03) 5467 2309

GRAND PYRENEES (FORMERLY CABERNET SAUVIGNON
Pyrenees $$$$

1995	16.7	2003	2007
1993	16.6	2001	2005
1992	16.5	2000	2004
1990	16.5	2002	2007
1989	15.0	1997	2003
1988	17.5	2000	2005
1987	13.5	1999	2004
1986	17.5	1991	1994

SHIRAZ
Pyrenees $$$

1997	17.2	2002	2005+
1996	16.7	2004	2008
1995	14.6	2000	2003
1994	16.5	1999	2002
1993	17.0	2001	2005
1992	18.0		2004+
1991	17.0	1999	2003

THE ONWINE AUSTRALIAN WINE ANNUAL 2000

Water Wheel

Raywood Road
Bridgewater-on-Loddon
Vic 3516
Tel: (03) 5437 3060
Fax: (03) 5437 3082

Region: Bendigo Winemakers: Peter Cumming, Bill Trevaskis
Viticulturist: Peter Cumming Chief Executive: Peter Cumming

In its Shiraz and Cabernet Sauvignon Water Wheel makes two of the most-recommended of all Australian red wines under $20, a price point under which they sit with great comfort. The wines are typically generous, plush and smooth, with a wonderfully bright, ripe mouthfeel of intense berry fruit and supportive chocolate oak.

CABERNET SAUVIGNON
Bendigo $$

1997	17.8	2002	2005+
1996	17.5	2001	2004
1995	17.0	2000	2003
1994	18.0	1999	2002
1993	18.0	1998	2001
1992	18.2	1997	2000
1991	18.0	1996	1999
1990	18.0	1995	1998

CHARDONNAY
Bendigo $$

1998	15.0	1999	2000
1997	17.8	1998	1999
1996	15.2	1997	1998
1995	16.0	1997	2000
1994	17.5	1996	1999
1993	16.8	1995	1998
1992	15.6	1993	1994

SAUVIGNON BLANC
Bendigo $$

1998	15.0		1999
1996	16.1	1998	2001
1995	16.0	1996	1997
1994	16.0	1996	1999
1993	16.5	1995	1998

SHIRAZ
Bendigo $$

1997	17.2	2002	2005
1996	17.7	2001	2004
1995	16.7	1997	2000
1994	17.4	1999	2002
1993	17.6	1998	2001
1992	18.2	1997	2000
1991	17.0	1999	2003
1990	16.5	1998	2002

Wignalls

**5384 Chester Pass Road
Albany WA 6330
Tel: (08) 9841 2848
Fax: (08) 9842 9003**

Region: Great Southern Winemaker: Bill Wignall
Viticulturist: Robert Wignall Chief Executives: Pat, Bill Wignall

Wignalls is a small specialist maker of cool-climate table wines from its base at Albany in WA's Great Southern region. Recent Pinot Noir releases are recovering some of the vineyard's early 1990s form, while the 1998 Sauvignon Blanc confirms my expectations that Wignalls should become a leading maker of this variety. More dependent on season, the Cabernet is a lighter style.

CABERNET

Great Southern $$$

1997	16.5	2002	2005+
1996	15.8	2001	2004
1994	17.8	2002	2006+

CHARDONNAY

Great Southern $$$

1997	15.0	1998	1999
1996	15.6	1998	2001
1995	15.0	1997	2000
1994	16.7	1996	1999
1993	17.7	1998	2001
1992	15.5	1994	1997
1991	18.0	1996	1999

PINOT NOIR

Great Southern $$$$

1998	16.5	2000	2003
1997	16.8	1990	1999
1996	16.8	2001	2004
1995	14.0	1996	1997
1994	14.0	1995	1996
1993	16.5	1995	1998
1992	18.3	1997	2005

SAUVIGNON BLANC

Great Southern $$$

1998	18.0	1999	2000
1997	15.0		1998
1996	16.8	1997	1998
1995	17.7	1996	1997
1994	18.0	1995	1996

Wildwood

St John's Lane Wildwood
Bulla Vic 3428
Tel: (03) 9307 1118
Fax: (03) 9331 1590

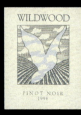

Region: Macedon Winemakers: Wayne Stott, Peter Dredge
Viticulturists: Peter Dredge, Wayne Stott Chief Executive: Wayne Stott

Wildwood is a small vineyard and winery near Bulla in Victoria's Macedon region which has proven capable of some delightfully intense fruit in its Shiraz, Cabernets blend and Pinot Noir.

PINOT NOIR

Macedon $$$

1998	17.0	2003	2006
1997	14.5	1999	2002
1996	15.0	1998	2001
1995	15.4	1997	2000
1994	15.3	1996	1999
1993	16.8	1998	2001
1992	16.8	1997	2000
1991	13.5	1993	1996
1990	14.0	1992	1995

Wilson Vineyard, The

Polish Hill River
Sevenhill via
Clare SA 5453
Tel: (08) 8843 4310

Region: Clare Valley Winemaker: Daniel Wilson
Viticulturist: Daniel Wilson Chief Executive: Daniel Wilson

Right out of the box, The Wilson Vineyard's wonderfully reserved 1998 Gallery Series Riesling simply oozes poise and style. Like most from this maker, it should cellar very gracefully indeed. While the Gallery Series Cabernet Sauvignon has slipped a little in recent vintages, the Hippocrene sparkling red remains a great source of fascination and pleasure.

GALLERY SERIES CABERNET SAUVIGNON

Clare Valley $$$

1996	15.2	2001	2004
1995	15.0	2000	2003
1994	17.9	2002	2006
1992	16.4	2000	2004
1991	16.8	1999	2003
1990	15.0	1995	1998
1989	16.0	1994	1997
1988	17.5	1996	2000
1987	18.0	1995	1999
1986	17.5	1994	1998

GALLERY SERIES RIESLING

Clare Valley $$

1998	18.7	2006	2010+
1997	16.0	2002	2005
1996	18.0	2004	2008
1995	18.5	2003	2007
1994	17.6	2002	2006
1993	17.3	1998	2001
1992	17.5	1997	2000
1991	17.6	1999	2003
1990	18.0	1998	2003
1989	15.0	1997	2001
1988	17.5	1993	1996

HIPPOCRENE

Clare Valley $$$

1994	15.0	1996	1999
Bin 93	14.5	1998	2001
Bin 92	15.0	1997	2000
Bin 91	17.7	1996	1999
Bin 90	18.2	1998	2002

Region: Southern Tasmania Winemaker: Andrew Hood
Viticulturist: Neil Snare Chief Executive: Neil Snare

Winstead is a postage stamp-sized vineyard near the small town of Bagdad, a little to the north of the bustling metropolis of Hobart. Its spicy, fruit-driven Pinot Noir is one of the finest from Tasmania, boasting true length and richness. Winstead's Rieslings from both 1997 and 1998 display qualities more familiar in better Alsatian riesling than those we are used to experiencing in Australian wine

Winstead

75 Winstead Road
Badgad Tas 7030
Tel: (03) 6268 6417
Fax: (03) 6268 6417

PINOT NOIR

Bagdad $$$$

1998	17.0	2000	2003
1997	16.3	1999	2002
1996	16.5	2001	2004
1995	17.2	1997	2000
1994	18.2	1999	2002

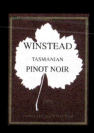

THE ONWINE AUSTRALIAN WINE ANNUAL 2000

Wirra Wirra

McMurtrie Road
McLaren Vale SA 5171
Tel: (08) 8323 8414
Fax: (08) 8323 8596

Region: McLaren Vale Winemaker: Ben Riggs
Viticulturist: Steve Brunato Chief Executive: Dr Tony Jordan

After a ten year stint setting up Domaine Chandon, Tony Jordan has joined the team at Wirra Wirra. This medium-sized McLaren Vale maker is widely known for the honesty and quality of its table wines, made across a steadily increasing number of varieties. Its most prestigious labels of RSW Shiraz and The Angelus Cabernet Sauvignon are almost uniformly excellent.

CHARDONNAY
McLaren Vale $$$

1997	16.8	1999	2002
1996	16.7	1998	2001
1995	16.0	1997	2000
1994	17.6	1996	1999
1993	17.5	1998	2001
1992	18.2	1997	2000
1991	18.0	1996	1999
1990	18.0	1995	1998

CHURCH BLOCK
McLaren Vale $$$

1997	18.2	2002	2005+
1996	16.0	1998	2001
1995	16.5	2000	2003
1994	18.0	1999	2002
1993	17.6	1998	2001
1992	16.8	1997	2000
1991	16.9	1996	1999
1990	18.0	1998	2002
1989	16.5	1994	1997
1988	17.0	1993	1996
1987	16.5	1992	1995
1986	16.0	1994	1998

HAND PICKED RIESLING
McLaren Vale $$

1998	15.6	2003	2006
1997	15.9	1999	2002
1996	15.0	1998	2001
1995	16.0	1997	2000
1994	16.5	1999	2002
1993	17.0	1998	2001
1992	17.9	2000	2004
1991	17.5		2003+
1990	16.5		2002+

RSW SHIRAZ

McLaren Vale $$$$

1996	18.9	2004	2008
1995	17.9	2000	2003
1994	18.5	1999	2002
1993	17.6	1998	2001
1992	18.2	2000	2004
1991	18.0	1996	1999
1990	18.3	1995	1998

SAUVIGNON BLANC

McLaren Vale $$

1998	15.3		1999
1997	16.0	1998	1999
1996	18.0	1997	1998
1995	17.6	1997	2000
1993	17.9	1994	1995

SCRUBBY RISE SEMILLON SAUVIGNON BLANC CHARDONNAY

McLaren Vale $$$

1998	16.0	2000	2003
1997	18.0	2002	2005
1996	17.0	2001	2004
1995	15.4	1997	2000
1994	17.3	1999	2002
1993	18.3	1998	2001
1992	17.6	1997	2000
1991	18.0	1999	2003
1990	16.0	1995	1998
1989	18.0	1994	1997

THE ANGELUS CABERNET SAUVIGNON

McLaren Vale $$$$

1996	18.6	2004	2008+
1995	17.5	2003	2007
1994	16.6	1999	2002
1993	18.2	2001	2005
1992	18.0	2000	2004
1991	18.2	1996	1999
1990	18.5	1998	2002
1989	16.5	1994	1997
1988	16.0	1990	1993

Wolf Blass

Bilyara Vineyards
Sturt Hwy
Nuriootpa SA 5355
Tel: (08) 8562 1955
Fax: (08) 8562 4127

Region: Barossa Valley   Winemakers: John Glaetzer, Wendy Stuckey
Viticulturist: Chief Executive: Ray King

A plethora of interesting new releases made and marketed on individual vineyards and varieties has helped breathe new life into this most popular of Australian brands. The new labels, which include a plush Barossa Valley Cabernet Sauvignon 1996 and 1998 Chardonnays from both the Adelaide Hills and Eden Valleys, don't make a clean break from the Blass house style, but certainly broaden its horizons.

BLACK LABEL DRY RED

South Australia $$$$$

1995	17.7	2003	2007
1994	16.7	2000	2003
1993	18.0	2001	2005
1992	18.5		2004+
1991	18.3	1999	2003
1990	18.4	2002	2010
1989	18.0	2001	2009
1988	18.5	1996	2000
1987	17.5	1995	1999
1986	18.3	1994	1998
1985	17.5	1993	1997
1984	18.2	1992	1996
1983	18.6	1995	2000
1982	17.0	1994	1999
1981	18.1	1993	1998
1980	18.4	1992	1997
1975	18.1	1995	2000

BROWN LABEL CLASSIC SHIRAZ

South Australia $$$$

1996	17.4	2004	2008
1995	16.0	2000	2003
1994	17.9	2002	2006
1993	16.7	1998	2001
1992	17.2	2000	2004
1990	17.7	1998	2002
1989	17.0	1997	2001
1988	18.1	1993	1996
1987	17.6	1995	1999
1986	18.4	1994	1998
1985	17.0	1993	1997
1984	18.1	1992	1996
1983	18.5	1991	1995
1982	17.0	1990	1994

GOLD LABEL RHINE RIESLING

Clare Valley, Eden Valley $$

1998	18.5	2003	2006
1997	17.5	2002	2005
1996	18.3	2004	2008
1995	16.0	1997	2000
1994	18.0	1999	2002

GREY LABEL DRY RED

South Australia $$$$

1996	17.3	2001	2004+
1995	18.0	2002	2007
1994	18.3	2002	2006
1993	16.8	2001	2005
1992	18.1	2000	2004
1991	18.3	1999	2003
1990	17.6	1995	1998
1988	17.5	1993	1996
1987	17.5	1992	1995
1986	18.3	1994	1998

RED LABEL DRY RED

South-Eastern Australia $

1997	16.0	1999	2002
1996	15.0	1997	1998
1995	15.7	1997	2000
1994	15.0	1996	2001

RHINE RIESLING

South Australia $$

1998	17.9	2000	2003
1997	16.0	1999	2002
1996	16.0	1998	2001
1995	16.0	1997	2000
1994	17.4	1999	2002
1993	17.8	1995	1998
1991	17.5	1993	1996
1990	17.4	1995	1998

Woodstock

**Douglas Gully Road
McLaren Flat SA 5171
Tel: (08) 8383 0156
Fax: (08) 8383 0437**

SHOW CHARDONNAY

South Australia $$$

1996	15.8	1998	2001
1994	17.0	1996	1999
1990	17.6	1992	1995

VINTAGE PINOT NOIR CHARDONNAY

Southern Australia $$$

1996	17.8	1998	2001+
1995	16.9	1997	2000
1992	16.4	1994	1997

YELLOW LABEL DRY RED

South Australia $$

1996	16.5	1998	2001
1995	16.2	2000	2003
1994	15.0	1996	1999
1993	16.0	1998	2001
1992	16.9	2000	2004
1991	16.0	1996	1999
1990	17.6	1995	1998

Region: McLaren Vale Winemaker: Scott Collett
Viticulturist: Scott Collett Chief Executive: Scott Collett

Woodstock's collection of McLaren Vale wines is led by its richly textured but consistently elegant best-of-vintage label known as The Stocks, which is either made from shiraz or cabernet sauvignon depending on the season. Its wines present flavours as generous as you'd anticipate from McLaren Vale, but are structured in a more restrained and supple fashion than many of its neighbours.

BOTRYTIS SWEET WHITE

McLaren Vale $$$

1997-98	14.8	2000	2003
1996	17.8	2001	2004
1995	18.2	2000	2003
1994	17.5	2002	2006
1993	17.1	1995	1998
1992	15.3	1994	1997
1991	16.6	1993	1996

CABERNET SAUVIGNON

McLaren Vale $$$

1997	16.7	2005	2009
1996	16.0	2001	2004
1995	16.2	2000	2003
1994	18.2	2002	2006
1993	17.5	2001	2005
1992	18.1		2004+
1991	18.6		2003+
1990	17.9	1998	2002

CHARDONNAY

McLaren Vale $$

1997	16.0	1999	2002
1996	18.0	2001	2004
1995	16.7	2000	2003
1994	17.6	1999	2002
1993	18.2	1998	2001
1992	17.8	1997	2000
1991	18.3	1996	1999

GRENACHE

McLaren Vale $$

1997	16.8	2002	2005
1996	16.4	1998	2001+
1995	15.7	1997	2000

SHIRAZ

McLaren Vale $$

1997	17.0	2002	2005+
1996	17.9	2004	2008
1995	15.8	2000	2003
1994	16.5	1999	2002
1993	18.2	2001	2005
1992	17.8	2000	2004
1991	16.4	1999	2003
1990	18.1	1998	2002
1989	17.5	1997	2001

THE STOCKS

McLaren Vale $$$$

1996	18.8	2004	2008
1995	17.9	2003	2007
1994	18.7	2002	2006
1993	18.0	2001	2005
1991	16.7	1999	2003

Wyndham Estate

**Dalwood Road
Dalwood NSW 2335
Tel: (02) 4938 3444
Fax: (02) 4938 3422**

Region: Lower Hunter Valley Winemaker: Robert Paul
Viticulturist: Stephen Guilbaud-Oulton Chief Executive: Andre Boucard

I never thought I'd be excited by Wyndham Estate's wines, since it appeared destined for mediocrity. Then came the Show Reserve Semillon and the Show Reserve Shiraz, including the wonderfully leathery 1993 vintage of this wine, a traditional Hunter classic!

BIN 111 VERDELHO

Lower Hunter Valley $

1998	15.3	2000	2003
1997	16.0	1999	2002
1996	15.8	1998	2001
1995	14.5	1999	2002
1994	15.5	1999	2002

BIN 444 CABERNET SAUVIGNON

Lower Hunter Valley $$

1996	15.0	1998	2001
1995	16.3	2000	2003
1994	16.0	1999	2002
1993	16.7	1998	2001
1992	16.7	1997	2000
1990	14.5	1991	1992
1989	16.5	1994	1997

BIN 888 CABERNET MERLOT

Lower Hunter Valley $$$

1997	17.2	2002	2005+
1996	16.7	2001	2004
1995	15.8	2000	2003
1994	17.0	2002	2006
1993	16.0	1998	2001
1992	16.8	1997	2000
1991	16.6	1993	1996

OAK CASK CHARDONNAY

Lower Hunter Valley $$

1997	15.3	1999	2002
1996	15.7	1998	2001
1995	15.2	1997	2000
1994	15.7	1996	1999
1993	17.0	1995	1998

SHOW RESERVE SEMILLON

Lower Hunter Valley $$$

1997	17.0	2005	2009
1996	17.2	2004	2009
1994	16.0	1999	2002

SHOW RESERVE SHIRAZ

Lower Hunter Valley $$$

1996	16.3	2001	2004+
1995	16.1	2000	2003
1993	18.6	2001	2005+

**Region: Coonawarra Winemaker: Peter Douglas until 1998
Viticulturist: Max Arney Chief Executive: Bruce Kemp**

Wynns Coonawarra is an icon in Australian red wine. Its principal quality label, the Black Label Cabernet Sauvignon, is a national benchmark and has never really been sold for its true worth. The 1996 is a fine, tight-knit cellar style. The Shiraz has a confusing and split personality, since vintages over the last decade and more have been relatively quick to develop, but mature vintages from the 'seventies backwards are rightly considered to be Australian classics. Of the two prestige labels, the John Riddoch Cabernet Sauvignon and Michael Shiraz, the Michael performed better in 1996, with the John Riddoch reverting to the rather souped-up and contrived style it has fallen back on in several warmer years.

CABERNET SAUVIGNON

Coonawarra $$$

1996	18.1	2004	2008
1995	17.2	2003	2007
1994	18.5	2006	2014
1993	18.0		2005+
1992	17.6	2000	2004
1991	18.6		2003+
1990	18.6	2002	2010+
1989	16.0	1991	1994
1988	18.3	1996	2000
1987	16.5	1992	1995
1986	18.2	1994	1998
1985	17.0	1993	1997
1984	16.4	1989	1992
1983	14.5	1985	1988
1982	18.1	1994	1999

Wynns Coonawarra Estate

**Memorial Drive
Coonawarra SA 5263
Tel: (08) 8736 3266
Fax: (08) 8736 3202**

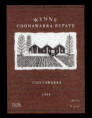

CABERNET SHIRAZ MERLOT (FORMERLY CABERNET HERMITAGE)

Coonawarra $$

1995	17.1	2000	2003
1994	16.8	1999	2002
1993	17.1	1998	2003
1992	17.8	2000	2004
1991	17.5	1996	1999
1990	18.0	1998	2002
1989	16.0	1991	2004
1988	18.3	1993	1996
1987	15.5	1989	1992
1986	18.5	1998	2003
1985	17.7	1990	1993

CHARDONNAY

Coonawarra $$

1998	16.8	2000	2003
1997	16.5	1999	2002
1996	16.0	1998	2001
1995	15.0	1997	2000
1994	17.8	1999	2002
1993	16.5	1998	2001
1992	17.6	1997	2000

JOHN RIDDOCH CABERNET SAUVIGNON

Coonawarra $$$$

1996	17.2	2004	2008+
1994	18.7		2006+
1993	18.3	2001	2005
1992	18.0		2004+
1991	18.3		2003+
1990	18.4		2002+
1988	17.4	2000	2005
1987	18.0	1999	2004
1986	18.4	1998	2006
1985	17.0	1993	1997
1984	16.7	1992	1996
1982	19.0	1994	2002

MICHAEL SHIRAZ
Coonawarra $$$$$

1996	18.5		2008+
1994	18.9	2006	2014
1993	18.8	2005	2013
1991	18.3	2003	2011
1990	18.4	2002	2010
1955	19.2	1975	1985

RIESLING
Coonawarra $

1998	17.2	2003	2006
1997	15.8	2002	2005
1996	17.2	2001	2004
1995	15.6	1997	2000
1994	17.5	1999	2002
1993	17.8	1998	2001
1992	17.0	1997	2000
1991	17.5	1999	2003

SHIRAZ
Coonawarra $$

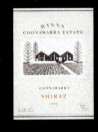

1997	16.5	2002	2005
1996	15.3	1998	2001
1995	16.8	2000	2003
1994	16.3	1996	1999
1993	16.5	1998	2001
1992	17.6	2000	2004
1991	16.8	1996	1999
1990	17.0	1995	1998
1989	16.5	1994	1997
1988	17.5	1996	2000

Yalumba

Eden Valley Road
Angaston SA 5353
Tel: (08) 8561 3200
Fax: (08) 8561 3393

Region: Barossa Winemakers: Simon Adams, Kevin Glastonbury, Louisa Rose
Viticulturist: Robin Nettelbeck Chief Executive: Robert Hill Smith

Yalumba is clearly playing a major role in the resurgence of the Barossa Valley, with a renewed focus on the wines that make this most important of Australian wine regions truly unique. The Signature blend of Cabernet Sauvignon and Shiraz has become of one of the country's most reliable premium reds, while the Octavius is a rowdy, attention-seeking wine of substantial quality and character. Meantime, the red Coonawarra blend of Menzies has not only joined the club to have 'The' in front of its name, but has turned out in typically fine form from 1996.

BAROSSA SHIRAZ

Barossa Valley $$$

1997	17.2	2002	2005
1996	15.8	1998	2001
1995	16.8	1997	2000

'D' METHODE CHAMPENOISE

Tasmania, Victoria, South Australia $$$

1996	17.5	2001	2004
1995	17.0	2000	2003
1994	18.5	1999	2002
1993	17.5	1998	2001
1992	14.8	1994	1997
1991	18.0	1995	1998
1990	18.2	1998	2002

GALWAY HERMITAGE

Barossa $

1998	15.0	1999	2000
1997	15.3	1999	2002
1996	15.0	1998	2001
1995	16.5	2000	2003
1994	14.5	1996	1999
1993	16.0	1998	2001
1992	16.3	1997	2000
1991	15.8	1996	1999
1990	17.0	1995	1998

LIMITED RELEASE VIOGNIER

Barossa Valley $$

1998	16.7	1999	2000
1997	16.7	1998	1999
1996	16.0	1997	1998

THE ONWINE AUSTRALIAN WINE ANNUAL

RESERVE CHARDONNAY

Barossa $$$

1996	17.1	1998	2001
1995	17.9	2000	2003
1994	18.1	1999	2002
1993	18.6	2001	2005
1992	17.9	1995	1998
1991	17.5	1993	1996
1990	16.0	1995	1998

THE MENZIES CABERNET SAUVIGNON

Coonawarra $$$

1996	18.4	2004	2008+
1995	16.8	2000	2003
1994	16.0	2006	2014
1993	16.8	2001	2005
1992	18.0	2000	2004
1991	18.5		2003+
1990	17.8		2002+
1989	18.0	1997	2003

THE OCTAVIUS

Barossa $$$$$

1995	18.0	2003	2007
1994	18.7	2002	2006+
1993	17.6	1998	2001
1992	18.6	2000	2004
1990	18.8		2002+

THE SIGNATURE (FORMERLY SIGNATURE RESERVE CABERNET SHIRAZ)

Barossa $$$$

1995	17.2	2003	2007
1994	18.5		2006+
1993	18.0	2001	2005
1992	18.7	2004	2012
1991	18.5		2003+
1990	18.5		2002+
1989	18.0	1994	1997
1988	18.3		2008+
1987	17.8	1995	1999
1986	17.5	1994	1998
1985	18.0	1997	2002
1984	16.0	1992	1996

Yarra Burn

60 Settlement Road
Yarra Junction Vic 3797
Tel: (03) 5967 1428
Fax: (03) 5967 1146

Region: Yarra Valley Winemakers: Stephen Pannell, Ed Carr, Emma Requin
Viticulturist: David Fyffe Chief Executive: Stephen Millar

BRL Hardy have a Yarra Valley base at Yarra Burn, whose wines have always been elegant, intensely-flavoured and ready to improve in the cellar. The new Bastard Hill range is a distinctively named addition to the folio, since the Pinot Noir and Chardonnay in question come from a particular slope within BRL Hardy's enormous Hoddle's Creek vineyard, whose name you can possibly guess. Time will tell if the very extractive Pinot Noir fleshes out a little. The 1997 Yarra Burn Pinot Noir offered exceptional value.

CABERNET
Yarra Valley $$$

1997	16.8	2002	2005
1995	18.3	2003	2007
1994	16.8	1999	2002
1993	16.8	1998	2001
1992	18.3	2000	2004
1990	16.0	1995	1998

CHARDONNAY
Yarra Valley $$$

1996	17.0	2001	2004
1995	15.7	1996	1997
1994	15.8	1999	2002
1993	17.7	1998	2001
1992	17.5	1994	1997

CHARDONNAY PINOT NOIR (FORMERLY PINOT NOIR METHODE CHAMPENOISE)

Yarra Valley $$$

1996	15.6	1998	2001
1993	16.0	1995	2000
1990	17.2	1995	1998
1989	16.7	1994	1997

PINOT NOIR
Yarra Valley $$$

1998	16.0	2003	2006
1997	17.8	2002	2005
1994	13.5	1999	2002

Yarra Edge

**Edward Road
Lilydale Vic 3140
Tel: (03) 9730 1107
Fax: (03) 9739 0135**

Region: Yarra Valley Winemaker: Tom Carson
Viticulturist: John Evans Chief Executives: Doug & Graham Rathbone

Yarra Edge is potentially one of the premier Yarra Valley vineyards. Today it's leased to Yering Station and its wines are made there by Tom Carson and team. Every now and again the Cabernets blend creates a wine of real style and finesse.

CABERNETS

Yarra Valley $$$$

1995	16.5	2003	2007
1994	18.7		2006+
1993	15.4	1998	2001
1992	18.3	2000	2004
1991	17.1	1999	2003
1990	18.1	1998	2002

CHARDONNAY

Yarra Valley $$$$

1997	15.2	1999	2002
1996	16.7	1998	2001
1995	18.0	2000	2003
1994	16.0	1999	2002
1993	16.3	1995	1998
1992	18.5	2000	2004
1991	16.2	1996	1999
1990	18.2	1998	2002

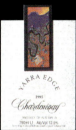

Region: Yarra Valley Winemaker: Rob Dolan
Viticulturist: Damien de Castella Chief Executive: Ray King

One of the most successful of the wide array of Mildara Blass brands, Yarra Ridge presents early-drinking, flavoursome and typically reliable table wines priced for the bistro market. Its Reserve wines offer an extra dimension of concentration and oak treatment. Many have done very well on the wine show circuit.

Yarra Ridge

**Glenview Rd
Yarra Glen Vic 3775
Tel: (03) 9730 1022
Fax: (03) 9730 1131**

CABERNET SAUVIGNON

Yarra Valley $$$

1998	16.3	1999	2002
1997	15.0	1999	2002
1996	15.3	1997	1998
1995	15.5	2000	2003
1994	17.7	1999	2002
1993	16.7	1998	2001
1992	16.0	1994	1997
1991	16.0	1993	1996
1990	17.0	1992	1995

CHARDONNAY
Valley $$$

1998	16.2	1999	2000
1997	16.7	1998	1999
1996	16.8	1998	2001
1995	16.5	1997	2000
1994	17.0	1996	1999
1993	17.3	1994	1995

MERLOT
Yarra Valley $$$

1997	16.8	1999	2002
1996	16.0	1998	2001
1995	18.1	1997	2000
1994	16.7	1999	2002
1993	15.0	1995	1998

PINOT NOIR
Yarra Valley $$$

1998	15.3	2000	2003
1997	16.0	1999	2002
1996	17.1	1998	2003
1995	17.6	2000	2003
1994	18.1	1999	2002
1993	15.6	1998	2001

RESERVE PINOT NOIR
Yarra Valley $$$$

1998	16.8	2000	2003
1997	16.7	1999	2002
1996	16.5	1998	2001

SAUVIGNON BLANC
Yarra Valley $$$

1998	15.4	1998	1999
1997	17.0	1998	1999
1996	17.8	1997	1998
1995	16.5	1996	1997

2000 THE ONWINE AUSTRALIAN WINE ANNUAL

Region: Yarra Valley Winemaker: Martin Williams
Viticulturists: Marcus and Troy Hill Chief Executive: Terry Hill

In its short history Yarra Valley Hills has made some stunning wines from chardonnay, pinot noir and sauvignon blanc, sourcing fruit from a number of small Yarra Valley vineyards. Its Cabernet Sauvignon tends towards the leafier end of the spectrum, but its Chardonnay can be a very smart cool climate wine indeed. The Semillon Sauvignon Blanc blend of 1998 has a musky tropical fragrance and a fresh, long palate with grassy passionfruit flavours and lively acidity.

Yarra Valley Hills

Delaneys Rd
Warranwood Vic 3134
Tel: (03) 5962 4173
Fax: (03) 5962 4059

CHARDONNAY
Yarra Valley $$$

1998	16.7	2000	2003
1997	15.0	1998	1999
1996	18.5	2004	2008
1995	18.3	2000	2003
1994	16.7	1999	2902
1993	18.2	1995	1998
1992	17.0	1994	1997

PINOT NOIR
Yarra Valley $$$

1998	16.7	2003	2006
1997	17.2	2002	2005
1996	18.0	2001	2004
1995	16.7	1997	2000
1994	18.3	1999	2002
1993	14.0	1995	1998
1992	16.0	1997	2000

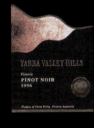

SAUVIGNON BLANC SEMILLON (FORMERLY SAUVIGNON BLANC)
Yarra Valley $$$

1998	17.3	2000	2003
1997	15.7	1998	1999
1996	18.2	1997	1998
1995	16.6	1997	2000
1994	16.2	1995	1996

Yarra Yarra

239 Hunts Lane
Steels Creek Vic 3775
Tel: (03) 9830 4180
Fax: (03) 9830 4180

Region: Yarra Valley Winemaker: Ian Maclean
Viticulturist: Ian Maclean Chief Executive: Ian Maclean & Anne Maclean

Yarra Yarra is a tiny Yarra Valley vineyard (not that you would have guessed) which specialises in dry red and white wines from the Bordeaux varieties. It is a welcome inclusion in this issue, since a tasting just days prior to going to print confirmed the extraordinary stature and consistency of its wines. From Ian Maclean's intended near-obscurity, his wine company should become an extremely high-profile brand sought after by those wanting the finer things in Victorian wine.

CABERNETS

Yarra Valley $$$$

1997	17.4	2002	2009+
1996	16.0	1998	2001+
1995	19.0		2007+
1994	18.2	2002	2006+
1993	17.3	2001	2005
1992	17.5	2000	2004+
1991	18.7	1999	2003+
1990	18.8	2002	2010+
1988	18.7	2000	2008
1987	17.6	1995	1999
1986	16.0	1994	1998
1985	17.2	1997	2005
1984	18.0	1996	2004

RESERVE CABERNET SAUVIGNON

Yarra Valley $$$$

1995	18.6		2007+
1994	16.9	2002	2006+
1993	16.8	1998	2001

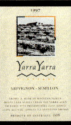

SAUVIGNON SEMILLON

Yarra Valley $$$$

1997	18.3	2002	2005
1996	17.8	2001	2004
1995	18.7	2003	2007
1994	16.3	1999	2002
1993	15.7	1995	1998
1992	18.7	2000	2004
1990	16.3	1995	1998
1989	16.6	1994	1997

Region: Yarra Valley **Winemaker:** Bailey Carrodus
Viticulturist: Bailey Carrodus **Chief Executive:** Bailey Carrodus

Yarra Yering
Briary Road
Coldstream Vic 3770
Tel: (03) 5964 9267
Fax: (03) 5964 9239

When they are good, they are very good indeed. Bailey Carrodus creates some of the most opulently concentrated and fine-grained of all Australian red wines, with a sweetness and balance all of their own. The best are simply great wines. I find Yarra Yering's white wines to be almost the most difficult in all of Australia to evaluate, since they seem at odds with some tenets of modern white wine production, yet from time to time make an assemblage of flavours and textures which complements food delightfully.

CHARDONNAY
Yarra Valley $$$$$

1994	16.5	1999	2002
1993	17.2	1998	2001
1992	17.1	1997	2000
1991	18.0	1996	1999
1990	17.0	1998	2002

DRY RED NO. 1
Yarra Valley $$$$$

1994	18.4	1999	2002
1993	18.5	2001	2005
1992	17.4	2000	2004
1991	18.6	1999	2003
1990	19.0	1998	2002
1989	17.5	1994	1997
1988	15.8	1993	1996
1987	16.5	1995	1999
1986	18.0	1994	1998+

DRY RED NO. 2
Yarra Valley $$$$$

1994	18.5	2002	2006
1993	18.0	1998	2001
1992	18.4	1997	2000
1991	18.0	1996	1999
1990	18.2	1998	2002
1989	17.5	1997	2001
1988	16.4	1990	1993
1987	15.5	1992	1995
1986	16.0	1991	1994
1985	17.5	1993	1997
1984	18.5	1992	1996

DRY WHITE NO. 1
Yarra Valley $$$$$ 4

1995	15.4	1997	2000
1994	17.2	1999	2002
1993	17.0	1998	2001
1992	15.9	1997	2000
1991	17.2	1999	2003
1990	15.3	1998	2002
1989	15.1	1991	1994

MERLOT
Yarra Valley $$$$$ 3

1994	18.8	2002	2006
1993	18.3	1998	2001
1992	17.6	1997	2000
1991	18.1	1996	1999
1990	17.3	1995	1998

PINOT NOIR
Yarra Valley $$$$$ 4

1996	14.5	1998	2001
1994	17.0	1999	2002
1993	16.6	1995	1998
1992	18.8	2000	2004
1991	18.7	1999	2003
1991	18.6	1996	1999
1990	17.0	1995	1998

UNDERHILL SHIRAZ
Yarra Valley $$$$$ 3

1994	17.0	1999	2002
1993	16.8	1998	2001
1992	18.9	1997	2000
1991	17.5	1993	1996

Region: Yarra Valley Winemaker: Claude Thibaut
Viticulturist: John Evans Chief Executives: Doug & Graham Rathbone

Yering Station has linked up with Devaux Champagne and its winemaker Claude Thibaut to fashion this very polished sparkling wine, made equally from Yarra Valley and Mornington Peninsula fruit. The wines each display a mouthfilling creamy texture, lingering flavours and clean, refreshing acidity.

YARRABANK CUVÉE

Yarra Valley, Mornington Peninsula $$$$

1995	18.6	2000	2003
1994	18.6	1996	1999
1993	18.2	1995	1998+

Yarrabank

**38 Melba Highway
Yering Vic 3775
Tel: (03) 9730 1107
Fax: (03) 9739 0135**

Region: Bendigo Winemaker: Nick Walker
Viticulturist: Lindsay Ross Chief Executive: Ray King

Yellowglen is one of the more ubiquitous mid-market to premium brands of Australian sparkling wine and at Smythesdale forms the headquarters of Mildara Blass' sparkling production. Even though its name suggests it might come from elsewhere than South Australia, I've always had a soft spot for the very elegant, classy Cuvée Victoria.

CUVÉE VICTORIA

South Australia (?!) $$$$

1995	17.0	1997	2000
1994	18.2	1996	1999
1993	17.0	1995	1998
1992	18.0	1994	1996

VINTAGE BRUT

South-Eastern Australia $$$

1996	16.7	1998	2001
1995	17.6	1997	2000
1994	16.0	1996	1999
1992	17.4	1994	1997

Yellowglen

**White's Road
Smythesdale Vic 3551
Tel: (03) 5342 8617
Fax: (03) 5333 7102**

Yering Station

38 Melba Highway
Yering Vic 3770
Tel: (03) 9730 1107
Fax: (03) 9739 0135

Yeringberg

Maroondah Highway
Coldstream Vic 3770
Tel: (03) 9739 1453
Fax: (03) 9739 0048

Region: Yarra Valley Winemaker: Tom Carson
Viticulturist: John Evans Chief Executives: Doug & Graham Rathbone

Yering Station has just finished its multi-multi-million dollar facelift and you can see at a glance where the money went. Fortunately enough went into wine production for this ambitious brand now truly delivers its promises of yesteryear with wines like the excellent 1998 Chardonnay and three superlative Reserve wines from 1997, made from Chardonnay, Pinot Noir and Shiraz.

CHARDONNAY
Yarra Valley $$$

1998	18.0	2000	2003+
1997	17.0	1999	2002
1996	14.5	1997	1998
1995	14.8	1996	1999
1994	14.4	1996	1999
1993	18.0	1998	2001
1992	18.1	1994	1997

PINOT NOIR
Yarra Valley $$$

1998	16.7	2000	2003
1997	16.0	1998	1999
1996	16.5	1998	2001

Region: Yarra Valley Winemaker: Guill De Pury
Viticulturist: Guill De Pury Chief Executive: Guill De Pury

It would come as a surprise to most Australian wine drinkers how well and for how long the comparatively refined wines of Yeringberg actually cellar, lasting in some instances for well over a century. If anything, Yeringberg's most recent releases have actually managed to lift the reputation of this stellar small vineyard to an even higher plane.

CHARDONNAY
Yarra Valley $$$$

1998	18.6	2003	2006
1997	18.3	2005	2009
1996	18.3	2004	2008
1995	17.8	2003	2007
1994	17.8	2002	2006
1993	18.6	2001	2005
1992	18.3	2000	2004
1991	17.5	1996	1999
1990	18.6	1998	2002
1989	16.0	1991	1994
1988	18.3	1993	1996

PINOT NOIR

Yarra Valley $$$$

1997	18.9	2005	2009
1996	18.4	2004	2008
1995	17.3	2000	2003
1994	17.8	2002	2006
1993	17.6	1995	1998
1992	18.0	1997	2000
1991	17.8	1996	1999
1990	18.5	1998	2002
1989	16.8	1994	1997
1988	16.7	1993	1996

(RED, FORMERLY CABERNET SAUVIGNON)

Yarra Valley $$$$$

1997	18.6	2005	2009+
1996	18.1	2004	2008
1995	16.6	2003	2007
1994	18.5	2006	2014
1993	17.6	2001	2005
1992	18.8		2012+
1991	17.3	1999	2003
1990	18.7	2002	2010+
1989	15.8	1994	1997
1988	18.7	2000	2008+
1987	15.6	1992	1995
1986	16.5	1994	1998
1985	17.0	1993	1997
1984	18.5	1996	2004
1983	15.2	1988	1991
1982	18.6	1994	2002
1981	16.6	1993	2001
1980	19.0	1992	2000
1979	18.8	1991	1999
1977	17.3	1989	1997
1976	18.6	1988	1996
1975	18.7	1987	1995+
1974	17.8	1986	1994

(WHITE, FORMERLY MARSANNE)

Yarra Valley $$$$

1998	18.0	2003	2006
1997	18.5	2005	2009
1996	17.5	2004	2008
1995	16.5	2003	2007
1994	18.3	2002	2006
1993	18.4	1998	2001
1992	17.9	1997	2000
1991	17.2	1993	1996
1990	17.5	1995	1998

Zema Estate

Riddoch Highway
Coonawarra SA 5263
Tel: (08) 8736 3219
Fax: (08) 8736 3280

Region: Coonawarra Winemakers: Matt & Nick Zema
Viticulturist: Nick Zema Chief Executive: Demetrio Zema

Zema Estate is a red wine specialist located in the heart of Coonawarra. Its wines are traditionally firm and long-living, with the Cluny blend of cabernet sauvignon and merlot providing an earlier-drinking alternative. The Zema family has its vineyard pruned by hand, thereby avoiding the intense leafy/mulberry flavours developed in several larger Coonawarra vineyards which regard traditional vine pruning almost as an afterthought. The Zemas have produced two excellent Family Selection Cabernet Sauvignons in 1994 and 1996.

CABERNET SAUVIGNON
Coonawarra $$$

1997	16.7		2002	2005
1996	16.0		2001	2004
1995	17.2		2000	2003
1994	17.8		1999	2002
1993	17.5		2001	2005
1992	18.3		2000	2004
1991	17.8		1999	2003
1990	18.0			2002+
1989	17.0		1997	2001
1988	17.5			2000+

CLUNY
Coonawarra $$

1997	16.2	2002	2005
1996	15.1	1998	2001
1995	16.6	2000	2003
1994	16.0	1999	2002
1993	15.4	1995	1998

FAMILY SELECTION CABERNET SAUVIGNON
Coonawarra $$$$

1996	18.3	2004	2008+
1994	18.4	2002	2006
1993	17.5	2001	2005
1992	16.8	2000	2004
1991	17.9		2003+
1990	16.8	1998	2002
1988	17.7	1996	2000

SHIRAZ
Coonawarra $$$

1997	16.0	1999	2002
1996	16.6	2001	2004
1995	17.0	2003	2007
1994	16.4	1999	2002
1993	18.4	2001	2005
1992	16.8	1997	2000
1991	18.0		2003+
1990	18.5		2010+
1989	16.7	1997	2003
1988	18.2		2000+

Key to Wine Entries

Name of wine: OLIVER ESTATE SHIRAZ

Grown in the Yarra Valley **region** — Yarra Valley $$

Wine Ranking of 3

Current vintage price between $12 and $17
Will improve. Drink from 2002 to 2008.

Vintage year	Wines scored out of 20.0		
1996	18.2	2002	2008
1995	16.0	1998	2000
1994	18.0	1996	1997

- Will improve. Drink from 2002 to 2008.
- Drink now. At its best between 1998 & 2000
- Possibly too old. Was best from 1996 to 1997

Wine Ranking Codes

Wine Ranking	Regular Score in Jeremy Oliver's Tastings	Medal Equivalent
1	18.8+	Top gold medal
2	18.3–18.7	Regular gold medal
3	17.8–18.2	Top silver medal
4	17.0–17.7	Regular silver medal
5	16.0–16.9	Top bronze medal

THE ONWINE AUSTRALIAN WINE ANNUAL